Mined-Land Rehabilitation

Mined-Land Rehabilitation

Dennis L. Law, ASLA
Kansas State University

VNR VAN NOSTRAND REINHOLD COMPANY

Copyright © 1984 by Van Nostrand Reinhold Company Inc.

Library of Congress Catalog Card Number: 83–19745
ISBN: 0–442–25987–5

Manufactured in the United States of America

Published by Van Nostrand Reinhold Company Inc.
135 West 50th Street
New York, New York 10020

Van Nostrand Reinhold Company Limited
Molly Millars Lane
Wokingham, Berkshire RG11 2PY, England

Van Nostrand Reinhold
480 Latrobe Street
Melbourne, Victoria 3000, Australia

Macmillan of Canada
Division of Gage Publishing Limited
164 Commander Boulevard
Agincourt, Ontario M1S 3C7, Canada

15 14 13 12 11 10 9 8 7 6 5 4 3 2 1

Library of Congress Cataloging in Publication Data

Law, Dennis L.
    Mined-land rehabilitation.

    Includes bibliographical references and index.
    1. Mineral industries—Environmental aspects—United
States.   2. Environmental protection—United States.
3. Revegetation—United States.   4. Reclamation of land—
United States.   I. Title.
TD195.M5L35   1984   631.6′4   83–19745
ISBN 0–442–25987–5

To my lovely wife Linda and to three beautiful children, Dwight, Andrea, and Brent, for undying love and support. To my parents who introduced me to God's creation and taught me to be a good steward of the land.

PROLOGUE

The Need to Rehabilitate

In 1973, a critical dilemma faced the United States in the form of an oil embargo imposed by the Arab oil-producing nations. Americans suddenly found themselves sitting in long lines to purchase gasoline for their automobiles. Many service station operators closed at noon and did not bother to open their doors on weekends. There was talk of rationing by the federal government of fuel purchases, as was done during World War II. California's rationing system obliged those with even-numbered license plates to make purchases on even-numbered dates. Since that time, the cost of fuel from all sources has multiplied many times over, inflating the cost of all goods and services—not only in our own nation, but throughout the world.

Solar greenhouses, solar homes, wood burning stoves, and fuel-efficient automobiles have become a status symbol. Our life-style now calls for lower winter temperatures, higher summer temperatures, 10-speed bicycles, and comfortable shoes. The desperate search for energy-related minerals has had its effect, not only on the nation's social structure, but on the economy and the environment as well.

In Gillette, Wyoming, the hub of the vast, coal-bearing Powder River Basin, the population—in 1980 at 15,600—is expected to rise some 28 percent in the next two years. By 1990, the city should double with a potential influx of 10,000 new workers. These workers will help man 12 new coal mines,

5 uranium operations, a power plant, and a synthetic fuels plant.[1]

Wyoming is the nation's third-fastest-growing state. Its population growth exceeds by far the state's ability to construct an adequate urban structure in which new citizens can find housing, education, and recreation. With additional population comes the need for roads, water supplies, and quality sewage treatment systems. "Homesteaders" are already living in tents in the Wyoming desert, moving back and forth between federal land and railroad right-of-way as officials drive them away. People sleep in their cars, moving from street to street in the cities of Green River and Evanston. In Rawlins, a man paid $350 in the summer of 1979 for a renovated chicken coop.[2]

In Littleton, Colorado, a Denver suburb, the main steet is closed to automobile traffic for up to five hours a day to allow coal trains to pass. Typically, a three bedroom house in Denver that sold six years ago for $35,000 will sell today for $105,000.[3] Some 3,000 oil companies of various sizes have offices in Denver. Its ever-growing skyline is reflective of these figures.

In July 1980, in Moab, Utah, some 500 people gathered in a city park for a rally where they listened to the national anthem on automobile stereos as the American Legion raised the American flag. Following speeches by three of the county's commissioners critical of federal land policy, the commissioners climbed aboard a bulldozer and proceeded to cut a destructive 200 yard-long swath through a proposed Bureau of Land Management wilderness area.[4] This action was part of what has come to be known as the "sagebrush rebellion," an attempt to wrestle the land away from federal government control.

In July 1981, the *Rainbow Warrior,* a converted trawler owned by a group of environmentalists called "Greenpeace," set sail from Boston to an off-shore drilling site near Cape Cod where a 12-story Shell oil rig had begun drilling after six years of delay and controversy. Greenpeace, concerned about potential pollution and oil spills, placed bumper stickers on the rig and left to continue its battle in court.[5]

Tales go on and on that outline the story of the conflict between environmentalists and industrialists—between mineral extraction and environmental and social integrity. However, one basic objective lies before us—we must produce as much energy as possible with a minimum impact on the environment. It is unrealistic to imagine the United States abandoning its commitment for self-sufficiency in energy production. We are simply too industrialized to swing in the other direction. Even agricultural products are dependent on fuel sources in the field as well as transport to our markets. It is equally unrealistic to imagine the mining and drilling companies removing the various minerals without some damage to the environment occurring. The challenge before us is by no means going to be easy. We must ensure that adequate rehabilitation standards are enforced.

The checks and balances that emerge in the conflict between such groups as Greenpeace, the Sierra Club, and the Audubon Society, and the oil and mining companies should be maintained in order to reach an acceptible mean. To turn the public lands over to the extracting industries without supervision could be disastrous. The *Wichita Eagle and Beacon* quotes Paul Driessen of the Rocky Mountain Oil and Gas Association stating that "wilderness areas, wildlife refuges, and parts of Yellowstone and other national parks should be opened to oil exploration."[6]

As our nation continues its desperate quest for energy self-sufficiency, the conflict between mineral extraction and the environment will broaden. What is badly needed is a realistic set of guidelines that will allow the mining and petroleum companies the latitude needed to remove the resource but with enough control that ensures proper rehabilitation. We also need thresholds or limitations on where oil or coal should be taken and where it should not be taken. I am not, quite frankly, anxious to see oil rigs or draglines sitting at the foot of the Tetons—no matter how desperate we get for oil and coal. Some things are just too sacred.

A careful balance must be maintained between the various forces of nature in our ecosystem. An area that has been disturbed must be rehabilitated as quickly as possible to ensure the balance of natural systems. This is especially critical in the arid and semiarid regions of the West where the balance is so intricate and sensitive. Success in this venture requires that the techniques of rehabilitation be studied and utilized.

A distinction should be made between the terms *restoration, reclamation,* and *rehabilitation.*

Restoration implies that the conditions of the site prior to the time of disturbance will be replicated after the action that disturbs the land is terminated. *Reclamation* implies that the site is habitable by organisms that were originally present or by others that are similar to the original inhabitants. *Rehabilitation* implies that the land will be returned to a form and level of productivity that conforms with a prior land use plan, including a stable ecological state that does not contribute substantially to environmental deterioration and that is consistent with surrounding aesthetic values.[7]

In western areas, complete restoration is rarely, if ever, possible. Reclamation and rehabilitation primarily depend on the goals set by society, which in turn are determined by what society wants and needs from its natural resources, by the physical and ecological conditions of the site, and the economic and social trade-offs involved in supplying those wants and needs.

Rehabilitation specialists, in order to be effective, need to have a knowledge of state and federal laws that relate to surface disturbances, mining and drilling processes, erosion and sedimentation control techniques, and revegetative processes. This book is meant to be an introduction to those topics considered to be basic to rehabilitation. It serves as the beginning of an educational process. The seed planted here, the author hopes, will someday blossom into a life of quality for all the living to enjoy—as well as those future generations that may benefit from our labors.

Dennis L. Law, ASLA
Associate Professor
Department of Landscape Architecture
Kansas State University

REFERENCES

1. "Gillette Area Boom Predicted," *The Wyoming Eagle,* Cheyenne, Wyo., July 27, 1981.
2. "Growing State Struggles with Urban Sprawl," *Kansas State Collegian,* Manhattan, Kans.: Kansas State University, December 2, 1980.
3. "Denver's Mile High Energy Boom," *Time,* August 13, 1979, p. 41.
4. "Utah 'Rebels' Bulldoze into Wilderness Study Area," *The Casper Star Tribune,* July 6, 1980.
5. "Oil Drills Hum off Cape Cod," *The Wyoming Eagle,* Cheyenne, Wyo., July 27, 1981.
6. "Energy-Rich West to Play Big Role in Nation's Goals," *The Wichita Eagle and Beacon,* October 14, 1979.
7. National Academy of Sciences, *Rehabilitation Potential of Western Coal Lands,* Ballinger Publishing Company, Cambridge, Mass., 1974, p. 11.

Contents

Mined-Land Rehabilitation

PART I
MINING PROCEDURES

1
Basic Mining Principles

INTRODUCTION

For thousands of years, man has been fascinated by gems and precious metals. Although some have appeared on the earth's surface, most have had to be reached by digging into the soil to remove the object or the ore. It has been estimated that mineral resources are unevenly distributed in only about 1 percent of the earth's crust.[1]

Mined products are used in our daily lives to a greater extent than most of us realize. Baking soda, for example, is mined from the desert floor in Wyoming. Our life-style and the nation's economy is dependent on the success of mining operations. Because of recent energy crises, the production of coal has taken on a renewed importance. Most of the discussions in this book, therefore, are primarily related to the mining and rehabilitation of coal lands.

Clements reports that the total United States has coal reserves of approximately 434 billion short tons that are economically and legally available.[2] With energy conservation, this reserve should supply the nation's needs for several decades. Nevertheless, even with a stable per capita use of fossil fuel, these energy sources are limited over time because of population growth. The Arab oil embargo of 1973 illustrates the fact that energy is both limited and expensive. Our dependence on domestic reserves for energy sources places a new demand on mineral-laden landscapes. The rates of natural, geological, and biological processes that replenish these resources are infinitesimally small when compared to consumption rates.

An understanding of rehabilitation processes must be preceded by a basic knowledge of mining principles. All the methods currently employed to remove minerals will not be discussed in this chapter, rather, only those methods having a significant impact on the earth's surface.

DEFINITIONS

Coal

Coal is classified into three types including *lignite, bituminous,* and *anthracite.* Each has unique characteristics, but can be evaluated most readily by its ability to produce energy. The content of coal relevant to its energy-producing potential can be expressed in terms of percentages of fixed carbon, volatiles, and water. Coals are rated according to the *fuel ratio,* which is the ratio of fixed carbon to volatile matter. Volatiles burn in the form of gas and produce a long, smoky flame. Fixed carbon produces a hot, smokeless flame. The anthracite coals have a high fuel ratio, bituminous, moderate, and lignite, low.

Lignite, often called *brown coal,* is extremely soft with a fibrous texture. In terms of geologic time, the lignite coals are not well developed. Bituminous coal, or *soft coal,* has evolved over a longer period of time than lignite. It has generally been buried deeper and thus, is more compressed. This accounts for the lower percentage of water contained in bituminous when compared to lignite.

Anthracitic coals have been compressed under tremendous weight for long periods of time. The coal is very hard and glassy in appearance. While anthracite is very valuable and of high quality, it is rare. Most of the reserves are found only in eastern Pennsylvania.

Bituminous coals are the most abundant and sometimes occur in extremely deep formations called *seams.* Those that can be economically mined vary from a few inches to over 60 feet in thickness.

Mining

The mining of coal employs two general methods—underground and surface—which will be discussed later in the chapter. In the process of mining, however, it should be noted that all the topsoil, rock, and other strata that lie above the coal seam, called *overburden,* must be removed. Once the overburden has been removed, it is usually placed in piles called *spoils.* Following the removal operations, the coal is then cleaned and milled to a consistent quality and texture. The residue from this milling process is stacked in piles that are known as *tailings.*

Not all coals are economically available for recovery. The feasibility of mining any given coal site is determined by the ratio of overburden to the thickness of the coal seam. The amount of overburden that lies over the coal is an indication of the expenses to be incurred in mining. The thickness of the coal seam is an indication of the expected profit. Other considerations should be taken into account such as the seam's *inclination* or the angle of slope in the formation. All the natural resources that affect the recovery of the coal will play a role in the economic feasibility of mining as well.

MINING PROVINCES

There is a wide range of differences throughout the United States in topography, geology, and mining techniques. For the purposes of discussing these differences, the United States has been divided into six mining provinces (shown in Figure 1.1), including:

A. Eastern province
B. Interior province
C. Gulf province
D. Northern Great Plains province
E. Rocky Mountains province
F. Pacific province

The variation in natural conditions from region to region creates the need to address mining methods and rehabilitation techniques that are unique to each.

The eastern province is characterized by rolling hills and steep slopes. Mining methods include contour and modified contour methods of removal. The interior and Gulf provinces possess generally flat terrain and thick overburdens. The methods most employed in these regions include box-cut and area stripping. The topography of the northern Great Plains, Rocky Mountains, and Pacific provinces varies from flat to mountainous. In these areas shallow overburdens and thick deposits are typically removed by area strip and open-pit mining methods. Underground mining can occur in all regions but has not been used in recent years to the extent of surface mining methods.

MINING METHODS

Underground Mining

Coal seams are usually locked between sedimentary types of rock formations. Therefore, the seams are usually relatively flat and extend horizontally or with some degree of incline because of geological uplift. In coal seams that lie deep below

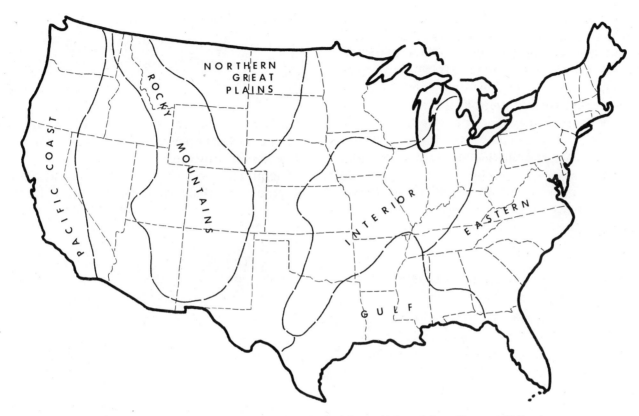

Figure 1.1. The six mining provinces of the United States (Adapted from Bureau of Mines).

the earth's surface, vertical shafts are constructed as an initial means to get to the seam. The coal is mined by extension of horizontal *drifts* or tunnels projected into the face of the seam. In mountainous terrain where the seam is exposed to the mountainside, the drifts can be driven directly into the formation.

Two basic methods are employed to remove the coal in the underground mine. The first is known as the *room-and-pillar* method in which approximately one-half of the coal is left in place as support pillars. The second method of underground mining is the long-wall system. In long-wall mining, all of the coal seam is removed centripetually inward from a large circle.

A large block of coal is left to support the shaft. In this system, the roof above the excavated area is allowed to settle as coal is removed.

In mining other types of minerals, especially some ores, the desired material flows along a *vein* embedded in igneous rock formations. Veins run horizontally, vertically, and in branches. Therefore, the underground mining must follow the vein. In mining for gold in the Rocky Mountains, the miners' tunnels may go to the left or right, or up and down to follow the lode wherever it may go. In most cases, the rock material excavated to get to the mineral is dumped at the entrance to the mine.

Surface Mining

Surface mining, also called strip mining, is employed whenever the coal seam has relatively shallow overburden, or when it outcrops along the hillside. There are four basic methods of strip mining including *area strip, contour strip, open pit,* and *mountaintop removal.*

Area Strip Mining.

Area strip mining occurs over large geographical areas typical of the interior and northern Great Plains provinces. It is characteristically used in areas with flat terrain, shallow overburdens, and thick seams. The mines require giant earth-moving equipment and must operate several years to justify the cost of the equipment.

The area strip method begins with an initial trench known as a *box cut.* The box cut exposes the seam to be removed. The excavated overburden is stockpiled to the side and will not be used to backfill until the mine is nearly completed. Successive parallel cuts are made, with the overburden cast into the box cut previously made (see Figure 1.2). The last cut leaves an exposed highwall and a deep trench until the rehabilitation process begins. The spoil piles are a parallel series of long peaks and valleys. Occasionally the seams occur in several layers separated by rock material known as *parting.* All the seams can be removed in each cut provided the seam is thick enough to justify the effort to get to it.

The process of mining with the area strip method begins with the removal of vegetation and topsoil located above the overburden. In some cases, where the vegetation is sparse, it is removed with the topsoil. The overburden is then blasted with an explosive charge, which fragments the material for ease of removal. The trenches and spoil banks are recontoured as the rehabilitation process begins. After the topsoil is spread, the mined area is then revegetated. This description of the process

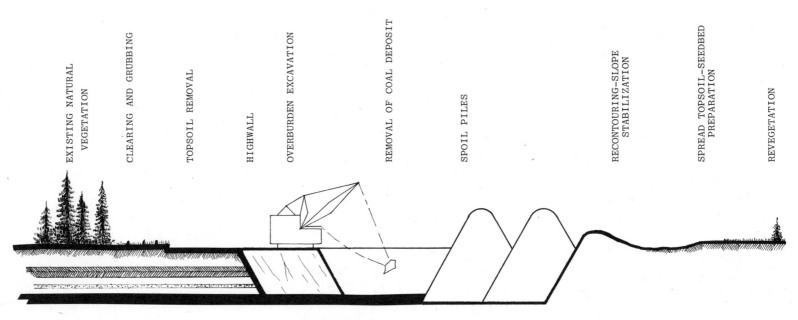

Figure 1.2. Area strip method of mining.

is offered in its most simplistic form. Considerations relative to soil chemistry, surface manipulation, and revegetation problems complicate the work in reality.

Conventional Contour Strip Mining. Contour strip mining is normally used in areas where the topography is rolling or mountainous. This method of surface mining establishes an initial cut into a hillside where an outcrop of coal or mineral seam occurs (see Figure 1.3). The *cut,* or excavation, continues along the hillside and resembles a contour line—hence the name of the method. The overburden in this method is cast on the downhill side in a variety of ways which will be discussed later. Once the overburden has been removed, the exposed, flat slope on which the seam lies is known as a *bench* or *shelf*. The bench is bordered on the downhill side by a spoil pile and on the uphill side by an exposed highwall up to 100 feet in height. The exposed highwalls and spoil piles destroy the vegetation and create tremendous visual intrusions on the landscape. Contour strip mining, for this reason, has been subject to quite a bit of criticism for environmental destruction.

The contour strip mining method buries the overburden of high quality beneath successive layers of low-quality overburden. The exposed overburden is often high in acidity and can produce disastrous pollution problems whenever it is exposed to high winds or heavy rains. With the highwall on one side and the spoil pile on the other, surface water often becomes entrapped. During heavy rains, these pools of stagnant water are more apt to enter the watershed and flow toward streams. Doyle indicates that there is an estimated 25,000 miles of contour bench in Appalachia. Of this figure, some 1,700 miles are affected by massive landslides.[3]

Open-pit Mining. Open-pit mines are essentially the opposite of contour mining in configuration. The open-pit mine has benches that are arranged in spirals or as levels with connecting ramps. The benches range in width from 25 to 125 feet. Safety considerations and the types of equipment employed in

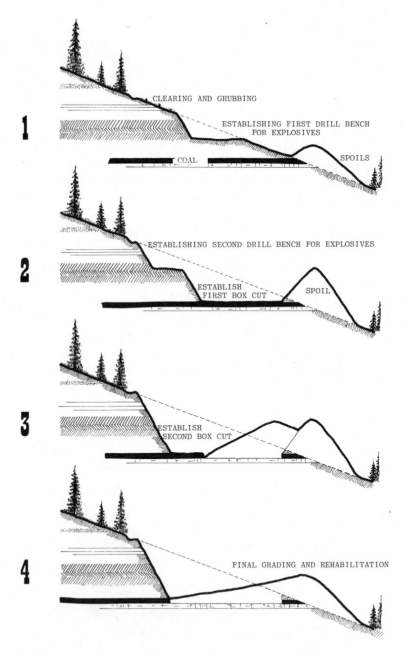

Figure 1.3. Conventional contour strip method of mining.

the mine are the determining factors in bench width. The length and gradient of the bench faces and working slopes are determined mostly by the type of rock formation found in the area. The impact of these operations can be overwhelming in scale. Ore production at a Utah open-pit copper mine approximates 100,000 metric tons per day.[4]

In open-pit mining, the non-ore material is stockpiled around the outside edges of the mine. Only when coal is found in extremely thick seams is the method used. Other forms of mining coal are generally more efficient. The open-pit mine is illustrated in Figure 1.4.

Mountaintop Removal. Mountaintop removal is a method of mining that removes the entire top of a mountain to expose a seam or mineral deposit (see Figure 1.5). It is basically the same method of area strip mining that has been adapted to mountainous or hilly terrain. In utilizing this method, a mining company is able to recover nearly 100 percent of the coal deposit. Excess overburden that cannot be retained on the site is placed in nearby valleys and depressions or on ridges.

This process begins initially with a box cut that is made parallel to the mountain ridge. A barrier at least 15 feet wide is left between the pit floor and the outslope. The barrier helps retain surface drainage and serves as an anchor for spoil piles. Overburden from the initial cut is removed and placed as described above. Overburden from successive cuts is placed in the previously excavated pit.

Chironis describes several distinct advantages that the mountaintop removal method offers, including: (1) No steep downslopes are created by the dumping of spoils; (2) highwalls are completely eliminated; (3) total resource recovery is realized; (4) rugged mountains are transformed into rolling hills and may be capable to future development; and (5) because of near total recovery, the site will not experience future mining disturbances.[5] The main disadvantage of this method is the impact of placing the overburden in the nearby valleys or *head-of-hollow* fills (see Figure 1.6).

The head-of-hollow fill is essentially a procedure whereby excess spoils are placed in nearby narrow, v-shaped, steep-sided hollows. The slopes created by this filling are then terraced to prevent erosion. Natural surface drainage is retained by employing a French drain of natural rock placed in layers on top of the original stripped surface. Downslopes are crown terraced and seeded every twenty feet to prevent erosion. The top of the entire fill is also crowned toward the highwall, if one exists.[6]

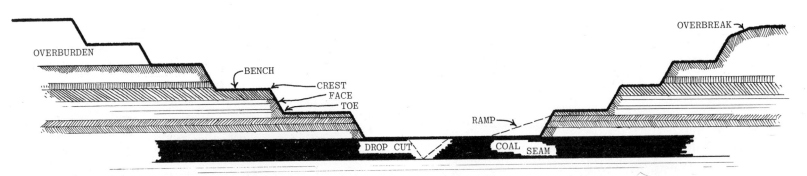

Figure 1.4. Open-pit method of mining (From Peters, W. C., *Exploration and Mining Geology*, New York: John Wiley, 1978).

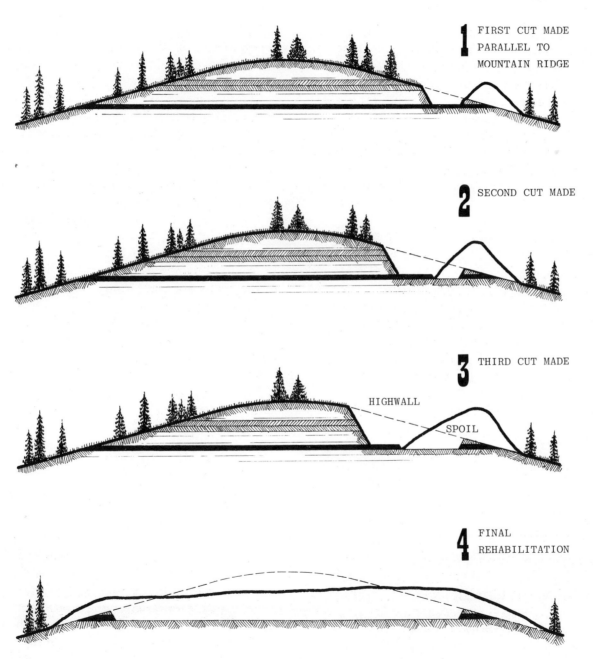

1 FIRST CUT MADE PARALLEL TO MOUNTAIN RIDGE

2 SECOND CUT MADE

3 THIRD CUT MADE

HIGHWALL

SPOIL

4 FINAL REHABILITATION

Figure 1.5. Mountaintop removal method of mining.

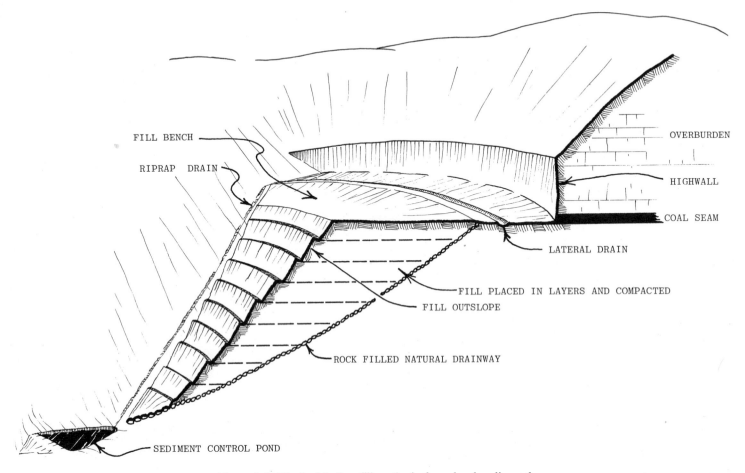

FILL BENCH

RIPRAP DRAIN

OVERBURDEN

HIGHWALL

COAL SEAM

LATERAL DRAIN

FILL PLACED IN LAYERS AND COMPACTED

FILL OUTSLOPE

ROCK FILLED NATURAL DRAINWAY

SEDIMENT CONTROL POND

Figure 1.6. Head-of-hollow fill method of overburden disposal.

Modified Forms of Contour Mining

There are scores of mining methods when one considers the variations and combinations of the alternatives listed above. The environmental impacts of the four basic forms of strip mining can be critical, especially from contour mining. Therefore, several attempts have been made to lessen the effects of contour mining by modifying the process in a variety of ways. Modified forms of contour mining include slope reduction, parallel slope, auger, modified block cut, and haulback technique.

Slope Reduction.   Ideally, by reducing the amount of spoil on and in the fill bench, the spoil is less likely to slide and erode. This theory serves as the basis for the slope reduction method as shown in Figure 1.7. In this method all of the overburden from the first cut is pushed downslope and graded to an angle less than that of the original slope. The spoils from

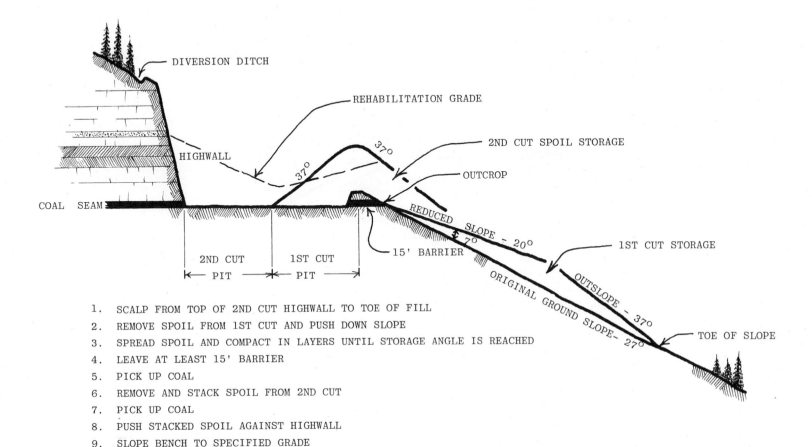

1.   SCALP FROM TOP OF 2ND CUT HIGHWALL TO TOE OF FILL
2.   REMOVE SPOIL FROM 1ST CUT AND PUSH DOWN SLOPE
3.   SPREAD SPOIL AND COMPACT IN LAYERS UNTIL STORAGE ANGLE IS REACHED
4.   LEAVE AT LEAST 15' BARRIER
5.   PICK UP COAL
6.   REMOVE AND STACK SPOIL FROM 2ND CUT
7.   PICK UP COAL
8.   PUSH STACKED SPOIL AGAINST HIGHWALL
9.   SLOPE BENCH TO SPECIFIED GRADE
10.   LEAVE AT LEAST 15' BARRIER INTACT.

Figure 1.7. Slope reduction method of mining—27° example (Adapted from Doyle, W. S., *Strip Mining of Coal,* Park Ridge, N.J.: Noyes Data Corporation, 1976).

the second cut are placed in the pit created from the first cut, as well as on the first cut pit and up against the highwall.

This method may also be used for a one cut operation, in which case 75 percent of the first cut is removed and pushed downhill and the remaining 25 percent is stacked on top of the first 75 percent. After mineral removal, the 25 percent spoil pile is pushed onto the bench and regraded in the same manner as the second cut method.

Parallel Slope. The parallel slope method is a simple modification of the slope reduction method. It begins with pushing the spoils downslope and compacting them in three foot layers at the same angle as the original slope (see Figure 1.8). The large friction plane between the original surface and the fill virtually resists any slides. Both methods, however, are subject to criticism from environmentalists lobbying for laws to prohibit the pushing of overburden on the downslope. Even

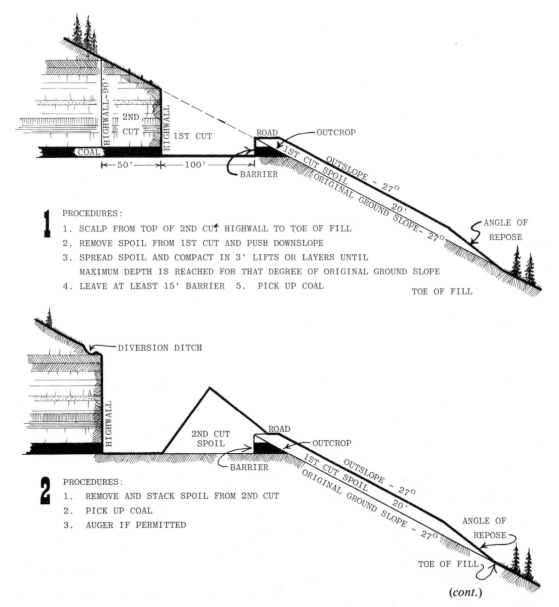

Figure 1.8. Parallel slope method of mining (Adapted from Doyle, W. S., *Strip Mining of Coal,* Park Ridge, N.J.: Noyes Data Corporation, 1976).

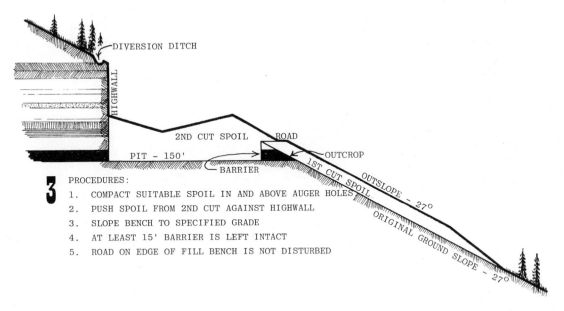

Figure 1.8. (*cont.*)

PROCEDURES:

1. COMPACT SUITABLE SPOIL IN AND ABOVE AUGER HOLES
2. PUSH SPOIL FROM 2ND CUT AGAINST HIGHWALL
3. SLOPE BENCH TO SPECIFIED GRADE
4. AT LEAST 15' BARRIER IS LEFT INTACT
5. ROAD ON EDGE OF FILL BENCH IS NOT DISTURBED

with the modified methods, the downslope fill material is non-retrievable and could likely erode into the watershed.

Auger Mining. The use of augers in mining is popular; they play a big role in contour mines, especially those located in the eastern province. Auger mining is used in conjunction with contour mining to recover additional amounts of deposit once the overburden-to-deposit ratio renders the mine incapable of producing a profitable output. Augers, which are up to 7 feet in diameter and 200 feet long, begin drilling horizontally into the seam from the bench. Because of the weight and length of these bits, the auger holes often slope downward causing portions of the deposit to be missed. Once the augering is complete, the holes must be backfilled or plugged by covering the lower portion of the highwall with spoils.[7]

Modified Block Cut Method. The modified block cut method of contour strip mining has great possibilities since it meets modern state and federal laws that prohibit pushing overburdens downslope. The initial block cut into the side of the slope establishes the width of cut, with the removal of overburden continuing until the deposit is exposed (see Figure 1.9). The spoils are placed above the highwall or spread along part of the downslope. Successive block cuts are approximately one-third the width of the initial cut and may proceed in both directions around the mountain simultaneously.

The overburden from each successive block cut is placed in the previously excavated adjacent pit as the mining continues around the mountain. Each block is mined as a separate unit, which allows concurrent regrading that nearly approximates the existing topography.

Block cut mining has many positive advantages. First, since

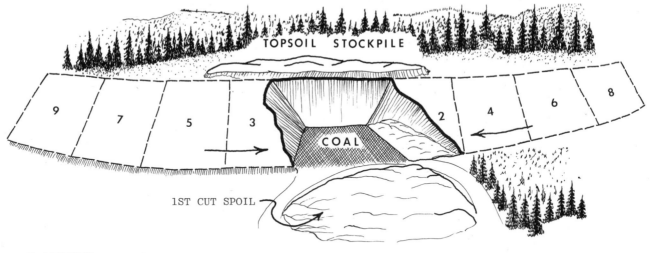

PROCEDURES:

1. SCALP FROM TOP OF HIGHWALL TO OUTCROP
    BARRIER. REMOVE AND STORE TOPSOIL.

2. REMOVE AND DISPOSE OF OVERBURDEN FROM
    CUT ONE.

3. PICK UP COAL, LEAVING AT LEAST A 15-FOOT
    BARRIER.

4. MAKE SUCCESSIVE CUTS AS NUMBERED.

5. OVERBURDEN IS MOVED IN DIRECTION OF ARROWS
    AND PLACED IN ADJACENT PIT.

6. COMPLETE BACKFILL AND GRADING TO THE APPROXIMATE
    ORIGINAL CONTOUR.

Figure 1.9. Modified block cut method of mining (Adapted from *Coal Age Operating Handbook of Coal Surface Mining and Reclamation,* Coal Age Mining Information Services, McGraw-Hill, Inc., 1978).

little or no spoils are pushed downslope, existing downslope trees can serve as a visual barrier to the operation. Second, the procedure disturbs approximately 60 percent less acres than any other technique now in use. Third, this method makes it possible to work on steeper slopes than conventional operations while still preventing slides and site disturbances. Fourth, since each block is mined individually and quickly revegetated, the environmental impacts are substantially less.

Haulback Method. This method, also known as *lateral movement,* is very similar to the modified block cut technique in that the rehabilitation and mining phase run concurrently. Overburden is stripped from one side of the cut to expose the mineral deposit. It is then placed on the other side of the cut under rehabilitation (see Figure 1.10).

The major advantage of this method is that the overburden must be handled once to accomplish the rehabilitation phase.

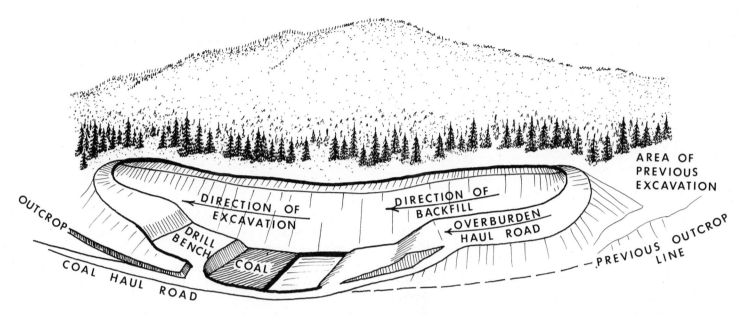

Figure 1.10. Haulback method of mining (Adapted from *Coal Age Operating Handbook of Coal Surface Mining and Reclamation,* Coal Age Mining Information Services, McGraw-Hill, Inc.).

It is of limited use, however, in areas where the gradient of the mountain is too steep to accomodate a haul road which must be constructed on the uphill side, as illustrated.

CONCLUSIONS

The art of mining is quite complicated and will vary with the type of material being mined, natural conditions in which the material is located, and the type of equipment available for use. It is beyond the scope of this chapter to acquaint the reader with all the aspects involved in mining operations. However, the more popular methods have been described and should serve as a foundation for understanding these methods and the vocabulary that one is likely to encounter in the field.

REFERENCES

1. Thomas, William L., Jr., *Man's Role in Changing the Face of the Earth,* vol. 2, Chicago: The University of Chicago Press, 1956.
2. Clements, Donald W., *Coal Surface Mining: Impacts of Reclamation,* ed. James E. Rowe, Boulder, Colo.: Westview Press, 1979.
3. Doyle, William S., *Strip Mining of Coal,* Park Ridge, N.J.: Noyes Data Corporation, 1976.
4. Peters, William C., *Exploration and Mining Geology,* New York: John Wiley & Sons, 1978.
5. Chironis, Nicholas P., *Coal Age Operating Handbook of Coal Surface Mining and Reclamation,* vol. 2, New York: McGraw-Hill, Inc., 1978.
6. Doyle, *Strip Mining of Coal.*
7. Ibid.

2
Mining Equipment

INTRODUCTION

The days of extracting minerals with ease are long past. Any resources lying close to the surface were removed long ago. The minerals in today's industry are located far below the surface of the earth or in difficult terrain. To facilitate recovery, sophisticated mechanized equipment is being used, capable of removing large chunks of rock and earth with a single bite creating tremendous impacts on natural, environmental systems.

In most mines, equipment is specially fabricated to handle specific jobs and makes the task of providing a complete inventory and analysis of all equipment impossible within the scope of this chapter. A basic understanding of various, prototypical equipment is necessary for the rehabilitation specialist to adequately plan operations with the highest degree of efficiency.

EQUIPMENT

The equipment described at this point is primarily used for mining. Equipment geared specifically for rehabilitation purposes will be described later. Mining equipment to be discussed includes:

A. Drilling rigs
B. Scrapers
C. Bulldozers
D. Front-end loaders
E. Shovels
F. Draglines
G. Bucketwheel excavators
H. Haul Trucks

Drilling Rigs

There are two general types of drilling rigs that will be discussed. The first is used to drill vertically. The second is the rig needed to drill horizontally in the auger mining operations described in Chapter 1.

Vertical Drills. In some cases, the overburden is composed of highly consolidated rock material that cannot be removed efficiently. In such cases, it is often desirable to fragment the overburden with explosives and blasting agents for easier removal. The charges must be placed into the overburden formation through the use of vertical drilling equipment. Mechanical drilling equipment comes in a wide variety of designs that range from small, hand-held models that could be used on small operations to large drills mounted on trucks, trailers, or crawlers (see Figure 2.1).

Most rigs use rotary drills with bits that either abrade, chip, or scrape the rock. Water flowing out of the bit forces the rock fragments up and out of the drilling hole. Rotary drills are em-

nitrate fuel oil (ANFO). This powdery material is detonated by using a booster of explosives, set off with electrical or non-electrical blasting caps. Blasting sequence and direction are important considerations in loosening the overburden material. The line of charges is known as an *explosive column* and is aligned along natural fissures in the rock formation. Detonation experts are needed to determine the precise placement and quantity of powder required to fracture the formation.

Horizontal Drills. The horizontal device used in auger mining operations is known as a *coal recovery drill.* This machine uses sections that are from 16 to 54 inches in diameter and up to 24 feet long. They have the capability of penetrating from 60 to 250 feet into the formation. The drills have a compound drilling head with both inner and outer cutters that are designed to remove soft coal in lumps. The coal, once removed by the auger, is conveyed on belts into trucks for transport off the contour bench.

Scrapers

Scrapers have been used in the construction industry for the last 50 years but are relatively new in surface mining, where they are used to remove and haul topsoil and overburden. Although scrapers can be loaded by other machines such as shovels or front-end loaders, they are primarily designed to be self-loading. In some mines, the scrapers and dozers are the only equipment involved in the stripping operation (see Figure 2.2).

There are two basic types of scrapers: the two axle and the three axle scraper. Each can have one diesel engine or two for more power. In steep grades, bottom-dump scrapers may have to be pushed with a bulldozer for extra power.

The most popular scraper runs with two engines and has four-wheel drive and an elevating conveyor. It is highly efficient except in areas with blocky or compacted material.

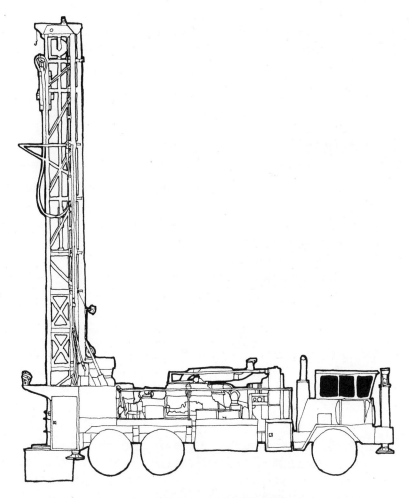

Figure 2.1. Wheeled vertical drilling rig.

ployed where deeper holes are necessary. For shallower holes, pneumatic drills may be used. These simply punch holes into the rock. Typical hole diameters range from 9 to 15 inches, with hole spacings that vary from 15 to 40 feet depending on how hard the formation becomes.

Once the holes have been drilled, they are loaded with explosives. The most common blasting agent is *ammonium*

Figure 2.2. (A) Single-engine, tandem scraper, and (B) twin-engine, tandem scraper.

Bulldozers

Bulldozers ("dozers") are essential in nearly all surface mining operations. They accomplish numerous tasks including the construction of haul roads, clearing terrain, leveling spoils and benches, pushing scrapers, ripping overburden, and rehabilitating the land.

There are two types of dozers: the tracked (crawler) and four-wheel drive, rubber-tired tractors. Crawler types are usually intended for excavation or heavy pushing. The popularity of large-wheeled tractors is increasing. The tracked types can work on steep grades and soft or muddy ground. Their main disadvantage is lack of speed, with 5 to 10 miles per hour as the maximum, which makes long hauls uneconomical.

The wheeled dozers attain a maximum speed of 20 to 30 miles per hour and are more maneuverable because of their articulated frames. They do, however, require a solid and near-level working base. Both types can be equipped with a variety of blades, buckets, and rippers. The design of the blade depends on the intended use of the machine (see Figure 2.3).

Front-End Loader

The front-end loader is an advanced development of a bulldozer that is primarily used for digging, lifting, and dumping rather than pushing. It is also called a shovel dozer, dozer shovel, tractor loader, end loader, front loader, or just loader. The loader may be carried by any type of tractor. Four-wheel drive and crawler tractors are used for heavy service. Smaller, two-wheel driver tractors are employed for lighter work. For added maneuverability, tandem models are becoming widely used (see Figure 2.4).

The relationship between the bucket size and power of a tractor is the major consideration in selecting a model for use in mining. Some tandem, four-wheel drive tractors have as

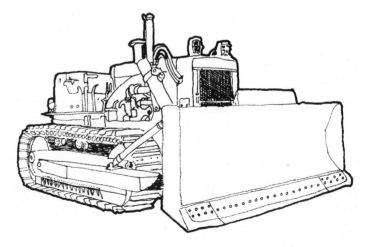

Figure 2.3. Standard bulldozer with pushing blade.

Figure 2.4. Tandem, rubber-tired front-end loader.

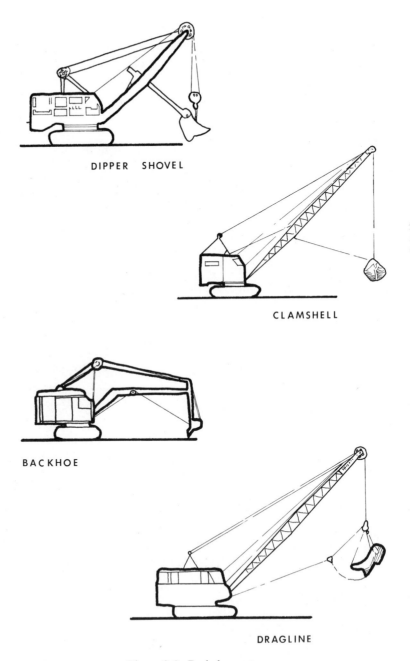

Figure 2.5. Basic boom types.

much as 1,200 horsepower. The buckets on the larger models are strongly reinforced and have a capacity of over 20 cubic yards. The bucket must be strong enough to take any punishment the tractor is able to deliver, but light enough to raise a big load without overbalancing the tractor and without absorbing too much lifting power.

The loader is used in the mine for a wide variety of tasks. It is most often used in situations where material must be loaded into trucks, usually coal but also rock and earth material not picked up by the overburden removal phase. It can also be used to transport material if the haul is not too lengthy.

Shovels

The stripping shovel has three structural parts. The top part is the revolving unit. The second part consists of the mounting or travel units, and the third, the boom attachments. The revolving and travel unit compose the "basic shovel." The four types of booms are known as dipper shovel (or dipper stick), backhoe, dragline, and clamshell (see Figure 2.5). Since draglines are major implements in mining and rehabilitation, they will be discussed separately.

The most popular shovel, other than the dragline, is the dipper attachment. The typical bucket on the dipper is a welded steel box that is open on the top and is closed on the bottom with a hinged door. Digging is accomplished by the front top edge which is reinforced by a lip. The bucket is subject to severe wear and is constructed of alloy steel. The teeth on the bucket are of manganese steel.

The largest shovels used in coal mines are powered by 7,200 volts of electricity. The power is fed to the machine through a *tail* or *trail cable* 5 inches in diameter and 5,000 to 15,000 feet long. The alternating-current motors that power the main generators total up to 9,000 horsepower. The machine uses as much electricity as a typical community of 15,000.[1]

The dipper has a capacity up to 220 cubic yards and a boom length up to 220 feet. The boom has a fixed angle of approximately 50 degrees and a maximum digging radius of 218 feet. The maximum dumping reach is 200 feet and dumping height is 140 feet. The shovel primarily operates at the bottom of the excavation.[2]

Shovels are most popular in shallow overburden and deposit removal. They can offer lower operating costs than draglines or bucketwheel excavators of equal size, where conditions are appropriate and operator skill is high. A high level of skill is mandatory in obtaining maximum production from the shovel.

Draglines

These huge machines operate from the top of highwalls to remove deep overburdens. They can effectively work large areas from one location because of their long boom length (up to 400 feet) and large-capacity buckets with a maximum of 220 cubic yards (see Figure 2.6).

The major differences between this machine and shovels are the method of mobility and extraction techniques. Shovels are mainly mounted on a large tracked base or crawler, whereas large draglines move by "walking." During overburden excavation, the dragline rests on a large ballast-filled "tub" which is up to 100 feet in diameter.

Once excavation is complete, two retractable pontoons are lowered to the ground. Pontoons for a medium-sized dragline may be 10 to 15 feet wide and 60 to 70 feet long. The pontoons are lowered in such a fashion that the support points fall behind the dragline's center of gravity. A hydraulic system can move the pontoons laterally from front to back as well as vertically. Once the pontoons begin to lift the dragline, it slides or walks forward. Large units can move up to 10 feet in one step. Like shovels, these draglines are also electrically powered.[3]

Bucketwheel Excavator

The bucketwheel excavator has been used in Europe, primarily Germany, for many years. Its use in the United States, however, has been uncommon until recently. These electrically powered machines are the largest, most complicated, and productive available in surface mining today. Under favorable conditions—soft overburdens or deep deposits—these continuous miners can excavate up to 2,000 cubic yards in one hour. Their extended conveyor system can allow spoils to be piled up to 400 feet away from the machine.

Bucketwheel excavators move on multiple crawlers and have two primary booms (see Figure 2.7). The digging boom carries the cutting wheel. The second boom has a discharge conveyor in which to dispose the cuttings. Both booms are mounted on a revolving superstructure. The booms may extend for hundreds of feet in both directions. The conveyor system can be extended and is capable of discharging the cuttings into a haul truck or to a spoil pile.

Haul Trucks

Trucks are the most versatile machine utilized in hauling mineral deposits in surface mines. They come in all shapes and sizes with some bottom dump models capable of carrying a

Figure 2.6. "Walking" dragline.

load of 150 tons or 175 cubic yards. Rear dump trucks for most mining situations, are in the 35 to 85 capacity, or 30 to 75 cubic yards.

Relatively new on the scene are trucks powered by electric wheels. These trucks have a diesel engine which powers a generator, which in turn powers an electric traction motor located in the tire hubs. This unique design eliminates U-joints, differentials, clutches, and power transmissions.

Figure 2.7. Bucket wheel excavator.

The operator controls are simplified to a foot-operated throttle; a dynamic and hydraulic brake; a range selector with three gears, forward, neutral, and reverse; and a steering wheel.

Other models employ four-wheel drive systems and articulated bodies. One unique hauler has an unusual steering unit allowing nonstop 180 degree turns. Suspended on nitrogen-filled compression chambers, it can attain speeds up to 40 miles per hour loaded and 55 miles per hour unloaded.

Generally, bottom dump trucks are used where ramps have gentle grades and long-distance hauling is involved. Rear dumps, on the other hand, are used where steep roads and tight maneuvers are necessary (see Figure 2.8). Rubber tires

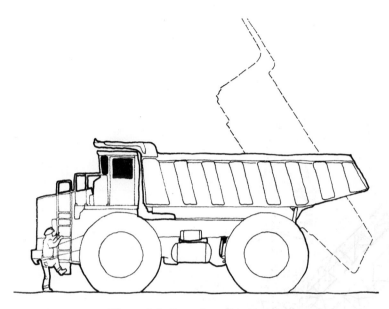

Figure 2.8. Rear dump haul truck.

are typical on most of the hauling trucks and can account for up to 20 percent of a truck's operating cost. In many tires, excess heat build-up due to high speeds can cause the tire to collapse. Goodyear Tire and Rubber Company has developed a speed formula that effectively reduces rubber tire problems.[4]

CONCLUSIONS

As a mining company begins to plan a mining operation, a major concern is what equipment is needed. The equipment represents a major capital outlay that must be expended prior to beginning the operation. Therefore, the most efficient equipment is employed—in some cases, having the capacity to move enormous volumes of rock and earth material. The danger of massive destruction of the area's natural resources should also be considered. Recent legislation has given as much priority to repairing the damage as to the removal of the resource.

In the next section, the environmental effects of various mining methods and equipment will be investigated. Knowledge of the machinery's capability can be used for rehabilitation as well as mineral extraction.

REFERENCES

1. Nichols, H. L., *Moving the Earth—The Workbook of Excavation,* 3d ed., Greenwich, Conn.: North Castle Books, 1976.
2. Chironis, *Coal Age Operating Handbook,* vol. 2. New York: McGraw-Hill, Inc., 1978.
3. Ibid.
4. Ibid.

PART II
ENVIRONMENTAL
IMPACTS OF MINING

3
Cultural Impacts of Mining

INTRODUCTION

The environmental impacts of mining operations are extremely complex. Entire volumes could be devoted to cover the subject, but this book will focus on three spheres that make up the environment. The first sphere, the subject of this chapter, is the cultural or anthropomorphic effects of mining. The next two chapters will discuss the geological and biological effects, respectively.

The reader must realize that this division is made to focus attention on each sphere independently. The environment, however, is composed of an intricate relationship among the three. The balance or well-being of any one depends on the well-being of the other two.

Longgood, in his book entitled *The Darkening Land,* describes the impact that past crimes against the environment by the mining industry have had on the quality of human life in the Appalachian region.

The assault on coal was particularly disastrous and permanent. Some of the delayed effects are only now being felt—and paid for. Exploitation of men and material was rampant as deep mines were dug and often collapsed because of the failure to provide safeguards. Hundreds of miners died ghastly deaths. No compensation was given those who became ill. Coal that could be taken cheaply and easily was removed and new cuts were begun elsewhere. Abandoned mines were left unsupported and often uncharted. Today these huge underground caverns and linking tunnels are caving in. Often they cause houses and buildings on the surface to collapse and foundations to crack.

Two million acres in twenty-eight states—much of it in Pennsylvania—have collapsed in this form of subsidence, according to the government. A million more acres are expected to sink by the year 2000. But there is no one to sue. The mine operators long ago made their fortunes, and decamped. Now the bill must be paid by the government—a delayed additional bounty to the mine owners from the taxpayers. Millions are being spent to relocate families. Millions more are being spent to fight the (underground) fires. The government has already spent over $15 million to control mine fires in the Appalachians. Two years ago Pennsylvania allotted $200 million to fill in abandoned strip mines and fight underground blazes. This is part of the hidden cost of the cheap goods produced from that cheap energy that American Industry boasts of."[1]

While recent legislation has curbed gross negligence, the rehabilitation specialist must realize that extreme care must be taken to lessen the effects of mining operations on a long-term basis. Three aspects of the cultural sphere of the environment will be discussed: economics, health, and aesthetics.

ECONOMICS

The mountains of Colorado are the home of many ghost towns—remnants of a past civilization devoted to the mining of various minerals found in the area. Why did these towns grow, blossom, and die? The answer lies in the intricate relationship among natural resources, economics, and human activity. The desire to extract minerals from the earth's surface has an economic impact on a community. Wali expressed some problems attendant on coal development as a response to the energy shortage in the model presented in Figure 3.1.[2]

Coal development and strip mining are a direct result of energy shortages which stimulate prices high enough for a predicted profit. As the mining operation gets under way, certain cultural and biological impacts begin to take place—some of which are long-lasting or even irreversible.

The human community has often been described as a complex living organism that is conceived, grows, matures, declines, and dies. Most authorities agree that the well-being of a community is directly related to economic factors. The author, in a previous study, developed a model (Figure 3.2) that illustrates the relationship among the natural resources of a community, economics, and human activity.[3] The various elements of the model are discussed below.

Natural Resources

Most urban economists agree that the extent to which a city is large and well-developed is directly related to its natural resources. Goodman points out that of the seven urban areas of the United Kingdom, six are located close to coal beds and the seventh, London, is a port open to the lowlands and Europe.[4]

Basic Industry

Foremost in the study of the model is *basic industry,* defined as those industries and services that produce goods for people living outside the region being studied and that brings in money to pay for food and raw materials that the area does not produce itself.[5] Basic industry is usually industry that extracts minerals, or processes them largely because of the industry's unique location to the source of raw materials. The location of a basic industry can also be determined by the market (exports) or the availability of a *nonbasic industry* (producers of goods and services).

Exports

Exports are developed out of need. In most cases, demand for a product develops because of two factors—scarcity and technology. The mining industry has recently blossomed because of energy shortages throughout the world. The impact on communities in the West, illustrated in the Prologue, is primarily the consequence of the energy crises of the seventies and eighties.

Technology has also had its impact. With the machinery described in Chapter 2, a mining enterprise has the opportunity to extract resources with a maximum of efficiency and profit.

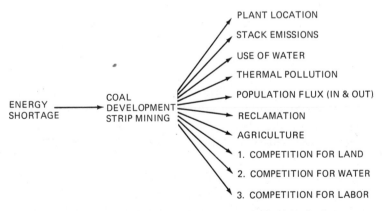

ENERGY SHORTAGE → COAL DEVELOPMENT STRIP MINING

- PLANT LOCATION
- STACK EMISSIONS
- USE OF WATER
- THERMAL POLLUTION
- POPULATION FLUX (IN & OUT)
- RECLAMATION
- AGRICULTURE
1. COMPETITION FOR LAND
2. COMPETITION FOR WATER
3. COMPETITION FOR LABOR

Figure 3.1. Impacts from energy shortages, (© Reprinted, with permission, from *Practices and Problems of Land Reclamation in Western North America,* ed. M. K. Wali, The University of North Dakota Press, Grand Forks, 1975).

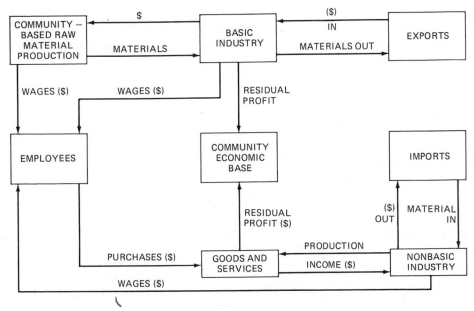

Figure 3.2. Community economic model.

Employees

Companies in basic and nonbasic industries hire employees because of their demand for the human resources necessary to turn raw-material into finished goods. It is the employees, both management and workers, that comprise the social and economic community. Employees are inspired by the anticipated wages of industry or the expected return on investment and will follow personnel demands created by industrial development.[6]

Nonbasic Industry

Nonbasic industry is composed of those businesses that exist for the purpose of offering goods and services to employees of basic industry and is usually a spinoff of the growth of basic industry. As basic industry grows, so does the need for goods and services. The system at this point becomes self-perpetuating when one element of the industrial whole attains the level necessary to maintain the other element.[7]

Community Economic Base

Community economic bases result from residual profits from the operations of basic and nonbasic industries. Residual profits are mean incomes produced above the expenses necessary for operation. It is, for example, money from exports that is equal to a sum greater than the sum needed in the basic industry for raw materials and wages for employees and executives.[8]

The economic base generally appears in two forms, one, investments, and the other, culture. Investments result in the expansion of industry, speculation, or capital building. As an industry's profits increase, certain decisions have to be made with regard to what is to be done with the earnings. The industry might use the money to expand its operations and ultimately raise the margin of profit. It might use the funds for speculative investments in the form of stocks, bonds, securities, and certain development enterprises, or for investment loans.

Culture only appears in communities that can devote time to promote its development, that is, communities that exist well above the level of mere necessity. A community that must devote its entire efforts to ensure its physical existence has neither energy nor time enough for the development of culture. Cultural forms include art, religion, and more complex forms of government, such as a welfare system.

In discussing the impacts of mining on the economic well-being of a community, one must realize the important balance that exists between the various elements within the economic model. Too many times, when a large mining operation opens, there is a lag between the development of basic industry and the development of nonbasic industry, which results in housing shortages, high prices at the supermarkets, crowded streets and avenues, crowded schools, poor sanitation systems, and so forth. Life cannot be comfortable until nonbasic and basic industries reach a state of equilibrium. This, in the author's opinion, is one of the major hazards to be associated with large-scale mining development in places, for instance, like Gillette, Wyoming.

The Aftermath

What happens to the economic environment when the basic industry goes flat? The residents of famous Battlement Mesa, Colorado, could probably address that question. In May 1982, Exxon Oil decided that the vast shale oil project near Battlement Mesa was too costly to realize a profit and closed the mining operation. As a result, the thousands of residents of that community, which was still under construction, pulled up stakes and left overnight. Battlement Mesa is now the most modern ghost town on the face of the earth. Without a basic industry extracting the natural resources, the other elements that comprise the model have no need to function.

HEALTH AND SAFETY

Downs describes the impact that mining has on the physical health of individuals by postulating two basic categories of hazards: direct and indirect.[9]

Direct Hazards

These hazards mostly affect the safety of miners or persons living in the immediate area of the mining operation. Past disregard for the safety of miners has brought about tremendous pressure to regulate the activities of the mine operator to insure the safety and welfare of the workers. However, public safety can still be threatened by the following hazards:

A. Sudden failure of certain mining facilities such as reservoirs, waste dumps, tailings lagoons, and open-pit sidewalls. On October 21, 1966, in Aberfan, South Wales, a huge spoil pile known as "tip 7" slipped down a 600 foot grade, killing 144 people. Of those killed, 116 were school children.

B. Major subsidence associated with underground mining. The major problem today lies with old abandoned mines whose stability or existence may be unknown.

C. Shafts, inclines, adits and open pits to which the public has access. Again, old mines that predate the legislation controlling such practices pose the most serious threat. They become particularly serious when water from the water table fills the caverns or pits.

D. The release of toxic effluents into either the air or waterways. Of particular interest in the Appalachian region of the United States is *acid mine drainage* (AMD). Acid mine drainage has deteriorated water quality along more than 10,000 miles of streams in the Appalachian area.[10] Problems occur when water and air react with sulfur-bearing minerals in mines or spoil piles to form sulfuric acid. AMD also contains toxic metals such as copper, lead, zinc, and cadmium. Sediment yields from strip mining operations in the United States may range up to 30,000 tons/mile^2/year.[11]

E. The use of explosives. *Flyrock,* the material propelled into the air by an explosion, poses a definite threat to persons living or working in the area.

F. Transportation hazards. Generally, the volume of traffic is greatly increased by mining operations involving large trucks or conflicts between rail and road.

Indirect Hazards

Less easy to detect are those hazards that if persistent over a period of time, can affect the health and safety of the general public. According to Downs, there are four factors that affect the extent of impact, including:

A. Size of operation
B. Geographical and locational factors
C. Method of mining
D. Mineral characteristics[12]

Major mining pollutants include:

A. Organic material (sewage)
B. Oils
C. Cyanides
D. Acids/alkalis
E. Base metals
F. Florides
G. Soluble salts
H. Processing reagents
I. Color
J. Suspended solids
K. Turbidity
L. Thermal
M. Radioactivity[13]

There are two types of pollution, including *point source* and *nonpoint source.* Point source pollution is identified as that pollution with concentrated emission from a particular point in the atmosphere or drainage system. Nonpoint pollution is emitted from a large area and its source is difficult to identify. These indirect hazards appear mostly in the form of air pollution and water pollution.

Air Pollution

The main pollutants from mining are suspended particulates —solid and liquid particles arising into the atmosphere from combustion, abrasion, or disturbance.[14] There are several types of suspended particulates including carbon monoxide (CO), hydrocarbons (HC), and oxides of nitrogen and sulfur (NO_x, SO_x). Carbon monoxide is a result of the incomplete combustion of hydrocarbons in internal combustion engines. Hydrocarbons arise from partial combustion of fossil fuels. Nitrates and sulfates are created by burning fossil fuels, especially those containing sulfur.

Water Pollution

Water pollution can occur in several ways. The dumping of effluents and wastes has already been discussed. However, water can be polluted by altering its state in ways, other than chemically, that are mostly process related, including such things as increasing sediment load, raising of water temperature discharged into streams, percolation, leaching, groundwater interception, and spillages. The effects of downstream distance on pollution concentration are shown in Figure 3.3. The kinds of water that can be polluted include flowing water,

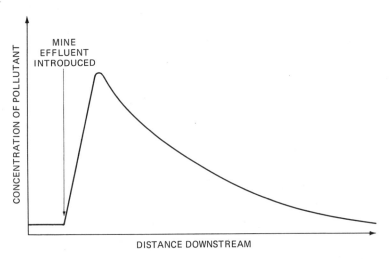

Figure 3.3. Effects of downstream distance on pollution concentration (From Downs, C. G. and J. Stocks, *Environmental Impact of Mining,* New York: John Wiley & Sons, 1977, p. 103).

standing water, and groundwater. The length of time that pollution remains in suspension varies with each type. Standing water retains pollution much longer than does flowing water. Dissolved pollutants that enter the groundwater system, as a general rule, are very long-lived and cannot be readily flushed out as with flowing water.[15]

AESTHETICS

The most obvious impact from mining is surface disturbance; some of the pollutants or hazards mentioned previously are not always visually obtrusive. Aspects of mining with a serious visual impact include excavations, spoil piles, plants, refining facilities, and increased linear disturbances, such as roads and pipelines.

Although landscape architects have been quite involved over the past decade in the search for an objective way to determine visual disturbances, much work and research in the area of visual resource analysis must still be done. Many public agencies, such as the Bureau of Land Management and the Forest Service, have developed standard methods to be used in connection with the land that they manage. It is the author's opinion that land being mined merits a unique system of visual resource analysis.

The process developed explicitly for the rehabilitation of oil and gas fields on Wyoming public lands is suggested. It should be noted that the visual environment has several elements which can be altered by man's mining activity, which include:

A. Landform
B. Vegetation
C. Water
D. Color
E. Adjacent scenery
F. Scarcity or uniqueness
G. Lack of disturbance or purity of scenery

Readers who wish to know the method used by the Bureau of Land Management to assess the visual impact of mining activities on these factors can write to the Bureau of Land Management, P. O. Box 1828, Cheyenne, Wyoming 82001, and ask for *REHAB: Oil and Gas Field,* Oil and Gas Technical Bulletin no. 1 by Dennis L. Law, Lester L. Linscott, and Richard L. Hopkins.

CONCLUSIONS

The economic, health, and aesthetic impacts of mining are of critical concern to the rehabilitation specialist. They can directly affect the well-being of man or can subtly play a role in an indirect manner. An attempt has been made to identify the issues, not how to mitigate the problems, which will be covered in later chapters. The rehabilitation specialist should have a well-established background in matters of economics, health, and aesthetics in order to make sound land use decisions since his actions can affect the lives of several generations.

REFERENCES

1. Longgood, William, *The Darkening Land,* New York: Simon and Schuster, 1972, p. 296.
2. Wali, M. K., *Practices and Problems of Land Reclamation in Western North America,* Grand Forks: University of North Dakota Press, 1975, p. 4.
3. Law, Dennis L., *A Methodology for Implementing a Downtown Pedestrian Mall for Plainview, Texas,* Master's thesis, Kansas State University, 1976, p. 5.
4. Goodman, Paul, and Percival Goodman, *Communitas,* New York: Random House, 1960, pp. 11, 12.
5. Blumenfeld, Hans, *The Modern Metropolis,* ed. Paul Spreiregen, Cambridge, Mass.: The M.I.T. Press, 1971, p. 335.
6. Goodman, *Communitas,* pp. 119–131.
7. Blumenfeld, *The Modern Metropolis,* p. 340.
8. Thompson, Wilbur R., "Growth and Development of Small Urban Areas," *Taming Megalopolis,* ed. H. Wentworth Eldridge, Garden City: Doubleday and Company, 1967.
9. Downs, C. G., and J. Stocks, *Environmental Impact of Mining,* New York: John Wiley & Sons, 1977, p. 13.
10. Canter, Larry W., *Environmental Impact Assessment,* New York: McGraw-Hill, Inc. 1977, p. 92.
11. Ibid.
12. Downs, *Environmental Impact of Mining,* pp. 20–26.
13. Ibid., p. 89.
14. Ibid., p. 59.
15. Ibid., p. 104.

4

Geological Impacts of Mining

INTRODUCTION

There is a strong relationship between changes in geology and the fate of various living organisms that inhabit the earth's surface. Whenever the outer geological mantle is disturbed by surface mining, there is a direct impact on the biological world. This chapter is devoted to a better understanding of what changes take place in the geological part of the environment. We shall see in the next chapter how these changes affect the biological world.

There are coal reserves under 128 million acres in the western United States. With current methods, 1.5 million acres can be economically surface mined.[1] To meet increasing coal consumption, 140 square miles will be disturbed by 1990. That figure will jump to 300 square miles by 2000.[2] Over 2,000 square miles have been disturbed to date in the eastern coal fields of the United States.[3] This figure represents a sizable impact on the geology of our nation.

There are two major categories of geological disturbances: *pedological* (having to do with soils) and *hydrological* (having to do with surface and ground water).

PEDOLOGICAL DISTURBANCES

Erosion

Surface mining's major impact on soils is *erosion*. Erosion is the group of processes whereby earthy or rock material is worn away, loosened, or dissolved, and removed from part of the earth's surface. It includes the processes of weathering, solution, corrosion, and transportation. Erosion is often classified by the appearance of the eroded area. Of all the eroding agents, water, which detaches and transports soil, is by far the most frequently encountered.

The impact of raindrops on a soil surface causes soil particles to be dislodged, especially under conditions of heavy rainfall. The detaching action of the raindrop is an important part of the erosion process. Raindrop impact and the resulting splash can throw a soil particle as high as two feet and move it horizontally four or five feet. A very heavy rain may detach as much as 100 tons of soil from an acre of exposed surface.[4]

The following terms are used to describe different types of water erosion:

Accelerated erosion: Erosion much more rapid than normal, natural, or geologic erosion, primarily a result of the influences of the activities of man or, in some cases, of other animals or natural catastrophes that expose base surfaces, such as fire.

Geological erosion: The normal or natural erosion caused by geological processes acting over long geologic periods and resulting in the wearing away of mountains and the building up of floodplains and coastal plains.

Splash erosion: The spattering of small soil particles caused by the impact of raindrops on wet soils. The loosened and spattered particles may or may not be removed subsequently by surface runoff.[5]

Sheet erosion: The removal of a fairly uniform layer of soil from the land surface by runoff water.

Rill erosion: An erosion process in which numerous small channels only several inches deep are formed. This occurs mainly on recently cultivated soils.

Gully erosion: The erosion process whereby water accumulates in narrow channels, over short periods, and removes the soil from this narrow area to considerable depths, ranging from 1 or 2 feet to as much as 75 to 100 feet.[6]

Soil particles become *sediment* when they are detached and moved from their initial resting place. If sediment washes into neighboring watercourses, it becomes a resource out-of-place and a pollutant by definition. The various types of erosion are illustrated in Figure 4.1.

The Impact of Erosion

Special efforts to prevent surface erosion are warranted, especially in view of the fact that repair of erosion damage is one of the most expensive recurring costs on rehabilitated sites. A representative rate of erosion at an abandoned surface mine is 2,400 tons per square mile, which is 100 times greater than an equal area of forest. The erosion at an active surface mine is 48,000 tons per square mile, 2,000 times greater than for an equal area of forest.[7] Sediment load originates from areas being cleared, grubbed, and scalped; roadways; spoil piles; areas of active mining; and areas being rehabilitated. It appears that erosion rates are highest during dump (spoil) construction and during the time from final shaping to the establishment of a protective vegetative cover. In the West, this typically takes one year. One of the most important threats to the physical in-

tegrity and ability of resurfaced spoils to support plant growth is surface erosion.

Soils that contain finer particles and are less compacted obviously will be subject to heavier erosion losses than coarse-textured or compacted soils. Topsoil is generally a little more stable than is spoil material because of aggregation.[8]

The detrimental effects from erosion runoff include:

A. Occupying water storage in reservoirs
B. Filling lakes and ponds
C. Clogging stream channels
D. Settling on productive land
E. Destroying aquatic habitats
F. Creating turbidity that detracts from recreational use of water and reduces photosynthesis
G. Degrading water for consumptive uses
H. Increasing water treatment costs
I. Damaging water distribution systems
J. Acting as a carrier of other pollutants such as insecticides, herbicides, and heavy metals
K. Acting as a carrier of bacteria and viruses[9]

The success of efforts to control erosion when operating on steep slopes is especially uncertain. The principal difficulty is stabilizing the spoil after mining. Although returning the material to its original position on the soil foundation of the bench increases the stability of the land cover, it still may have a greater tendency to slide or erode than in its previous undisturbed state. There appears to be substantial doubt as to whether slopes greater than about 25 percent can be permanently restored. About one-third of Appalachian strip-mined output came from slopes steeper than 25 degrees in 1971. About 80 percent of the strippable reserves in that region appear to be on slopes of under 25 degrees.[10]

At area strip mines, the spoil cast below the outcrop line usually has the greatest potential for causing off-site sediment damage. Contour mines have a narrow linear geometry and, therefore, more spoil area drains directly into the off-site

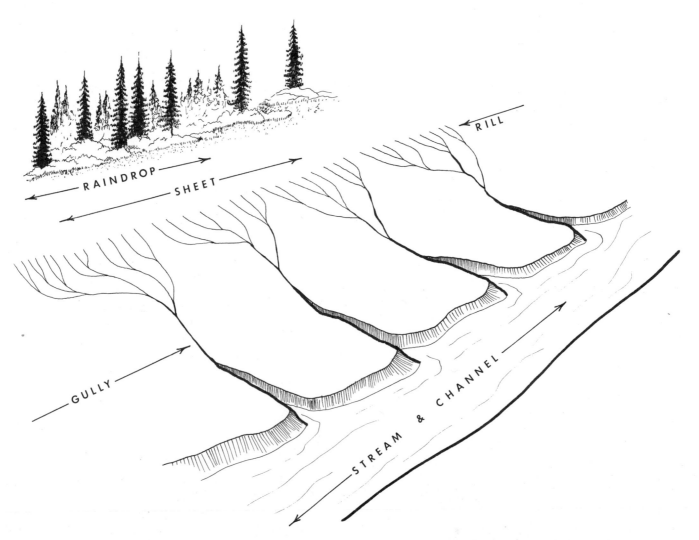

Figure 4.1. Types of erosion (Adapted from *Michigan Erosion and Sedimentation Control Guidebook,* Lansing, Mich.: Department of Natural Resources, 1975, p. 8).

drainage system. The bench area being actively mined often drains directly into the off-site drainage system.[11]

The most critical areas at a mountaintop removal site are the spoil slopes around the perimeter of the site, roadways ex-tending from the mine and valley, or head-of-hollow fills. The fills are especially critical because they are placed in drainage-ways, and, consequently, are highly susceptible to *piping* (sub-surface removal of soil) and landslides.[12]

Roadways constructed outside the actual mine site to gain access to the operation are a major source of sediment pollution and erosion over the life of the mine, and often beyond, if proper control measures are not employed. Long access roads significantly disrupt the natural drainage system. They intercept, concentrate, and divert surface runoff.

The Environmental Protection Agency has estimated that an unmined watershed will typically yield 28 tons of sediment per square mile. A spoil bank will yield 27,000 tons per square mile, and a haul road, 57,000 tons per square mile.[13]

Topsoil

Topsoil is defined as the presumed fertile soil material capable of supporting substantial vegetative growth. It is a unique geobiological environment capable of supporting not only vegetation, but a wide variety of other living organisms including microorganisms.

Topsoil is either synthetic or geologic. Synthetic topsoils can include sand, stone chips, flyash, sawdust, or manure which is not usually a part of the geological process. Geologic, or weathered topsoil, is created by weathering of parent rock material throughout geologic time. Geologic topsoil forms in two directions. As parent rock material weathers, topsoil is formed downward. A build-up of organic material as debris from vegetation and animals builds topsoil from above (see Figure 4.2). Topsoil construction is an extremely long process. How valuable topsoil is can be measured by the centuries that it takes to form. It should be preserved at all costs.

The handling of topsoil is crucial in the rehabilitation process, and its stockpiling has been the subject of a lot of research in the past few years. According to Downs, topsoil undergoes a marked deterioration and acidification whenever it is stored improperly or for too long a period of time. The deterioration is caused by anaerobic decay of the organic matter in the stockpile.[14]

Overburden

It is generally recognized that total destruction of the current soil pattern is an inevitable result of mining. It is impossible for the soils to be preserved or reconstructed to their original form once mining has been completed.

Soils are classified by the percentage of sand, silt, or clay they contain and vary widely across the United States. Soil classification is determined by texture. In the western United States, fine-textured soils prevail for the most part. Clay soil predominates in the Midwest and the East. Each of these soil classifications is characterized by certain chemical properties, which influence the chemical reactions that occur as a result of mining. The fine-textured soils of the West are high in sodium and have a high pH. Those in the Midwest and the East have acid clays, sandstones, or shales, and toxic levels of metals.

In mine rehabilitation, the establishment of plant material and the protection of surface and groundwater supply from chemical pollution are of highest priority in rehabilitating the site. The chemical analysis of the spoil or overburden is critical to rehabilitation. Guidelines for chemical analyses and standards for toxicity levels are established by each state, although Montana's guidelines are used by many states.

Generally, soil analyses take the following into account:

A. pH
B. Electrical conductivity
C. Base-saturation percentage
D. Exchangeable-sodium percentage
E. Texture
F. Cation exchange capacity
G. Organic matter

pH.   The pH of a soil is the indicator of its level of acidity or alkalinity. pH ranges on a scale from 0 to 14 with 7.0 being neutral. If the pH is lower than 7.0, the soil is considered to be acid. If the pH is higher than 7.0, the soil is basic or alkaline.

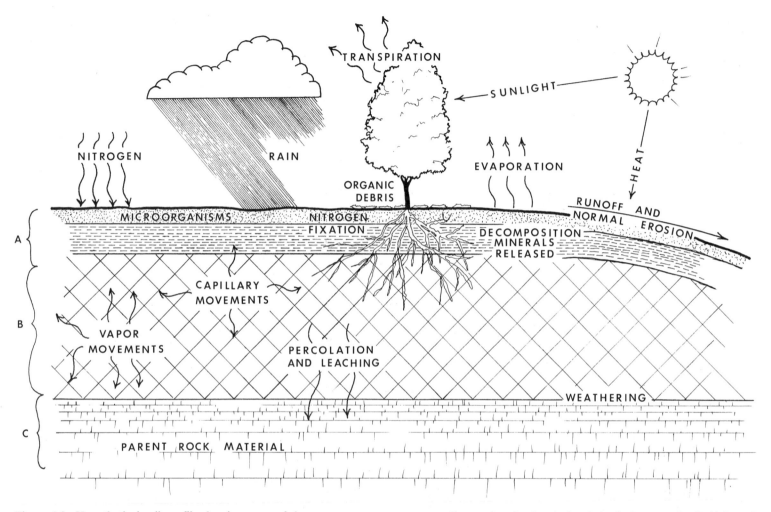

Figure 4.2. Hypothetical soil profile showing some of the more common processes tending to alter the chemical and physical nature of soils (Adapted with permission of Macmillan Publishing Co., Inc., from *Basic Concepts of Ecology* by Clifford B. Knight, Copyright © 1965 by Clifford B. Knight).

Most plants prefer slightly acid soils. However, in the West, some of the native vegetative species require alkaline soils. Most rehabilitation problems occur when the pH is below 3.0 or greater than 8.5. The pH scale is logarithmic. The intensity of acidity of alkalinity changes tenfold with each unit change in pH. For example, a pH of 9.0 is ten times more alkaline than the pH of 8.0 and a pH of 10.0 is 100 times more alkaline than a pH of 8.0.[15]

The most critical soil characteristic in determining revegetative practices is the pH. Nutrient levels are dependent on certain pH thresholds. The acceptable pH ranges for plants being considered for revegetation should be identified.

Electrical conductivity. The electrical conductivity is a measure to determine if the soil is *saline-sodic* (containing salts). There are four classifications for electrical conductivity, presented in Table 4.1.

Table 4.1. Classifications for Electrical Conductivity.

0–4 millimhos/centimeter	none to slight
4–8 millimhos/centimeter	moderate[a]
8–16 millimhos/centimeter	strong[b]
>16 millimhos/centimeter	very strong

[a]Many grasses are affected in this range.
[b]Only use salt-tolerant grasses.
Source: USDA Agriculture Handbook no. 60, 1954.

Base-saturation percentage. Soil is made up of molecules that are electrically charged called *ions*. Ions with a positive charge are called *cations,* and those with a negative charge, *anions*. Atoms with a positive charge are attracted to atoms with a negative charge. In soils, this concept is important when considering the ability of a certain type of soil to attract or release elements.

Of particular interest are two groups of absorbed cations that have opposing effects on soil acidity and alkalinity. One group, made up of hydrogen and aluminum atoms, tends to dominate acid soils and contribute to the concentration of $H+$ ions in the soil solution. All other cations comprise the second group. These are called *exchangeable bases* and have the ability to neutralize soil acidity. The proportion of the cation exchange capacity occupied by these bases is called the base-saturation percentage. Therefore, if the percentage base saturation is 60, three-fifths of the exchange capacity is satisfied by the bases and two-fifths by hydrogen and aluminum.

There is a strong relationship between the base-saturation percentage of a soil and its pH. As the base-saturation percentage is reduced by the drainage of calcium and other metallic constituents, the pH is also lowered. This is why leaching leads to more acidic soils.

Exchangeable sodium percentage. The exchangeable sodium percentage is a criterion used to differentiate an alkaline from a nonalkaline soil. The exchangeable sodium percentage must be greater than 15 for the soil to be classified as alkaline. Again, revegetation decisions are based on this criterion, especially in plant material selection.

Texture. The texture of soils is based on the size distribution of the particles comprising the soil. Texture is classified into three kinds; clays, silts, and sands. The percentages of each of these in a particular soil determines that soil's texture.

Texture governs two critical factors. The first is the *water-holding capacity* and *permeability*. Clay soils are so tight that they retain nearly 100 percent of water, whereas sand retains very little. Both extreme conditions are detrimental to plant life. The pores within the soil are important because they not only hold water but also gases essential to plant life. Pores are divided into two groups: *macropores,* which are large like those contained in sand, and *micropores,* which are small, like those typically found in clay. Sandy soils are composed mainly of macropores that supply needed gases but cannot hold adequate water, which leads to dehydration. Clay soils will hold adequate water, but not the gases necessary to plant growth. This is why *loamy,* or mixed, soils are best for plant growth.

Cation exchange capacity. *Cation exchange capacity* is a measure of the soil's ability to absorb cations. Cations, held on the surface of the soil particle by a weak bond, are readily available to plants as nutrients for growth. The higher the cation exchange capacity, the greater amount of nutrients and, thus, the better the plant growth.

Organic matter. Organic matter in the soil promotes structure and is a source of nutrients for plants. Soil is divided into four classes based on percentage of organic matter: 0 to 1% is considered low; 1.1 to 3.0%, medium; 3.1 to 10%, high; and greater than 10%, very high. Organic material serves as a nitrogen source and is necessary to good soil structure.

Suspect levels. The state of Montana has established a series of *suspect levels,* or levels that approach a serious pollution or health hazard. These levels, which are presented in Table 4.2, have been used by other states in establishing tolerance thresholds. These thresholds should be used in testing overburden material to prevent degradation of water quality and plant production.

HYDROLOGICAL DISTURBANCES

Water Cycle

Water bodies cover approximately two-thirds of the earth's surface. Proportionately, this amount is needed to maintain sufficient water vapor for overland condensation, which we know as *precipitation*. The water evaporates and is moved inland by prevailing winds, as illustrated in Figure 4.3. According to Leopold, there are three basic causes for condensation:

A. Water vapor is cooled to the *dew point,* or temperature at which the vapor becomes liquid, when the air mass containing the vapor moves over mountains into cool air zones.

B. A vapor-laden warm air mass collides with a cool or cold air mass.

C. Vapor-laden air is warmed sufficiently to cause it to rise vertically to higher, cooler temperature zones.[16]

In addition to evaporation, water also enters the atmosphere through *transpiration*. Transpiration is the movement of water into the atmosphere from plants. Plants offer tremendous sources of water vapor supply. Leopold, for example, suggests that an acre of corn gives off to the air approximately 3,000 to 4,000 gallons of water each day.[17]

Once water vapor has reached the dew point and falls to the earth's surface, it reaches the ocean by two primary routes. First, it flows downward through underground streams called

Table 4.2. Montana Department of State Lands Guidelines for Suspect Levels in Overburden Material.[a]

ANALYSIS	SUSPECT LEVEL
Conductance	> 4–6 mmhos/cm
Sodium absorption ratio	> 12
Mechanical analysis	clay > 40%
	sand > 70%
Saturation	none
pH	> 8.8–9.0
PO_4-P	none
NO_3-N	> 10–20 ppm
NH_4-N	> 10–20 ppm
Cd	> 0.1–1.0 ppm
Cu	> 40 ppm
Fe	unknown
Pb	pH < 6, > 10–15 ppm
	pH > 6, > 15–20 ppm
Mn	> 60 ppm
Hg	> 0.4–0.5 ppm
Se	> 2.0 ppm
Mo	> 0.3 ppm
B	> 8.0 ppm
Zn	> 30–40 ppm
Ni	DTPA extraction, > 1.0 ppm
	acid extraction, > 5.0 ppm

[a] From Dollhopf, D. J., W. D. Hall, W. M. Schafer, E. J. DePuit, R. L. Hodder, *Selective Placement of Coal Stripmine Overburden in Montana,* vol. I, Bozeman, Mont.: Montana Agricultural Experiment Station, 1977, p. 43.

aquifers, and second, it flows overland in streams and rivers. After water enters the ocean, the cycle begins anew. Usable water can only be retrieved whenever the water is on the land surface or in the ground. The water cycle is like an intricately balanced system. Life as we know it depends on both the quantity and quality of fresh water. This system must be maintained in its natural state as much as possible. Tampering with it could lead to disaster. The two primary forms of water flow will be studied and the effects of mining on the system will be explored.

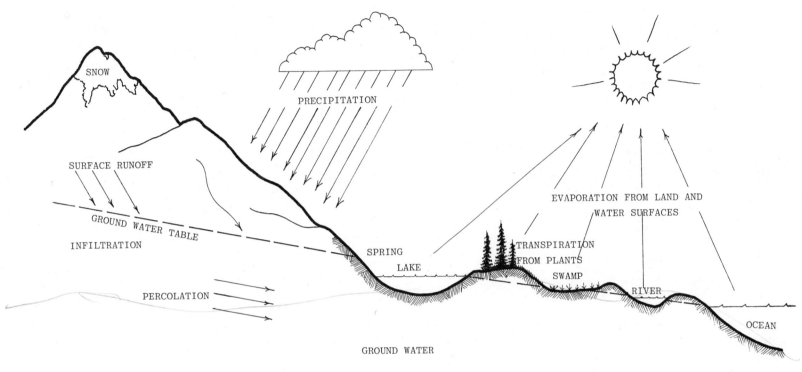

Figure 4.3. The hydrologic cycle.

Groundwater

Surface water becomes groundwater whenever it enters the ground through infiltration. The areas with geologic formations conducive to infiltration are called *aquifer recharge zones* (see Figure 4.4). A recharge zone promotes infiltration primarily because of its type of soil. Coarse-textured, porous soils have the highest infiltration rate as shown in Table 4.3. The porous soil or rock formation must also be stratified in such a way as to slope into the aquifer. Water moves into and through an aquifer by two primary forces, *capillarity* and *gravity*. Capillarity is the tendency for water to cling to the surface of a particle because of surface tension. The water moves, therefore, from surface to surface and gradually saturates the particles. This movement can be upward and outward as well as downward. Sandstone is one of the primary geological rock formations that serves as an aquifer. The

Table 4.3. Relation of Soil Texture to Infiltration Rate.

SOIL	INFILTRATION RATE OF WET SOIL (INCHES PER HOUR)
Sandy loam	1.42
Sandy clay loam	1.22
Clay loam	1.07
Clay	0.86

Source: Leopold, Luna B., *Water: A Primer,* San Francisco, Calif.: W. H. Freeman & Co., Copyright © 1974.

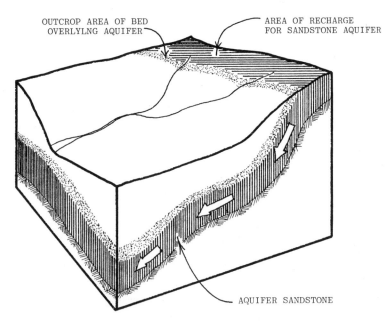

OUTCROP AREA OF BED
OVERLYLNG AQUIFER

AREA OF RECHARGE
FOR SANDSTONE AQUIFER

AQUIFER SANDSTONE

Figure 4.4. Relation of recharge area to aquifer. Water bearing layer, or aquifer, is shown both underground and where it crops out at the earth's surface (U.S. Geological Survey).

water table is the top of the zone of saturation within the aquifer.

The National Academy of Sciences reports that in most western coal fields, the coal beds that lie close to the surface are also aquifers.[18] By removing the coal, the mining operation would intersect the aquifer, cutting off the source of water for wells in the immediate area. The intersection of an aquifer can result in several adverse impacts that are worth noting. First, the flow patterns in the aquifer can be changed, and in some places, the aquifer can become dewatered. Second, if the aquifer is exposed in the highwall, water can flow into the mining pit and then have to be pumped out. Overland flow causes increased erosion, especially for water flowing in *ephemeral* streams (a channel that only flows after a storm). Third, water quality can deteriorate both in the aquifer and in surface flow.

Of particular concern would be the preservation of aquifer recharge zones. The entire groundwater system is dependent on the replenishment of the water source. If the recharge area is destroyed, the aquifer is doomed. These areas should be identified and protected in order to preserve this part of the sensitive hydrological cycle.

Surface Water

Precipitation can occur in many forms including rain, snow, ice, or dew. Its form is directly related to the way the water re-enters the atmosphere. Snow, for example, is the most likely form of water to enter an aquifer because its runoff and evaporation are slow. Rain, however, has an immediate run-off and is likely to flow into a series of channels to make its way back to the ocean.

Streams are generally classified into three types. The *ephemeral stream* channel is usually dry, only flowing with water after a storm. The second classification includes *intermittent streams,* which flow during certain seasons of the year. Third, water flows in *perennial stream* channels year-round, with the possible exception of an occasional brief dry period.

The *watershed,* or *drainage area,* is that area from which water drains to a single point. It is made up of a series of dendritic patterns of channels that are divided into segments called *orders.* The initial channel high in the watershed is called a *first-order stream.* Two or more first-order streams flow together to form a *second-order stream.* This gives rise to third-order streams, which flow together to form fourth orders, and so on (see Figure 4.5).

Water tends to flow in sheets until a sufficient quantity of water with enough volume and velocity gives rise to channelization. Flowing water has a tremendous effect on the landscape. The sediment that it delivers is abrasive to the earth's surface, and as the water flows, there is a continual cutting and depositing. The meander of a stream creates a tremendous amount of energy against the outside of the curve. The outside

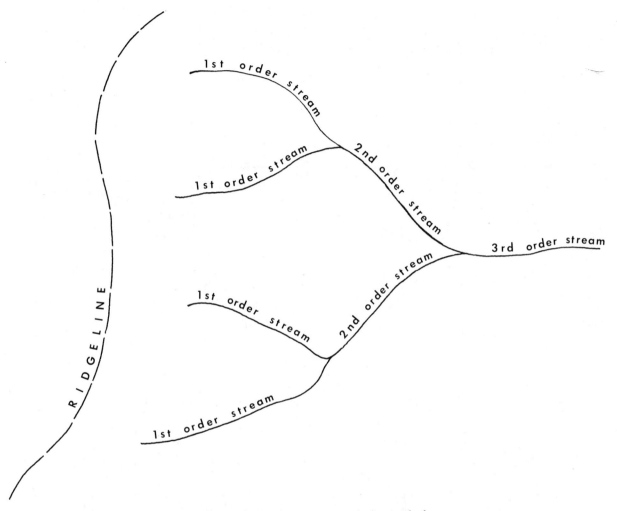

Figure 4.5. Stream orders of a typical watershed.

of the curve, therefore, continues to be cut, while on the inside of the curve, *alluvial soils* are deposited (see Figure 4.6).

Erosion and deposition are natural phenomena. The forces that give rise to channelization tend to be in dynamic equilibrium with the forces that resist channelization. Therefore, any mining process that alters the surface flow interferes with the natural processes involved in hydrology. The off-site impacts from surface mining include:

A. Changes in surface flow volume. This includes both increases and decreases. Increased flow contributes to:
 1. Downcutting and widening of stream channels

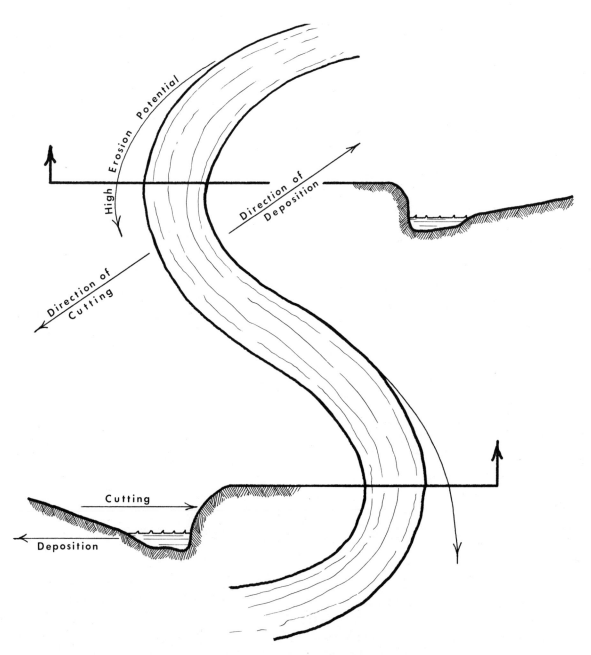

Figure 4.6. Cutting/deposition forces on typical stream meander.

2. Depleting tributary channels of water because the flow elevation of major streams has been downcut
3. Increased sediment load
4. Increase in flow velocity
5. Destruction of aquatic habitat

B. Deterioration of water quality
C. Channel changes caused by an increase in sediment yield
D. Increase in endemic diseases among users of water that has been contaminated by the mining operation

It is imperative that surface flow remain undisturbed as much as possible. Alluvial valley floors and stream channels must be left intact. Alluvial deposits are particularly susceptible to erosion because the soil material is unconsolidated. The removal of alluvium from a valley floor creates a situation where the water table is lowered and the protective vegetation cover is destroyed. Both these results drain soil moisture, with potentially catastrophic effects.

REFERENCES

1. National Academy of Sciences, *Rehabilitation Potential of Western Coal Lands,* Cambridge, Mass.: Ballinger Publishing Co., 1974, p. 2.
2. Ibid.
3. Ibid.
4. Environmental Protection Agency, *Erosion and Sediment Control, Surface Mining in the Eastern U.S.,* vol. I, *Planning,* EPA Technology Transfer Seminar Publication. Washington, D.C.: Government Printing Office, 1976, p. 23.
5. U.S. Department of Agriculture (USDA), *User Guide to Soils Mining and Reclamation in the West,* USDA Forest Service General Technical Report INT-68, Ogden, Utah: Intermountain Forest and Range Experiment Station, 1979, p. 69.
6. Ibid.
7. Environmental Protection Agency, *Erosion and Sediment Control,* p. 5.
8. U.S. Department of Agriculture, *User Guide to Soils,* p. 60.
9. Environmental Protection Agency, *Erosion and Sediment Control,* p. 23.
10. Mintz, Robert, *Ecology Law Quarterly,* vol. 5, no. 3, 1976, p. 461.
11. Environmental Protection Agency, *Erosion and Sediment Control,* p. 10.
12. Ibid., p. 11.
13. Ibid., p. 7.
14. Downs, *Environmental Impact of Mining.*
15. Vogel, Willis G., *A Guide for Revegetating Coal Minesoils in the Eastern United States,* USDA Forest Service General Technical Report NE-68, Broomall, Pa.: Northeast Forest Experiment Station, 1981, p. 11.
16. Leopold, Luna B., *Water, A Primer,* San Francisco, Calif.: W. H. Freeman and Co., 1974, p. 5.
17. Ibid., p. 6.
18. National Academy of Sciences, *Rehabilitation Potential,* p. 45.

5
Biological Impacts of Mining

INTRODUCTION

The biological world is a complex and highly varied system of organisms whose population patterns are held in intricate balance. A discussion of all the realms of biology and ecology as they relate to mining is certainly beyond the scope of this chapter and could well be a book by itself. To understand rehabilitation processes, however, certainly requires a basic knowledge of ecological principles. The rehabilitation specialist should become intimately familiar with the various interrelationships that compose the biological community in the area in which he is working. This chapter, which is dedicated to basic principles, will address two general bodies of knowledge, including biotic communities and ecosystems.

BIOTIC COMMUNITIES

Ecological Succession

The earth's surface is constantly changing in a variety of ways. Forest or range fires cause sudden changes in the vegetative community and thus affect soils, hydrology, and wildlife. An earthquake or landslide exposes large portions of parent rock material to the atmosphere which cannot immediately support vegetation without an organic base. And mining, especially strip mining, can have the same effect. Whatever the cause, the familiar biological world at first appears to have been

banished from these disturbed areas. After a long series of changes the biological world eventually reaches a stage of stability wherein natural changes, called *succession,* are rare. When disturbed lands are reoccupied, the first organisms to do so are called *pioneers*. The first pioneer species are quite opportunistic and serve an extremely valuable purpose. The establishment of initial pioneer species alters the immediate environment. The pioneers provide shade, organic debris, and an altered soil structure. These, in turn, provide an opportunity for other organisms to become established that would not have done so immediately following the disturbance.

There are two types of succession. *Primary succession* takes place when the ground has been disturbed to such an extent that viable soil has been destroyed or is nonexistent. *Secondary succession* results when the land has been disturbed but the soils basically left intact. On minded lands, successions generally start with ground-up rocks and qualify as primary succession unless the topsoil has been stockpiled and redistributed. This factor is the single greatest distinguishing characteristic of rehabilitation processes that are secondary and of those that are primary. In terms of the successional time required to establish a stabilized plant community, the use of topsoil can save decades or even centuries of work by the biological community.

Without topsoil, ground-up rock lacks the qualities of soil and will not become soil until it becomes chemically weathered to free the nutrients needed by plants and until humus from plant and animal debris becomes abundant. This is a much slower process than the case of secondary succession. It must be emphasized that soil is the most critical factor. It comprises a mineral component and both inert and living organic components. The degree of a soil's development limits the biotope it supports.[1]

Pioneer communities are made up of a limited number of species types. Over time, plant species best adapted to the altered microenvironment will establish themselves and become dominant. As other, more permanent species establish themselves, the pioneer species will decrease. Species that invade an abandoned mine site are usually found in the vicinity of the disturbed area.

Ecological Stability

Changes within the biotic makeup of an area will continue to occur until it reaches a stage of dynamic equilibrium that persists over long periods of time. This point is called *climax* and can be recognized by a relatively constant species composition and structure.[2] Generally speaking, stable communities are self-perpetuating and possess the ability to withstand considerable environmental stress without a dramatic change in floristic composition or community structure. Climax communities generally have high species diversity. Unstable, primitive communities are highly susceptible to stress because of the low diversity in species populations. These factors are particularly important in selecting revegetation species during the rehabilitation processes.

Vertical Stratification

The location of a plant or animal within the community is called a *niche*. Temperature, light, and oxygen demands vary from organism to organism and play a major role in the development of niches. It must be pointed out that niches are three-dimensional in form. Organisms not only occupy space in land area, but also occur in vertical, stratified layers (see Figure 5.1). These give rise to overstory, understory, and ground-covers in the plant kingdom. The plants requiring greater sunlight and dryer environments will occupy the upper strata while those plants requiring shade and high humidity will occupy the lower strata. The same stratification holds true for animals such as fish in a lake. The basic requirements for wildlife include food, water, cover, and living space (territory). The availability of each of these dictates the type of niche that will exist for a particular organism.

Latitude and Elevation

There is a definite correlation in niche development between latitude on the earth's surface and elevation above sea level. There is a striking difference in plant and animal species as one moves north or south from the equator. The same principle occurs when one moves into higher elevations (see Figure 5.2).

The two main factors that account for this correlation are temperature and precipitation. As one moves up a mountain in the tropics, vegetation can be found that also exists on a valley floor further north.

The principles of ecological succession, stability, stratification, and latitude/elevation reflect the complicated nature of natural plant and animal placement within the environment. With successful revegetation efforts in rehabilitation, wildlife should succeed rather well. The rehabilitation specialist should make every effort to create a biologically balanced environment by use of native material whenever possible. This prescription will be discussed in greater detail in Chapter 10.

Case Example

In an area that has been mined and abandoned with the overburden spoils left intact, the successional process is extremely slow. The initial invader species in the primary succession

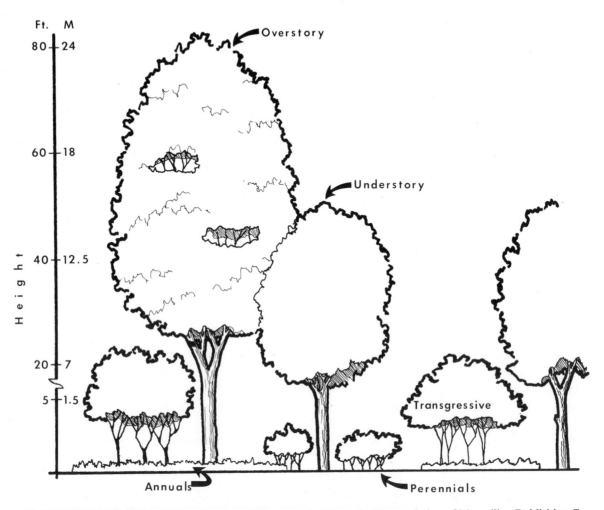

Figure 5.1. Stratification of vegetation in a deciduous stand (Adapted with permission of Macmillan Publishing Co., Inc., from *Basic Concepts of Ecology* by Clifford B. Knight, Copyright © 1965 by Clifford B. Knight).

would be a series of lichens such as *Grimmia laevigata*. Acids produced by the lichens would help weather the rock and, along with the debris and soil blown into the voids, develop a situation where moss (*Polytrichum sp.*) could invade. Eventually, a large variety of small annuals would invade followed by biennials and finally perennial grasses such as *An-dropogon*. Following the establishment of grasses, small shrubs such as sumac (*Rhus sp.*) become common. If environmental conditions, especially climatic, are ideal, coniferous evergreens such as Eastern Red Cedar (*Juniperus virginiana*) or Eastern White Pine (*Pinus strobus*) become the next inhabitants.

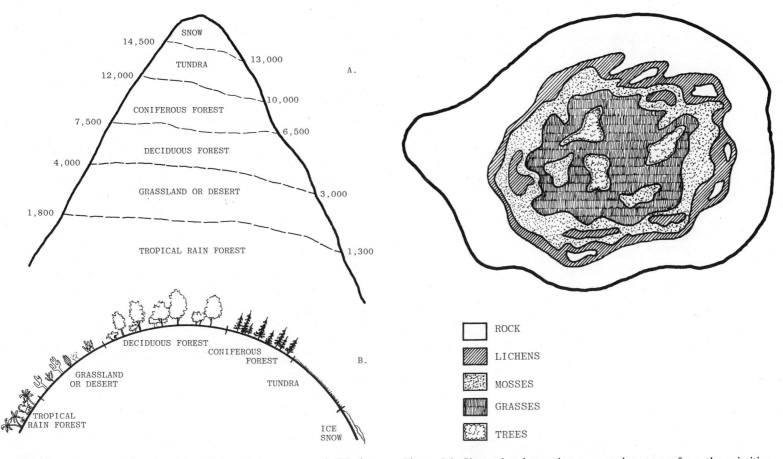

Figure 5.2. Vegetational zonation in (A) montane areas, and (B) the similarities with latitudinal zonation. Note that vegetational zones vary in altitudinal extent and location, depending on whether they are located on a north- or south-facing slope. Elevations in (A) are in feet (Adapted with permission of Macmillan Publishing Co., Inc., from *Basic Concepts of Ecology* by Clifford B. Knight, Copyright © 1965 by Clifford B. Knight).

Figure 5.3. Vegetational zonation on a rock outcrop from the primitive pioneer community of lichens around the outer edge to more advanced stages (trees) located in the center of the outcrop where the soil is thickest (Adapted with permission of Macmillan Publishing Co., Inc., from *Basic Concepts of Ecology* by Clifford B. Knight, Copyright © 1965 by Clifford B. Knight).

The final, climax community would be made up of a hardwood forest composed of oak-hickory varieties. The successional process takes place in concentric circles as pointed out by Knight.[3] This concept is illustrated in Figure 5.3. This example assumes that the surface material left after mining is only rock material. This whole process can take from 6 to 10 centuries to occur. The time of succession can be greatly reduced if some soil material is left in the area. It can be further reduced if topsoil is placed on the site immediately after mining. The process might only take 1/5 of the time needed without topsoil. The successional sequence can also be short-circuited by sowing or planting desirable species that are high in the successional ladder. This remains as one of the rehabilitation specialist's major goals—to shorten the necessary time required to achieve a climax or near-climax community.

ECOSYSTEMS

The makeup of various ecological communities is determined by several factors. They include:

A. Climate
B. Atmosphere
C. Temperature
D. Light
E. Soil
F. Soil water
G. Physiography
H. Biotic composition
I. Fire

Climate

Climate is defined as the average course or condition of the weather at a particular place, over a period of many years, as exhibited by the absolute extremes, the means, and the frequencies of given departures from these means of temperature, wind velocity, precipitation, and other weather elements.[4] Of all the climatic variables, two emerge as having significant, primary roles in ecological development: precipitation and precipitation patterns.

Precipitation. Effective precipitation depends on six factors: intensity, duration, distribution, air and ground temperature, wind velocity, and relative humidity.[5] The rehabilitation specialist would be ill advised to use annual precipitation as the only criterion for selecting plant materials for rehabilitation. The six factors given above should all be taken into account. The relative importance of each of these may vary with geographic location, physiography, physical soil factors, and plant cover.

Precipitation patterns. In most areas of the United States, precipitation rates vary from season to season. Along the West Coast, for example, precipitation rates are highest in the winter and very low during the summer. In the northern Great Plains, however, the opposite is true. Most of the precipitation there comes in June and tapers to a low in the winter. This information becomes important as one selects the time of year in which planting or seeding should take place in revegetation efforts.

Atmosphere.

Composition. The atmosphere is composed of several gases including nitrogen (78.09%), oxygen (20.93%), argon (0.93%), and carbon dioxide (0.03%).[6] Nitrogen is essentially nonusable by plants or animals in its molecular form. Nitrogen compounds, however, are formed from the air and made available to plants. The plants that absorb nitrates create a much more complex protein molecule.[7]

Carbon dioxide, though not abundant in the atmosphere, serves as a critical ingredient in the photosynthetic process. Oxygen is also a product of the photosynthetic process. It is given off in the presence of light (transpiration), whereas carbon dioxide is continually given off. The rehabilitation specialist can do little to simulate or duplicate the chemical composition of the atmosphere. However, the atmosphere can be polluted to such a degree from noxious fumes that alter its composition that the specialist would have to consider plant materials with appropriate tolerances.

The atmosphere also contains water vapor, whose concentration can vary from just below 1 to as much as 4 percent.

Water vapor is not the same thing as humidity, which is minute droplets of condensed vapor. *Relative humidity* is the amount of moisture in the air expressed as a percentage of the amount the air can hold at any given temperature. Any temperature change will affect the relative humidity. Moisture is one criterion that can be manipulated in rehabilitation. Many projects, in order to insure a degee of success, irrigate whenever either the relative humidity or other forms of precipitation is too low.

Temperature

Lapse rate. Air temperature decreases as altitudes increase at a rate of approximately 1°F per 300 vertical feet.[8] This is known as the *lapse rate* and is due primarily to two reasons. First, as it moves away from the earth, the air is also moving away from its major source of heat. Second, there is a decrease in the density of air molecules as the altitude increases. The molecules, therefore, are less likely to warm each other or collide, creating heat-producing friction. This accounts for the species differentiation as one moves up a mountain slope. Humphrey suggests that the temperature variations could decrease at a rate of 10°F per thousand foot difference.[9]

Soil temperatures. Germination rates are most dependent on soil temperatures which may vary for several reasons, including:

A. Soil color
B. Soil moisture
C. Aspect or exposure
D. Insolation (receiving of solar radiation)
E. Plant cover
F. Snow cover
G. Frost heaving

The rehabilitation specialist should make every effort to determine the germination season for a particular site in selecting varieties and planting dates.

Light

Light is defined as the portion of the radiant-energy spectrum that is visible to the human eye[10] and that ranges from 400 to 700 millimicrons. The entire radiant-energy spectrum varies in length from 290 to 5,000 millimicrons.[11] Because photosynthesis also takes place in the 400 to 700 millimicron range, light is critical to revegetation.

Plants vary in their ability to efficiently use light. Those that thrive in bright light are called *heliophytes*. Those that require shade are called *skiophytes*. If the desired climax species on a rehabilitation project are skiophytes, the revegetation efforts must first be directed to fast-growing heliophytes and the successional process allowed to naturally take place. In certain seed mixtures, one may attempt to mix in a few skiophytes with the heliophytes to speed up the successional process.

Soils

It is certainly beyond the scope of this portion of the chapter to adequately describe the complex role of soils in the ecological development of a certain site. We will attempt, however, to briefly describe the various soil types, soil nutrients, and rehabilitation considerations.

Soil types. Soils are classified according to genesis or development and include three primary types: *zonal, intrazonal,* and *azonal*. Soils are developed from an interplay between several forces, including such things as geology, climate, vegetation, relief, wildlife, and age.

Zonal soils. Most soils are zonal in nature and reflect climate and vegetation in their development. There are basically three types of zonal soils. First, soils typically found in forested areas, particularly conifers and conifer-hardwood mixes, are called *podzol soils*. The second group of soils, known as *chernozem soils,* are found in grasslands and are developed under climatic and early pyric conditions.[12] These soils are deep and abundant in humus. The third zonal soil is called *desert soils.* These develop in areas where climate prevents abundant plant growth.

Intrazonal soils. These soils are quite often found associated with zonal soils and occupy limited or restricted areas. They are mostly formed by local factors including parent material or physiography. Intrazonal soils include *bog soils, planosol soils,* and *rendzina soils.* Bog soils develop in swampy regions with poor aeration; planosols in flat, humid to sub-humid regions where an underlying hardpan develops, and rendzinas in limestone regions adapted to grasses.

Azonal soils. These soils differ from zonal and intrazonal soils in that they possess no marked distinguishing morphological characteristics. This is probably due to an insufficient amount of time in which to develop or from a climate or parent material not conducive to soil maturity.

The soils genesis or classification can be quite specific to a particular site. This, in the author's opinion, is the single most important criterion to be used in the revegetation process. A detailed soils analysis is a must, as is a consultation with a soil scientist to adequately plan rehabilitation processes.

Soil nutrients. Plants require certain elements from the soil for plant growth. These include nitrogen, phosphorus, potassium, carbon, oxygen, hydrogen, sulfur, calcium, iron, and magnesium. In addition, there are some microtrace elements that are needed including boron, copper, molybdenum, cobalt, iodine, selenium, and zinc. The rehabilitation specialist needs to have a thorough knowledge of revegetation plant requirements and to correlate them with the available nutrients. Needed elements can be easily added to insure proper plant establishment.

Soil Water

Water is an essential part of the soil composition. Soil is basically composed of matter in three states: solids, liquids, and gases. The solid portion remains rather constant while the liquids and gases fluctuate in reciprocal fashion. As liquids increase, the gases decrease.

Water exists in the soil in several states including gravitational water, capillary water, hygroscopic water, bound water, and water vapor.

Gravitational water and field capacity. When soil is completely saturated to such an extent that it can no longer hold additional water, it is said to have reached *field capacity.* Additional water, that which runs off the surface by gravitational pull, is called *gravitational water.*

Capillary water. At field capacity, there is an adhesive or cohesive force called capillary tension that attracts water molecules to the soil particles. *Capillary water* is what is mostly used by plants. Capillary water is constantly moving, although very slowly. The water moves from areas of low tension forces to those of higher tension forces. It can also be said that water moves from high vapor-pressure (relatively wet) areas to low vapor-pressure (relatively dry) areas. The movement of capillary water can occur in any direction. When capillary water is removed from the soil because of evaporation or transpiration and is no longer available to plants, the soil is said to have reached the *wilting point.*

Hygroscopic water. There is a thin film of water that clings to the soil particle even when all the capillary water has been removed. This water is known as *hygroscopic water.* It is not normally available to plants. It can, however, evaporate and condense in the soil as capillary water.

Water vapor. Water vapor moves from warm soils to cold soils. As a gas, it will condense into a liquid whenever it comes in contact with a cool soil particle or rock. Plants cannot survive once the wilting point has been reached. In many cases, the wilting point does not occur because of the cyclic condensation of water vapor as the soil becomes cooled in the evenings. This is critical in some of the arid areas where rainfall is below 10 inches per year. As land becomes disturbed during the mining process, those pockets of space in the soil structure are opened up and areas where water vapor is generally locked in place are exposed. The unconsolidated soil in regraded spoils has a much higher tendency to become dry for longer periods of time.

Physiography

Physiography is the science of landform or configuration of the earth's surface. It pertains to elevation, topography, direction of exposure, and insolation. Physiographic factors affect plant and animal life indirectly through their effects on such factors as light, temperature, moisture, and soils.

Biotic Factors

Biotic factors have been presented in the earlier portions of this chapter. However, it is significant to point out here that there is a variety of interdependencies which account for the success of biological life. An example would be the intricate relationship that plants and animals have with each other in the food chain. All animals ultimately depend on plants for survival. Even carnivores depend on prey that are herbivores. The rehabilitation specialist should have a thorough knowledge of the relationship of one organism to another.

Fire

Certain plant species are able to survive fire, whereas others are destroyed by it. It must be remembered by the reader that fire is a natural phenomenon. In the author's opinion, there needs to be research conducted as to the effects fire has in the rehabilitation process as a means to selectively eliminate unwanted species. Until such research is conducted, man will probably not know the extent of its constructive use in rehabil-

itation and may even slow the revegetative processes down with haphazard use.

CONCLUSIONS

Mining creates impacts on nearly all aspects of natural biological life. Opportunistic species, which first colonize disturbed lands, are followed by successively more equilibrated species. If the process continues without disturbance over a period of time, a self-perpetuating climax community often develops. In the latter stages, species richness increases, food webs become more complex, and the transfer of energy and the cycling of materials tend to become more efficient. During mining disturbances, the equilibrial species suffer disproportionately, and communities revert back to earlier, less-diverse successional stages that are dominated by opportunists. The rehabilitation specialist should make an attempt to shorten the time it takes to reach climax in the various biological communities.

REFERENCES

1. Curry, Robert R., "Biogeochemical Limitations on Western Reclamation," *Practices and Problems of Land Reclamation in Western North America,* ed. Mohan K. Wali, Grand Forks: University of North Dakota Press, 1975, p. 21.
2. Mueller-Dombois, Dieter, and Heinz Ellenberg, *Aims and Methods of Vegetation Ecology,* New York: John Wiley & Sons, 1974.
3. Knight, Clifford B., *Basic Concepts of Ecology,* New York: Macmillan Company, 1971, p. 280.
4. Humphrey, Robert R., *Range Ecology,* New York: The Ronald Press Co., 1962, p. 6.
5. Ibid., p. 7.
6. Ibid., p. 19.
7. Ibid., p. 20.
8. Ibid., p. 26.
9. Ibid., p. 27.
10. Ibid., p. 40.
11. Ibid.
12. Ibid., p. 53.

PART III
REHABILITATION:
SURFACE
MANIPULATION

6
The Impact of Erosion

INTRODUCTION

Erosion control is one of the most expensive recurring costs in the rehabilitation of mined lands and warrants special efforts to minimize its effects. Occasionally, state and federal laws govern the amount of sediment loss that is acceptable. In these cases, the sites have to be carefully monitored to insure compliance with the standards dictated by the law.

Table 6.1 provides insight into the impact of erosion from mined sites relative to the impact of other sources of sediment pollution. Mined sites, along with construction sites, are highest in sediment yield when compared to other types of surface disturbances. They are, in fact, 2,000 times higher in erosion loss than a typical, undisturbed forest site. Sediment generally comes from the areas being cleared, grubbed, and scalped in a mining operation. Erosion also is prevalent along roadways, on spoil piles, or areas being rehabilitated.

Steep, bare unrevegetated soils are subject to high rates of erosion by both water and wind. The effect is a lessening of the stability of the site and, just as important, removal of the valuable topsoil that has been redistributed on the mined area. Slope steepness, slope length, drainage provided, control structures, lack of vegetation of the slope, and the types of spoils and soils material on the site will affect the amount of wind and water erosion that will occur.

Most research has concerned water erosion rather than wind

Table 6.1. Representative Rates of Erosion for Various Land Uses.

LAND USE	METRIC TONS PER KM^2 PER YEAR	TONS PER MI^2 PER YEAR	RELATIVE TO FOREST = 1
Forest	8.5	24	1
Grassland	85.0	240	10
Abandoned surface mines	850.0	2,400	100
Cropland	1,700.0	4,800	200
Harvested forest	4,250.0	12,000	500
Active surface mines	17,000.0	48,000	2,000
Construction	17,000.0	48,000	2,000

Source: Methods for Identifying and Evaluating the Nature and Extent of Nonpoint Sources of Pollutants, EPA-4030/9-73-014, Washington, D.C.: U.S. Environmental Protection Agency, Oct. 1973.

erosion, whose impact, though sometimes neglected, is quite significant. The Intermountain Forest and Range Experiment Station in Ogden, Utah, reports that wind over a western phosphate field produced fugitive dust that has been estimated at one-half pound per ton of material mined.[1]

Table 6.2 gives wind erodibility indexes measured at mined sites in North Dakota. As shown in the table, wind erosion indexes indicate moderate to minimal wind erosion susceptibility for mined materials. Stockpiled soil materials, however, are more susceptible to wind erosion than mine spoil but less susceptible than fallow soils from adjacent nonmined areas. Gee, et al. attributes the low wind erodibility of mine spoil materials to a high sodium absorption ratio which creates compacted, crusted surfaces.[2]

The Intermountain Forest and Range Experiment Station in Ogden, Utah, points out that soils that contain finer particles and are less compacted obviously will be subject to heavier erosion losses than coarse-textured or compacted material. Because of aggregation, topsoil is generally a little more stable than is spoil material.[3]

SOURCES OF SEDIMENT FROM SURFACE MINING

As mentioned previously, sediment originates in a variety of locations within the mine. Table 6.3 gives comparative rates of erosion for locations within the mine. Despite the attention given to spoil banks or highwalls, haul roads are critical concerns for the rehabilitation specialist. Along with roads, other areas within the mine will discussed in this chapter.

Roadways (Haul and Access Roads)

As indicated in Table 6.3, roadways contribute over 2,000 times the sediment yield as an unmined watershed. There are several factors that contribute to soil loss from roadways and offsite areas affected by the roadways. The Environmental Protection Agency lists several factors, including the following:

A. Poor location and alignment of the roadway, which results in one or more of the following adverse conditions:

Table 6.2. Wind Erodibility Data for Mined Surfaces and Fallowed Land in Western North Dakota (sampled in April 1976).

SAMPLE	NO. OF SAMPLES	NONERODIBLE MATERIAL(%)[a]	WIND ERODIBILITY INDEX (I)[b]	WIND ERODIBILITY GROUP (WEG)[c]
Fallowed soil[d]	16	40(20–60)[e]	119(0–237)	5(2–7)
Topsoil-stockpiled	9	50(33–66)	90(27–166)	6(3.5–7)
Topsoil-respread	10	53(41–72)	76(22–116)	6(5–7)
Spoil (with SAR 30)	5	98(97–99)	0(0)	7(7)

[a]Aggregates 0.84 mm equivalent diameter
[b]Refers to wind erodibility relative to a standard plot. Expressed in metric tons/ha per year.
[c]Erodibility class: 2-high, 7-low.
[d]Fallowed soils included Arnegard, Belfield, Chama, Flaxton, Rhoades, Temvik, Veber, and Williams.
[e]Mean values are reported. Numbers in parentheses reflect the range for the tested materials.
Source: Reproduced from *Reclamation of Drastically Disturbed Lands, 1978,* p. 680 by permission of the American Society of Agronomy, Crop Science Society of America, and Soil Science Society of America.

Table 6.3. Comparative Rates of Erosion.

AREA	YIELD (TON/MI²)	FACTOR
Unmined watershed	28	1
Mined watershed	1,930	69
Spoil bank	27,000	968
Haul road	57,600	2,065

Source: Environmental Protection Agency, *Erosion and Sediment Control, Surface Mining in the Eastern U.S.,* vol. I, *Planning,* EPA Technology Transfer Seminar Publication, Washington, D.C.: Government Printing Office, 1976, p. 7.

1. The presence of excessively long or steep grades. This concentrates runoff and increases flow velocity.
2. Disturbance by cutting and filling operations on unstable slopes or areas having a high groundwater table. This often results in landslides, muddy roadbed conditions, and revegetation problems.
3. Failure to maintain adequate vegetative filters along waterways. This allows sediment flow from the road into a stream.
4. Creation of unnecessary, or unstable stream crossing.

B. If the case is one of improper construction of the roadbed, the following can result:
   1. Failure to provide adequate load capacity and/or subsurface or surface drainage. The roadway will become rutted and saturated, which leads to gully erosion and landslides.
   2. Failure to provide an erosion-resistant surface.

C. Improper layout and construction of drainage structures:
   1. Failure to properly size, align, shape, and stabilize ditches.
   2. Improper disposal of concentrated runoff such as water flowing through culverts and other types of conduits.

D. Poor maintenance practices, including:
   1. Failure to control fugitive dust during times of low precipitation.
   2. Raising the flow line of ditches by poor placement of fill material from excavations.

E. Inadequate stabilization of cut and fill slopes:
   1. Slopes constructed with a gradient in excess of 2 to 1 on cut or 3 to 1 on fill are usually erodible for most soil types.
   2. Poor revegetation stands resulting from improper plant material selection, planting techniques, and application of soil supplements and mulches.[4]

Areas Being Cleared, Grubbed, and Scalped

The Environmental Protection Agency also points out several factors that contribute to soil loss and sedimentation as a result of clearing and grubbing operations. These include:

A. Failure to develop perimeter drainage control measures prior to the start of the clearing and grubbing operation.
B. Exposure of soils, without cover, on steep slopes.
C. Overclearing, or the clearing and grubbing of an area too far ahead of the mining operation or too far below the outcrop line.
D. Improper placement and/or protection of stockpiled topsoiling material.
E. Creation of a soil surface during the clearing and grubbing operation that impedes infiltration. This often results in a concentration of surface runoff that initiates rills and gullies.[5]

Areas of Active Mining

The discussion regarding erosion potential is directly related to the type of mining operation being used. The main source of problems of each mining method is as follows:

A. Contour strip mines
   1. Surface drainage from the disturbed area generally has uninterrupted access to the adjoining drainage system, which presents serious downstream sedimentation problems.
   2. Contour mines have a narrow, linear geometry and, therefore, more spoil area drains directly into the offsite drainage system.
   3. The bench area of a contour mine that is being actively mined, unlike the pit area of an area strip mine, often drains directly into the offsite drainage system.
   4. The receiving waterway of a contour mine is generally closer to the source of sediment and separated from the source by relatively steep terrain.
B. Area strip mines. Though the erosion loss from an area strip mine is significantly less than that from a contour mine, a potential hazard exists in area strip mining from the spoil that is cast below the outcrop line because of its great potential for causing off-site sediment damage.
C. Mountaintop removal. The potential for off-site sediment damage is likely to be less than for a contour strip mine disturbing an equal area of land. This is especially true if surface drainage is internally controlled within the site. These advantages, according to the Environmental Protection Agency, could be offset by problems with chemical and acid pollution and landslides. Problems in erosion that are unique to the mountaintop removal mine are as follows:
   1. The fills, which are placed in natural drainageways, are particularly susceptible to *piping* (subsurface removal of soils).
   2. A great potential for sediment loss exists from rainfall and runoff on the face of the fill slope.[6]

Areas Being Rehabilitated

Most people consider rehabilitation as beneficial to landscape stability. However, the land surface between the beginning of the grading operations and the establishment of adequate vegetation is highly susceptible to runoff damage because of extended periods of exposure. In the past, too little attention was given to surface manipulation or the creation of adequate drainage networks that more nearly match premine conditions.

CONCLUSION

In human terms, the effects of strip mining and erosion can mean desolate physical surroundings, risk of property damage, and injury from landslides and flooding, contamination of water supply, and a stark and intolerable degradation of the quality of life in local communities.

The answer to the causes and impact of erosion from surface mining is coming from study and work already done to heal the wounds by grading and replanting, finding new uses for the land, assessing the past work done, and trying new ways to make the damaged land acceptable and useful.

REFERENCES

1. U.S. Department of Agriculture, *User Guide to Soils, Mining, and Reclamation in the West,* USDA Forest Service General Technical Report INT–80, Ogden, Utah: Intermountain Forest and Range Experiment Station, Forest Service, 1980, p. 59.
2. Gee, G. W., Armand Bauer, and R. S. Decker, "Physical Analyses of Overburden Materials and Mine Land Soils," *Reclamation of Drastically Disturbed Lands,* Madison, Wis.: American Society of Agronomy, 1978, p. 680.
3. U.S. Department of Agriculture, *User Guide to Soils,* 1980, p. 60.
4. Environmental Protection Agency, *Erosion and Sediment Control, Surface Mining in the Eastern U.S.,* vol. I, *Planning,* EPA Technology Transfer Seminar Publication, Washington, D.C.: Government Printing Office, 1976, p. 69.
5. Ibid., p. 6.
6. Ibid., p. 10.

7
Sculpturing the Surface

INTRODUCTION

Slope stabilization and revegetation constitute the basic components of rehabilitation. Although the next chapter is devoted to physical and botanical devices that are employed to control erosion and sedimentation, sculpturing the slopes remains the most critical concern. In the past, rehabilitation earthwork procedures transformed most topographic configurations into smooth, uniformly sculptured landforms. In most cases, however, the slopes were not responsive to natural drainage systems prevalent in premining landscapes.

Recent research has indicated that the creation of properly aligned channels in rehabilitation processes is crucial to successful erosion control. Control mechanisms are wasted efforts in many cases if the landform has not been properly graded. It is the purpose of this chapter to offer some guidelines relative to landform sculpture.

The factors related to erosion are so numerous that quantitative determinants are difficult to anticipate. Therefore, slope design is a complicated exercise.

DEFINITIONS

The following are definitions and principles that can assist the reader to deal with basic design concepts.

Channelization Equilibrium

Natural forces create erosion and channel development. Examples of erosive forces include the rate of runoff and the gradient of a slope. There are also forces that resist erosion or channel development, such as soil sheer strength. In the natural setting, the forces that give rise to channel development are said to be in dynamic equilibrium with the forces that resist channelization. It is only occasionally that one finds an area with accelerated erosion that has not been disturbed by man or by some unusual natural event.[1]

Dendritic Channel Patterns

Dendritic channel patterns are the random branching pattern of natural stream configurations that are exemplified by a hierarchy of channels ranging from numerous small rills flowing together into larger gullies which collectively flow together to form streams.

Drainage Density

Drainage density is defined as the cumulative length of channel segments in a unit of area, commonly expressed in miles of channel segments per square mile of land surface.[2] Representative natural drainage density values are given in Table 7.1.

Table 7.1.   Natural Drainage Density (Dd) Values

LOCATION	Dd MILES/MILES^2
Ozark Plateau, Missouri	17
Gulf Coast Plain, Louisiana	5
Coastal Plain, Virginia	6
Appalachian Plateau, Kentucky	56
Ozark Plateau, Illinois	15
Verdugo Hills, California	26
Badlands, Perth Amboy, New Jersey	650
Badlands, Petrified Forest, Arizona	260
Coastal Range, California	17
Cumberland Plateau, Tennessee	5
Glaciated, North Wisconsin	1.5

Courtesy OES Publications, University of Kentucky, and Professor David J. Barr, University of Missouri, Rolla.

Stream Order Segments

Streams are made up of a hierarchy of channel segments called *orders,* as described in Chapter 4. Definitions of the various orders will be described in greater detail including:

First-order segment.   The smallest or "fingertip" channels that are the uppermost portion of a stream watershed. These are generally dry but do carry wet weather flow.

Second-order segment.   A stream segment that is formed by the junction of any two second-order streams.

Third-order segment.   The stream segment that is formed by the junction of any two second-order streams. The various orders are illustrated in Figure 4.5.

The Universal Soil Loss Equation (USLE)

The universal soil loss equation considers all the various contributing factors in determining the gross movement of soil that occurs as sheet and rill erosion.[3] The equation is:

$$A = RKLsCP$$

where,

A = Computed soil loss in tons/acre/year
R = Rainfall factor
K = Soil erodibility factor
Ls = Slope length/slope gradient factor
C = Cover management factor
P = Erosion control practice factor[4]

These factors will be described in greater detail under the *Design Concepts* section later in the chapter.

Zero-Order Watershed

A zero-order watershed is defined as the minimum drainage area whose runoff has sufficient force to initiate channel development.[5]

SLOPE TYPES

There are basically four types of slopes illustrated in Figure 7.1. Profiles along the slopes in the figure have quite a variable rate of erosion susceptibility. The studies dealing with the susceptibility of the various slopes to erosion can be summarized as follows:

A. Slopes that are concave are the least affected by erosion, yield the least amount of sediment, and change shape faster than most other profiles.[6]
B. Slopes that are convex erode very rapidly, yield the most sediment, and change shape faster than most other profiles.[7]
C. Complex and uniform slopes are affected to an intermediate degree, although long, uniform slopes can be severely eroded in a single rain storm.[8]
D. Slopes developed on reclaimed material will tend to

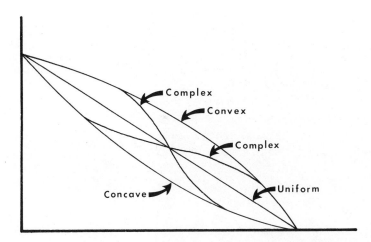

Figure 7.1. Basic slope profile shapes of slopes (Courtesy OES Publications, University of Kentucky, and Professor David J. Barr, University of Missouri, Rolla).

develop concave profiles in their mid to lower sections given sufficient time.[9]

E. The steepness of the toe of the slope is the major factor affecting the amount of sediment yield and the rate at which the slope will change shape.[10]

DESIGN CONCEPTS— UNIVERSAL SOIL LOSS EQUATION

Using the Universal Soil Loss Equation (USLE)

In the development of a grading plan for the rehabilitation of slopes disturbed by mining processes, the USLE is useful for rating the area's need for certain rehabilitation processes. The USLE was developed for agronomic purposes and was never geared to the complexities of mined land rehabilitation. Therefore, it must be realized that its usefulness is definitely limited and its products only a guide for making decisions, which are at best only educated guesswork. Research is currently being conducted to develop a system that will give more

realistic solutions to the needs of a particular site. Prior to its completion, the USLE will suffice, provided the rehabilitation specialist realizes its drawbacks.

The equation $A = RKLsCP$ takes into consideration all those factors that contribute to soil loss. The procedures for determining factorial quantities will be described in the next few sections.

Rainfall Factor (R and Rt)

The R-factor is a direct conversion from the two year–six hour isopluvial provided by the National Weather Service for a particular area, usually statewide in scale. This factor considers two rainfall characteristics: the kinetic energy and the maximum 30 minute intensity of a rainstorm. The values are the annual sum of these products.[11] Figure 7.2 indicates the R-factors for the state of Wyoming. Maps of the other states can be secured from each state's soil conservation district. The Rt-factor is not available in many states. It reflects the erosion from snow melt runoff in addition to the energy intensity units from rainfall.[12]

Of all the factors within the USLE, the R-factor, in the author's opinion, is one whose values can be called into question. Not all the maps supplied by the Soil Conservation Service (SCS) have the same degree of detail nor do the isopluvials match up when one aligns a map from one state to its adjoining state. States such as Utah, Colorado, and Montana have maps that seem to be highly detailed, taking higher elevations and steep terrain into consideration.

Soil Erodibility Factor (K)

The K-factor is determined from direct soil loss measurements on selected soils. The relative erodibility for most soil types has been determined for sediment yield in tons per acre per unit of rainfall erosion potential. Tables 7.2 and 7.3 are general guidelines that can be used to determine the K-factor for topsoils and subsoils, respectively.

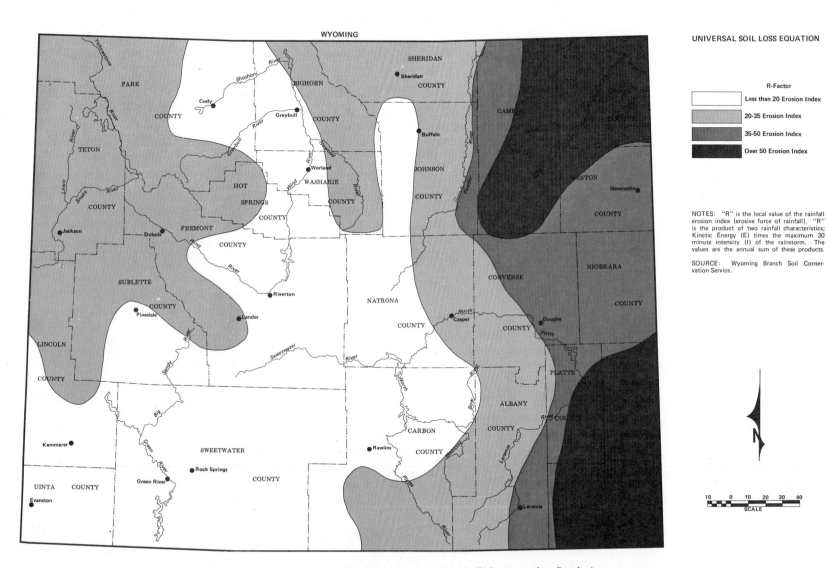

Figure 7.2. R-factors for the state of Wyoming (From Wyoming Branch Soil Conservation Service).

Table 7.2.   K Values for Topsoil.

TEXTURE OF SURFACE LAYER	ESTIMATED K VALUE
Clay, clay loam, loam, silty clay	.32
Fine sandy loam, loamy very fine sand, sandy loam	.24
Loamy fine sand, loamy sand	.17
Sand	.15
Silt loam, silty clay loam, very fine sand loam	.37

Source: Soil Conservation Service, *Water Management and Sediment Control for Urbanizing Areas,* Columbus, Ohio, 1978, p. 79.

Table 7.3.   K Values for Subsoil.

GENERALIZED SOIL CATEGORY (TEXTURE OF MATERIALS)	ESTIMATED K VALUE OF EXPOSED SUBSOIL MATERIAL
A. Outwash soils	
Sand	.17
Loamy sand	.24
Sandy loam	.43
Gravel, fine to mod. fine subsoil	.24
Gravel, med. to mod. coarse subsoil	.49
B. Lacustrine soils	
Silt loam and very fine sandy loam	.37
Silty clay loam	.28
Clay and silty clay	.28
C. Glacial till	
Loam, fine to mod. fine subsoil	.32
Loam, med. subsoil	.37
Clay loam	.32
Clay and silty clay	.28
D. Loess	.37
E. Residual	
Sandstone	.49
Siltstone, nonchannery	.43
Siltstone, channery	.32
Acid clay shale	.28
Calcareous clay shale or limestone residuum	.24

Source: Soil Conservation Service, *Water Management and Sediment Control for Urbanizing Areas,* Columbus, Ohio, 1978, p. 79.

Soils with K values of less than .23 are generally classified as low erodibility, whereas soils rated between .24 and .40 are considered to have moderate erodibility, and soils with a value above .41 are considered to have high erodibility. Using the general soils association map of a state or county as an initial basis, and taking slope ranges and soil permeability as additional criteria, one can often determine erodibility zones. In all cases, where slopes are to be sculptured for rehabilitation and stabilization, it is recommended that the soil be tested on a site-specific basis. For most soil types, the guidelines offered in Table 7.4 can be used to determine slope thresholds. Slopes in excess of the thresholds require additional devices such as erosion control blankets or riprap.

Slope Length/Slope Gradient Factor (Ls)

Soil erosion is affected by the length of a slope as well as its grade. By using Table 7.5 as a basis, a single topographic factor (Ls) can be determined. The rehabilitation specialist should only determine slope length by on-site observations of the area under consideration. The equation is only valuable for erosion caused by water moving in a thin sheet across the ground. Water usually moves only in thin sheets for short distances and then concentrates to form rills or gullies. The slope lengths should be computed then to the distance water moves in a thin sheet down slope before it enters a defined channel.[13]

In establishing values for the Ls-factor, the Soil Conservation Service (SCS) has arbitrarily assigned a value of 1.0 to a 9

Table 7.4.   Maximum Slope Thresholds.

K-FACTOR	CUT SLOPES	FILL SLOPES
Low	1:1	1½:1
Mod. low	1½:1	2:1
Moderate	2:1	3:1
Mod. high	3:1	4:1
High	4:1	5:1

Table 7.5.   Soil Loss Ratio (Ls).

percent slope (s)

LENGTH OF SLOPE (L) +	0.2	0.3	0.4	0.5	1.0	2.0	3.0	4.0	5.0	6.0	8.0	10.0	12.0	14.0	16.0	18.0	20.0	25.0	30.0	40.0	50.0	60.0
20 +	.05	.05	.06	.06	.08	.12	.18	.21	.24	.30	.44	.61	.81	1.0	1.2	1.6	1.8	2.6	3.5	5.5	8	10
40 +	.06	.07	.07	.08	.10	.15	.22	.28	.34	.43	.63	.87	1.2	1.4	1.8	2.2	2.6	3.5	5.0	8	11	15
50 +	.07	.08	.08	.08	.11	.17	.25	.33	.41	.52	.77	1.0	1.4	1.8	2.2	2.6	3.0	4.5	6.0	10	14	18
80 +	.08	.08	.09	.09	.12	.19	.27	.37	.48	.60	.89	1.2	1.6	2.0	2.6	3.0	3.5	5.5	7	11	16	21
100 +	.08	.09	.09	.10	.13	.20	.29	.40	.54	.67	.99	1.4	1.8	2.2	2.8	3.5	4.0	6.0	8	13	18	23
110 +	.08	.09	.10	.10	.13	.21	.30	.42	.56	.71	1.0	1.4	1.8	2.4	3.0	3.5	4.5	6.0	8	13	19	24
120 +	.09	.09	.10	.10	.14	.21	.30	.43	.59	.74	1.0	1.6	2.0	2.6	3.0	4.0	4.5	6.0	9	14	20	25
130 +	.09	.09	.10	.11	.14	.22	.31	.44	.61	.77	1.2	1.6	2.0	2.6	3.0	4.0	4.5	7	9	14	20	26
140 +	.09	.10	.10	.11	.14	.22	.32	.46	.63	.80	1.2	1.6	2.2	2.8	3.5	4.0	5.0	7	9	15	21	27
150 +	.09	.10	.11	.11	.15	.23	.32	.47	.66	.82	1.2	1.6	2.2	2.8	3.5	4.0	5.0	7	10	15	22	28
160 +	.09	.10	.11	.11	.15	.23	.33	.48	.68	.85	1.2	1.8	2.2	3.0	3.5	4.5	5.0	7	10	16	23	29
180 +	.10	.10	.11	.12	.15	.24	.34	.51	.72	.90	1.4	1.8	2.4	3.0	4.0	4.5	5.5	8	11	17	24	31
200 +	.10	.11	.11	.12	.16	.25	.35	.53	.76	.95	1.4	2.0	2.6	3.0	4.0	5.0	6.0	8	11	18	25	33
300 +	.11	.12	.13	.14	.18	.28	.40	.62	.93	1.2	1.8	2.4	3.0	4.0	5.0	6.0	7	10	14	22	31	40
400 +	.12	.13	.14	.15	.20	.31	.44	.70	1.0	1.4	2.0	2.8	3.5	4.5	5.5	7	8	12	16	25	36	46
500 +	.13	.14	.15	.16	.21	.33	.47	.76	1.2	1.6	2.2	3.0	4.0	5.0	6.0	8	9	13	18	28	40	52
600 +	.14	.15	.16	.17	.22	.34	.49	.82	1.4	1.6	2.4	3.5	4.5	5.5	7	8	10	14	19	31	44	57
700 +	.15	.16	.17	.18	.23	.36	.52	.87	1.4	1.8	2.6	3.5	5.0	6.0	8	9	11	16	21	33	47	61
800 +	.15	.16	.17	.18	.24	.38	.54	.92	1.6	2.0	2.8	4.0	5.0	6.0	8	10	12	17	22	36	50	65
900 +	.16	.17	.18	.19	.25	.39	.56	.96	1.6	2.0	3.0	4.0	5.5	7	9	10	12	18	24	38	53	69
1000 +	.16	.18	.19	.20	.26	.40	.57	1.0	1.6	2.2	3.0	4.5	5.5	7	9	11	13	19	25	40	56	73
1100 +	.17	.18	.19	.20	.27	.41	.59	1.0	1.8	2.2	3.5	4.5	6.0	8	9	11	14	20	26	42	59	77
1200 +	.17	.18	.20	.21	.27	.42	.61	1.0	1.8	2.4	3.5	4.5	6.0	8	10	12	14	20	28	44	62	80
1300 +	.18	.19	.20	.21	.28	.43	.62	1.2	2.0	2.4	3.5	5.0	7	8	10	12	15	21	29	46	64	83
1400 +	.18	.19	.21	.22	.29	.44	.63	1.2	2.0	2.6	3.5	5.0	7	9	11	13	15	22	30	47	67	87
1500 +	.19	.20	.21	.22	.29	.45	.65	1.2	2.0	2.6	4.0	5.5	7	9	11	13	16	23	31	49	69	90
1600 +	.19	.20	.21	.23	.30	.46	.66	1.2	2.2	2.6	4.0	5.5	7	9	11	14	16	24	32	51	71	93
1700 +	.19	.21	.22	.23	.30	.47	.67	1.2	2.2	2.8	4.0	5.5	7	9	12	14	17	24	33	52	73	95
2000 +	.20	.22	.23	.24	.32	.49	.71	1.4	2.4	3.0	4.5	6.0	8	10	13	15	18	26	36	57	80	104

Contour limits—2 percent, 400 feet; 8 percent, 200 feet; 10 percent, 100 feet; 14–24 percent, 60 feet. The effectiveness of contouring beyond these limits is speculative.

When the length of slope exceeds 400 feet and (or) percentage of slope exceeds 24 percent, soil loss estimates are speculative as these values are beyond the range of research data.

Source: Soil Conservation Service, *Water Management and Sediment Control for Urbanizing Areas,* Columbus, Ohio, 1978, p. 81.

percent slope with a length of 73 feet. The effects of slope steepness and length have been combined in the Ls values for uniform slopes shown in Table 7.5. The Ls values vary, as shown in the table. For example, a 5 percent slope 100 feet in length has an Ls value of .54, whereas a 14 percent slope 300 feet in length has an Ls value of 4.0.

If a slope steepens or flattens significantly toward the lower end or is composed of a series of convex and concave segments, its overall average gradient and length do not correctly indicate the topographic effect on soil loss. The successive slope segments cannot be evaluated as independent slopes when runoff flows from one segment to the next. When the rehabilitation specialist encounters irregular slopes, the values read from Table 7.5 must be adjusted to account for effects of the gradient changes. The SCS points out that convex slopes of the same percentage and length as concave slopes will have a significantly higher erosion hazard.[14]

Making adjustments depends on two basic assumptions:

A. The change in gradient is not sufficient to cause upslope deposition, and
B. The irregular slope can be divided into a small number of equal-length segments with the general gradient within each segment being uniform. In most cases, three segments should be sufficient.[15]

Procedure. Divide the convex, concave, or complex slope into three *equal* segments as shown in Figure 7.3 and ascertain the percent slope for each segment. Find the *total slope length* in Table 7.5 and read the Ls value corresponding to the steepness of each of the three slope segments. Be sure to compute the slope percentage for each segment for the total length of the slope. Multiply the chart value for the upper segment by 0.58, the middle segment value by 1.06, and the lower segment value by 1.37 (factors obtained from Table 7.6). The average of the three products is then a good estimate of the effective Ls value for that slope. If the slope has been divided into a

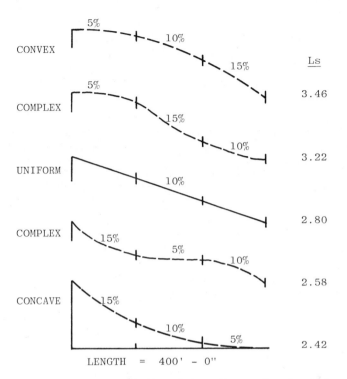

Figure 7.3. Demonstration of effect of slope shape on Ls value (Adapted from Soil Conservation Service, *Water Management and Sediment Control for Urbanizing Areas,* Columbus, Ohio, 1978, p. 83).

**Table 7.6.   Factors to Adjust Ls Chart Values
for Successive Segments of a Slope
Where the Slope-length Exponent Equals 0.5.**

SEGMENT NO. (TOP TO BOTTOM)	NUMBER EQUAL-LENGTH SEGMENTS INTO WHICH THE SLOPE IS DIVIDED FOR EVALUATION OF Ls			
	2	*3*	*4*	*5*
1	0.71	0.58	0.50	0.45
2	1.29	1.06	0.91	0.82
3		1.37	1.18	1.06
4			1.40	1.25
5				1.42

Source: Soil Conservation Service, *Water Management and Sediment Control for Urbanizing Areas,* Columbus, Ohio, 1978, p. 83.

number of segments other than 3, substitute the appropriate adjustment factors from Table 7.6.

Example.   Assume a convex slope 400 feet long for which the upper third averages a 5 percent slope; the middle third, 10 percent; and the lower third, 15 percent (Figure 7.3). Find *the 400 foot total slope length* in Table 7.5 and copy the values shown in that line for slopes of 5, 10, and 15 percent: 1.0, 2.8, and 5.0, respectively. Multiply the three values by the previously mentioned adjustment factors from Table 7.6: 0.58, 1.06, and 1.37, respectively, and average the products. In tabular form, the computations are as follows:

SEGMENT NO.	SLOPE %	TABLE 7.5 VALUE	TABLE 7.6 VALUE	SEGMENT Ls
1	5	1.0	0.58	.58
2	10	2.8	1.06	2.96
3	15	5.0	1.37	6.85

Average = 3.46

Cropping Management Factor (C)

Most values for the C-factor were derived from experiments on agricultural croplands. These have very little value for typical revegetation practices in rehabilitation. Recent work by the SCS provides values for uncultivated range and woodlands but is hardly appropriate for the rehabilitation of mined sites where the exposed overburden spoils must be controlled from erosion. Perhaps the most realistic values can be taken from Table 7.7 using the ''bare areas'' category. One could, however, question the validity of using a C-factor value of 1.0 on all mine sites. This is certainly one area in which much research needs to be conducted to establish more realistic values.

Table 7.7.   C-factor for Various Quantities of Mulch.

MULCH ADEQUATELY CRIMPED INTO SOIL	C-FACTOR
Bare area	1.0
1/4 ton straw mulch per acre	.52
1/2 ton straw mulch per acre	.35
3/4 ton straw mulch per acre	.24
1 ton straw mulch per acre	.18
1–1/2 ton straw mulch per acre	.10
2 ton straw mulch per acre	.06
3 ton straw mulch per acre	.03
4 ton straw mulch per acre	.02

Source: Soil Conservation Service, *Universal Soil-Loss Equation*, Agronomy Note #50, Colorado SCS, 1977, p. 15.

Erosion Control Practices Factor (P)

The final criterion to be considered in the USLE governs the various techniques employed to prevent erosion by cultural practices. Most of the research in this area has again centered on agricultural activities including contour tillage, cross-slope farming, and contour strip cropping. These are all techniques used to diminish the velocity of the overland flow of surface water, which, in turn, increases the opportunity for water to permeate the soil and decreases the danger of carrying suspended particles away from the area. However, very little research has been conducted relative to normal rehabilitation practices. Terraces and diversions do not qualify as P-factor values since they are considered part of the length of the slope factor Ls.[16] Table 7.8 provides for the P-factors for a variety of circumstances. In most rehabilitation circumstances, the up and down hill column with a value of 1.0 would apply. Notice, however, that utilizing the P-factor involves two limitations. First, the maximum slope in Table 7.8 is 24 percent. The slope length, as noted in the footnotes to Table 7.5, for up and down hill practices between 14 and 24 percent would have to be under 60 feet in length. Second, the values for up and down hill are 1.0 no matter what the slope percentage may be. In the

Table 7.8. P-factors for Conservation Practices.

SLOPE (PERCENT)	UP & DOWN HILL	CROSS-SLOPE FARMING WITHOUT STRIPS	CONTOUR FARMING	CROSS-SLOPE FARMING WITH STRIPS	CONTOUR STRIP CROPPING
2.0– 7.0	1.0	0.75	0.50	0.37	0.25
7.1–12.0	1.0	0.80	0.60	0.45	0.30
12.1–18.0	1.0	0.90	0.80	0.60	0.40
18.1–24.0	1.0	0.95	0.90	0.67	0.45

Source: Soil Conservation Service, *Universal Soil-Loss Equation,* Agronomy Note #50, Colorado SCS, 1977, p. 15.

author's opinion, these values should increase appreciably as the slopes increase.

IMPLEMENTING THE USLE

The primary objective of using the USLE for rehabilitation work is to develop some guidelines to lessen the rate of erosion to a limit tolerable to the soil type. The product of the USLE, sediment load in tons per acre per year, can be compared to the soil loss tolerance (T-factor) to see where conflicts occur.

Several USLE factors are fixed and cannot be manipulated. However, the Ls, C, and P factors can, to a certain degree, be manipulated to control the USLE product. The Ls factor, for example, can be altered by constructing terraces or waterbars to cut down on the slope length.

The T-factor, which is secured by an adequate soil survey, should be matched by the USLE product if at all possible in order to make rehabilitation decisions.

Sample Problem

An oil well pad in Sweetwater County, Wyoming, is to be reclaimed. The operator will grade the slopes back to the original 20 percent, uniform grade. The length of the slope midway across the pad is 200 feet. The dominant soil on the pad is Rentsac-Blackhall with a K-factor of .32. What is the predicted average annual soil loss in tons per acre?

Solution. With the USLE, A = RKLsCP, as a basis, the next six steps should be followed:

Step 1. Determine R-factor from Figure 7.2. R = 20.0.
Step 2. Determine K-factor from SCS soils description. K = .32.
Step 3. Determine Ls-factor from Table 7.5. Ls = 6.0.
Step 4. Determine C-factor from Table 7.7, bare areas with no vegetal cover. C = 1.0.
Step 5. Determine P-factor from Table 7.8, up and down slope. P = 1.0.
Step 6. Multiply (R = 20) × (K = .32) × (Ls = 6) × (C = 1.0) × (P = 1.0). The product of these factor values indicates that approximately 38.4 tons/acre/year of sediment loss occurs on the pad.

Rehabilitation Planning Considerations. The soil loss tolerance, T-factor, for Rentsac-Blackhall soils as determined by the SCS is 1.0, which means that they can tolerate a sediment loss of 1 ton/acre/year. The predicted soil loss on the well pad of 38.4 tons/acre/year is extremely excessive and in order to reduce the sediment yield to an acceptable tolerance, mitigating measures must be undertaken. The following measures should be employed to reduce sediment yield:

A. Reduce the slopes and slope runs by developing a series of terraces and diversions.
B. Install plant cover, preferably grasses with fibrous root systems, in an effort to reduce the value of the C-factor. The use of mulches should be employed as a temporary control until the grasses become established. If all factors remain the same, the use of 2 tons of straw mulch

per acre would reduce the C-factor value to .06 (see Table 7.7), which would reduce the USLE value to 2.3 tons/acre/year, twice the acceptable tolerance. The alteration of slopes with the use of terraces will probably get the product to an acceptable level. This procedure illustrates the use of the USLE as a land management tool in rehabilitation practices.

DESIGN CONCEPTS— SCULPTURING THE LANDFORM

Erosion is a natural process, which when uncontrolled is harmful because of its destruction of productive landforms and its creation of sedimentation deposits. In the higher portions of a watershed, gullies begin when water cuts through the

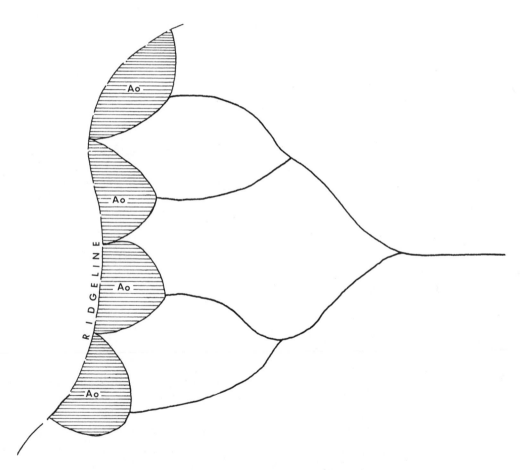

Figure 7.4. Zero-order watersheds.

soil on overland flow. The natural phenomenon prevalent in channelization equilibrium (defined earlier in the chapter) can be duplicated by cultural practices during rehabilitation earthwork operations. The art of sculpturing the land to develop channelization equilibrium seems to lie in the ability to duplicate the drainage density that existed prior to mining, or, if those data are not available, the drainage density prevalent in the same watershed.

The drainage network can be designed with proper density by using the zero-order watershed concept as produced by the equilibrium condition.[17] The zero-order watershed, which is the minimum drainage area from which the runoff produced has sufficient force to initiate channel development, is illustrated in Figure 7.4. The rehabilitation specialist could implement land form sculpturing by insuring that no surface area larger than zero-order watershed (A_0) exists without being drained by a well-defined channel.[18]

Several techniques could be used to develop a value for A_0. The simplest method would involve values derived from maps and aerial photos of premine conditions. If these data are not available, the drainage density and the size of A_0 are generally the same within the same major watershed. Therefore, the drainage density in another area within the watershed could be measured and used as a basis for determining the size of A_0.

Drainage channels should be constructed to resemble natural channels with parabolic cross-sections. The depth of the channels should grade from shallow (0.5 feet ±) at the top of the slope to several feet deep for trunk collector channels. Schaefer suggests that top bank widths should range from perhaps 12 feet wide on small tributaries to broader channels in the trunk streams. He further suggests that the flow line of the channels be concave in configuration, if possible, with the gradient steepest at the head-end with flattening toward the mouth of the primary trunk stream.[19]

Unless the rehabilitation planners consider replicating the premine drainage patterns by duplicating the size of the zero-order watershed and drainage density, there will be tremendous soil loss over the time span necessary for the site to reach natural, dynamic equilibrium. This could be the single most important factor in returning the site to a stable condition at the earliest possible time.

REFERENCES

1. Schaefer, Melvin, B. Elifrits, and D. J. Barr, "Sculpturing Reclaimed Land to Decrease Erosion," *Symposium on Surface Mining Hydrology, Sedimentology, and Reclamation,* Lexington, Ky.: University of Kentucky, 1979, p. 99.
2. Barr, David J., and John D. Rockaway, "How to Decrease Erosion by Natural Terrain Sculpturing," *Weeds, Trees, and Turf,* January 1980, p. 31.
3. U.S. Department of Agriculture, Soil Conservation Service, *Universal Soil Loss Equation,* January 1976, p. 1 (hereafter cited as *USLE*).
4. Ibid.
5. Schaefer, Elifrits, and Barr, "Sculpturing Reclaimed Land," p. 101.
6. Ibid., pp. 100–101.
7. Ibid.
8. Ibid.
9. Ibid.
10. Ibid.
11. U.S. Department of Agriculture, Soil Conservation Service, *USLE,* p. 3.
12. Ibid.
13. Ibid., p. 4.
14. Ibid.
15. U.S. Department of Agriculture, Soil Conservation Service, *Water Management and Sediment Control for Urbanizing Areas,* Columbus, Ohio, 1978, p. 81.
16. U.S. Department of Agriculture, Soil Conservation Service, *USLE,* p. 5.
17. Schaefer, Elifrits, and Barr, "Sculpturing Reclaimed Land," p. 101.
18. Ibid.
19. Ibid., p. 106.

8
Erosion Control Devices

INTRODUCTION

The universal soil loss equation discussed in Chapter 7 identifies the various contributing factors that create an erosive situation. Knowledge of these factors, including rainfall energy, soil types, slope length and gradient, cover, and practices, help the rehabilitation specialist realize the variables that must be manipulated to control the destructive forces of erosion. For example, if he is working in an area with highly erodible soils, the rehabilitation specialist must consider what can be done to offset the potential for accelerated erosion.

Rehabilitation of the land is primarily centered around activities that will stabilize the slopes and revegetate the soils. These often go hand-in-hand since the most effective erosion control device available is a good stand of vegetation. There is a discrepancy, however, between the time that the slopes are groomed and the time when vegetation establishes itself sufficiently to promote equilibrium. In these instances, other cultural practices must be employed to assist in erosion control until the vegetation becomes adequately established.

Erosion is a result of excesses in either the volume or velocity of water movement. If either volume or velocity can be held within reasonable limits, erosion will be checked. Although this chapter provides guidelines for the several devices commonly used to reduce erosion, anything can be used that will reduce the volume or concentration of water in small areas, or that will reduce the velocity of the water as it moves over the land's surface.

The Michigan Department of Natural Resources lists five basic principles that should be followed for erosion control:

A. Keep disturbed areas small.
B. Stabilize and protect disturbed areas as soon as possible.
C. Keep storm water runoff velocities low.
D. Protect disturbed areas from storm water runoff.
E. Retain sediment within the corridor or site area.[1]

Erosion control systems can generally serve four purposes including *diversions, conveyance, stabilizers* and *dissipators,* and *retension.* Each of these will be discussed in detail.

DIVERSION SYSTEMS

A diversion can be defined as any device that moves surface water from its natural flow pattern to a controlled outlet. The purpose of moving the water is to ensure that the flow is directed to a stable outlet. Diversions can serve to impede the velocity of the water and often concentrate its flow.

Mechanical Diversions

Among the types of mechanical diversions are such devices as dikes, ditches or channels, or a combination of dike and ditch. In rehabilitation work, many of the devices are temporary in nature, only serving to stabilize the soil until vegetation can become established.

Dikes.   Figure 8.1 illustrates the use of an earthen dike placed upgrade from a rehabilitated, recontoured area. The surface flow is directed away from the disturbed area and across the undisturbed, stable soil. After one or more growing seasons, sediment will fill the upslope side of the dike while the downslope edge of the dike begins to settle. The vegetation should become enough established that the need to divert the water is alleviated.

Ditches or Channels.   Open diversions are defined as any drainage course open to the atmosphere. A storm water drainage system is a collection of both diversions and conveyance systems that act together in dendritic patterns to drain a watershed. The construction of a channel, illustrated by Figure 8.2, is measured by the following:

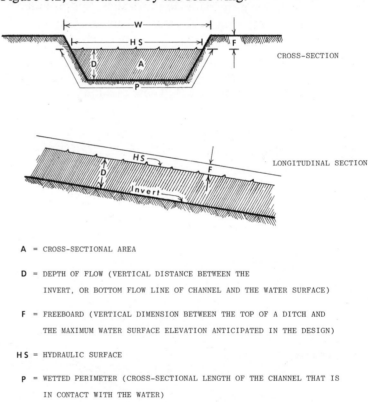

CROSS-SECTION

LONGITUDINAL SECTION

A = CROSS-SECTIONAL AREA

D = DEPTH OF FLOW (VERTICAL DISTANCE BETWEEN THE
  INVERT, OR BOTTOM FLOW LINE OF CHANNEL AND THE WATER SURFACE)

F = FREEBOARD (VERTICAL DIMENSION BETWEEN THE TOP OF A DITCH AND
  THE MAXIMUM WATER SURFACE ELEVATION ANTICIPATED IN THE DESIGN)

HS = HYDRAULIC SURFACE

P = WETTED PERIMETER (CROSS-SECTIONAL LENGTH OF THE CHANNEL THAT IS
  IN CONTACT WITH THE WATER)

W = WIDTH OF CHANNEL

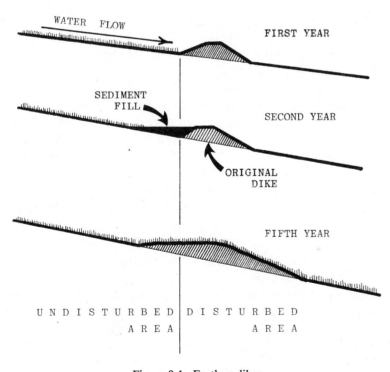

Figure 8.1. Earthen dikes.

Figure 8.2. Ditch relationships.

A. *Depth of flow* (D) which is the vertical distance between the *invert,* or bottom flow line, of the channel and the water surface.
B. *Wetted perimeter* (P) which is defined as the cross-sectional length of the channel that is in contact with the water.
C. *Hydraulic radius,* defined as the ratio between the cross-sectional area of the channel and the wetted perimeter.
D. *Freeboard* (F) which is defined as the vertical dimension between the top of a ditch and the maximum water surface elevation anticipated in the design. It is provided to prevent overtopping because of unforeseen circumstances.

The geometry of a channel can vary between one of three types as illustrated in Figure 8.3. These include:

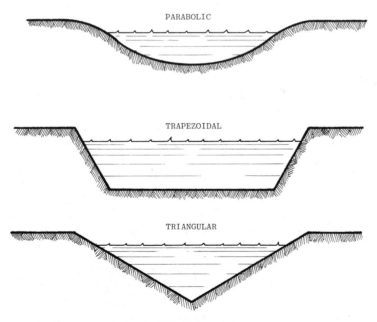

Figure 8.3. Types of ditch geometry.

A. Parabolic
B. Trapezoidal
C. Triangular

Design concepts.   Generally speaking, the parabolic ditch is the most efficient in that it resists scouring and flows with less surface resistance than other forms. Those channels that have constant cross-sections and slopes will have uniform flow. The relationship of velocity of flow to cross-sectional area and volume is expressed as:

$$Q = V a$$

where

Q = volume of flow in ft³/sec
V = velocity in ft/sec (average)
a = cross-sectional area of the channel in sq ft (Ref. 2)

This formula provides a basis for choosing a particular ditch geometry and size needed to carry the volume of water flowing into the area. For earthen ditches, the velocity should be kept to 2 to 4 feet per second. The velocity for paved ditches should be kept between 2 and 8 feet per second. Earthen ditches should be planted with grass to resist scouring and erosion. Ditch gradient should be kept to a minimum of 1 percent and a maximum of 3 percent. If ditch gradient should be in excess of 3 percent, stabilizing devices such as riprap should be employed.

One of the most complex problems associated with rehabilitation concerns the design of systems to handle water flow, especially storm water. Developing an easy method of measuring the amount of flow for ditch and culvert design is nearly impossible. The objective of this book, to assist the rehabilitation specialist in accurate selection of proper, efficient drainage systems, is best served by keeping the method as simple as practical. This allows a greater use of the system and, it is hoped, better techniques in controlling erosion and sedimentation. Factors that play a role in computing water flow are as follows:

A. Size of watershed
B. Topographical features within the watershed
C. Drainage density
D. Surface texture of land and channel
E. Rainfall intensity
F. Design frequency (if one designs for a 100 year storm, the system would be much larger than if a 2 year storm were considered)
G. Time of runoff from the high point in the watershed to point of the design
H. Elevation above sea level of the watershed

The design of drainage systems demands a variety of computed products including:

A. Volume of discharge (quantity) of water in the watershed.
B. Velocity of water flowing through a channel or system. Optimum velocity range for grass-lined ditches is 2 to 4 feet per second. Enclosed channels or paved ditches should be designed for a velocity range of 2 to 6 feet per second.
C. Capacity of channels or systems
D. Ditch or culvert gradient.

Quantities of surface water flow can be calculated for areas under 4 acres in size by using the *rational formula*

$$Q = CIA$$

where
Q = quantity of discharge
C = coefficient of roughness (surface texture of ditch or culvert)
I = intensity of rainfall in inches/hour for a period equal to the time of concentration
A = area of watershed in acres

Figure 8.4 provides the one-hour isopluvials for various time intervals. The figures for the geographical locations found on the map can be used in the formula. The coefficient values are found in Table 8.1. This formula is likely to be inaccurate for areas larger than 4 acres, but is often used because of its simplicity. The product is generally going to be higher than necessary, which results in overdesign and a system more expensive than necessary.

In some states, the state highway department has developed more accurate methods for determining flow quantity. It would be advisable for the rehabilitation specialist to consult the highway department to determine if this is true and which formulas might apply.

Once the quantity of flow is determined, the size and geometry of the ditch needed to divert or convey the surface water can be selected using Figures 8.5 through 8.17.

Dike and ditch.   Temporary diversions above disturbance areas can often take the form of a combination of dikes and ditches. These are especially valuable on steep slopes where the fill from the ditch can be cast downslope to increase the capacity of the ditch. The dike may have to be compacted to prevent piping, or subsurface erosion. Dike and ditch diversions are illustrated in Figure 8.18.

Conclusions.   Diversions serve to temporarily solve drainage problems, but cannot be used for long-term solutions. The reason for this primarily lies in the fact that the surface flow becomes concentrated within the transportation system and, thereby, increases the erodibility of the soil in the outlet areas.

If possible, the diversion systems should be vegetated to lessen the erosive force of moving water. Those ditches that exceed acceptable thresholds should be lined with riprap.

Table 8.1 Coefficient Values for the Rational Formula.

VALUES OF C $= \dfrac{\text{RUNOFF}}{\text{RAINFALL}}$			VALUE PROPOSED		VALUE BY OTHER AUTHORITY	
Surfaces			Min.	Max.	Min.	Max.
Roofs, slag to metal			0.90	1.00	0.70	0.95
Pavements	Concrete or asphalt		0.90	1.00	0.95	1.00
	Bituminous macadam, open and closed type		0.70	0.90	0.70	0.90
	Gravel, from clean and loose to clayey and compact		0.25	0.70	0.15	0.30
Railroad Yards			0.10	0.30	0.10	0.30
Earth Surfaces	*Sand,* from uniform grain size, no fines, to well graded, some clay or silt.	Bare	0.15	0.50	0.01	0.55
		Light vegetation	0.10	0.40	0.01	0.55
		Dense vegetation	0.05	0.30	0.01	0.55
	Loam, from sandy or gravelly to clayey.	Bare	0.20	0.60		
		Light vegetation	0.10	0.45		
		Dense vegetation	0.05	0.35		
	Gravel, from clean gravel and gravel sand mixtures, no silt or clay to high clay or silt content	Bare	0.25	0.65		
		Light vegetation	0.15	0.50		
		Dense vegetation	0.10	0.40		
	Clay, from coarse sandy or silty to pure colloidal clays.	Bare	0.30	0.75	0.10	0.70
		Light vegetation	0.20	0.60	0.10	0.70
		Dense vegetation	0.15	0.50	0.10	0.70
Composite Areas	City, business areas		0.60	0.75	0.60	0.95
	City, dense residential areas, vary as to soil and vegetation		0.50	0.65	0.30	0.60
	Suburban residential areas, vary as to soil and vegetation		0.35	0.55	0.25	0.40
	Rural districts, vary as to soil and vegetation		0.10	0.25	0.10	0.25
	Parks, golf courses, etc., vary as to soil and vegetation		0.10	0.35	0.05	0.25

Note: Values of "C" for earth surfaces are further varied by degree of saturation, compaction, surface irregularity and slope, by character of subsoil, and by presence of frost or glazed snow or ice.
Source: Seelye, Elwyn E., *Data Book for Civil Engineers,* vol. I, *Design,* 3d ed., New York: John Wiley & Sons, 1957.

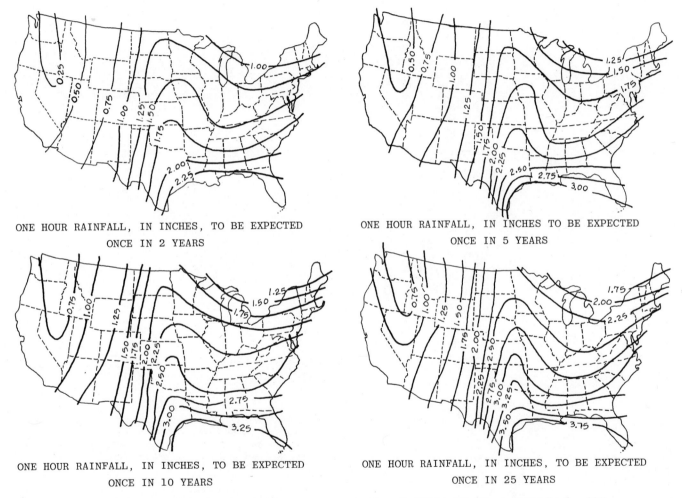

ONE HOUR RAINFALL, IN INCHES, TO BE EXPECTED
ONCE IN 2 YEARS

ONE HOUR RAINFALL, IN INCHES TO BE EXPECTED
ONCE IN 5 YEARS

ONE HOUR RAINFALL, IN INCHES, TO BE EXPECTED
ONCE IN 10 YEARS

ONE HOUR RAINFALL, IN INCHES, TO BE EXPECTED
ONCE IN 25 YEARS

Figure 8.4. Rainfall intensity probability (From D. L. Yarnell, USDA Miscellaneous Publication 204).

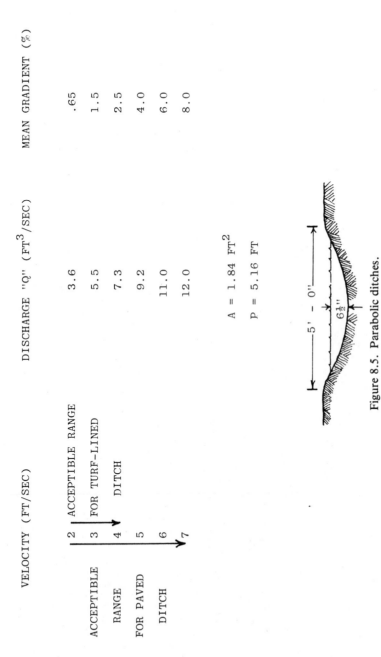

VELOCITY (FT/SEC)		DISCHARGE "Q" (FT^3/SEC)	MEAN GRADIENT (%)
2	ACCEPTABLE RANGE	3.6	.65
3	FOR TURF-LINED	5.5	1.5
4	DITCH	7.3	2.5
5		9.2	4.0
6		11.0	6.0
7		12.0	8.0

ACCEPTABLE

RANGE

FOR PAVED

DITCH

A = 1.84 FT^2

P = 5.16 FT

Figure 8.5. Parabolic ditches.

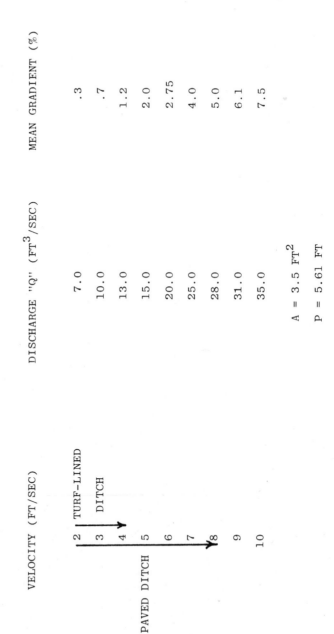

VELOCITY (FT/SEC)		DISCHARGE "Q" (FT^3/SEC)	MEAN GRADIENT (%)
2	TURF-LINED	7.0	.3
3	DITCH	10.0	.7
4		13.0	1.2
5		15.0	2.0
6		20.0	2.75
7		25.0	4.0
8		28.0	5.0
9		31.0	6.1
10		35.0	7.5

PAVED DITCH

A = 3.5 FT^2

P = 5.61 FT

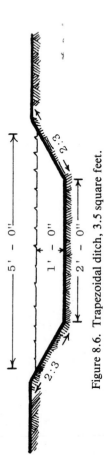

Figure 8.6. Trapezoidal ditch, 3.5 square feet.

VELOCITY (FT/SEC)	DISCHARGE "Q" (FT³/SEC)	MEAN GRADIENT (%)
2 — TURF-LINED	8	.3
3 — DITCH	12	.7
4	14	1.3
5	20	2.0
6	24	2.8
7	28	3.8
8	32	5.0
9 — PAVED DITCH	35	6.5
10	40	7.5

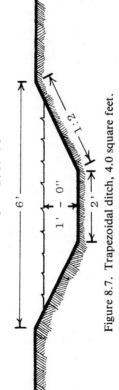

$$A = 4.0 \ FT^2$$
$$P = 6.47 \ FT$$

6' 1' – 0" 2'

Figure 8.7. Trapezoidal ditch, 4.0 square feet.

VELOCITY (FT/SEC)	DISCHARGE "Q" (FT³/SEC)	MEAN GRADIENT
2 — TURF-LINED	10	.32
3 — DITCH	14	.72
4	20	1.5
5	25	2.0
6	30	3.8
7 — PAVED DITCH	35	4.0
8	40	5.0
9	45	6.5
10	50	8.0

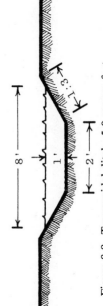

$$A = 5.0 \ FT^2$$
$$P = 8.32 \ FT$$

8' 1' 2' 1:.3

Figure 8.8. Trapezoidal ditch, 5.0 square feet.

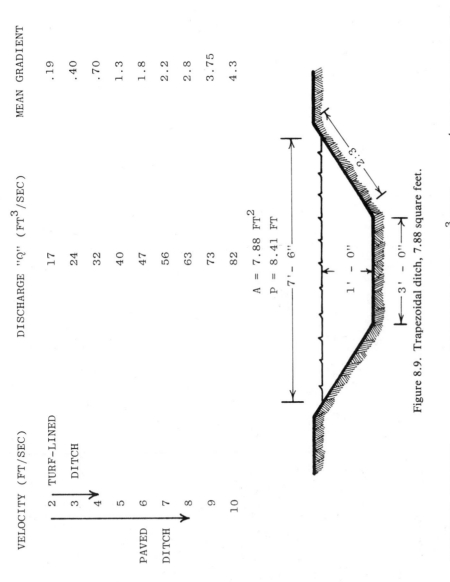

Figure 8.9. Trapezoidal ditch, 7.88 square feet.

VELOCITY (FT/SEC)		DISCHARGE "Q" (FT^3/SEC)	MEAN GRADIENT
2	TURF–LINED	17	.19
3	DITCH	24	.40
4		32	.70
5		40	1.3
6		47	1.8
7		56	2.2
8		63	2.8
9		73	3.75
10		82	4.3

PAVED DITCH

$A = 7.88 \ FT^2$

$P = 8.41 \ FT$

7' – 6"

1' – 0"

3' – 0"

2:3

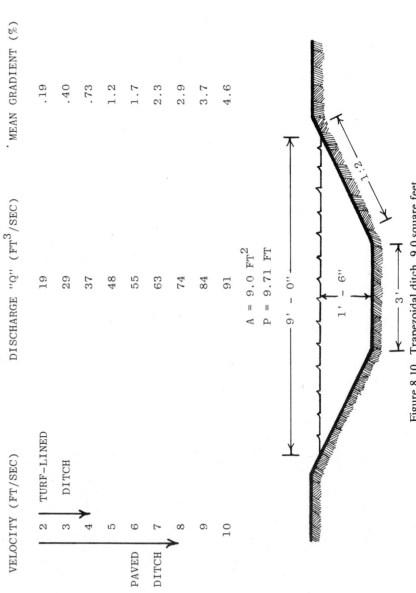

Figure 8.10. Trapezoidal ditch, 9.0 square feet.

VELOCITY (FT/SEC)		DISCHARGE "Q" (FT^3/SEC)	MEAN GRADIENT (%)
2	TURF–LINED	19	.19
3	DITCH	29	.40
4		37	.73
5		48	1.2
6		55	1.7
7		63	2.3
8		74	2.9
9		84	3.7
10		91	4.6

PAVED DITCH

$A = 9.0 \ FT^2$

$P = 9.71 \ FT$

9' – 0"

1' – 6"

3'

1:2

VELOCITY (FT/SEC)	DISCHARGE "Q" (FT³/SEC)	MEAN GRADIENT (%)
2	22	.2
3	37	.41
4	47	.8
5	56	1.2
6	67	1.7
7	80	2.3
8	90	3.0
9	100	3.8
10	115	4.7

TURF-LINED DITCH

PAVED DITCH

$A = 11.25 \ \text{FT}^2$

$P = 17.49 \ \text{FT}$

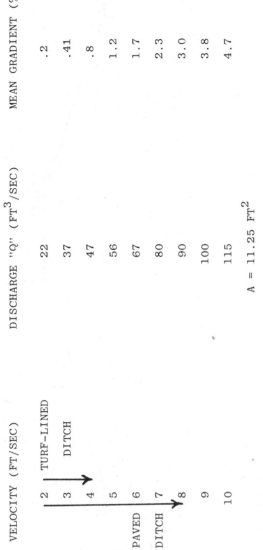
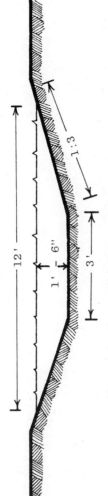

Figure 8.11. Trapezoidal ditch, 11.25 square feet.

VELOCITY (FT/SEC)	DISCHARGE "Q" (FT³/SEC)	MEAN GRADIENT (%)
2	25	.15
3	37	.30
4	49	.51
5	60	.80
6	71	1.2
7	85	1.7
8	97	2.1
9	110	2.7
10	130	3.1

TURF-LINED DITCH

PAVED DITCH

$A = 12 \ \text{FT}^2$

$P = 10.21 \ \text{FT}$

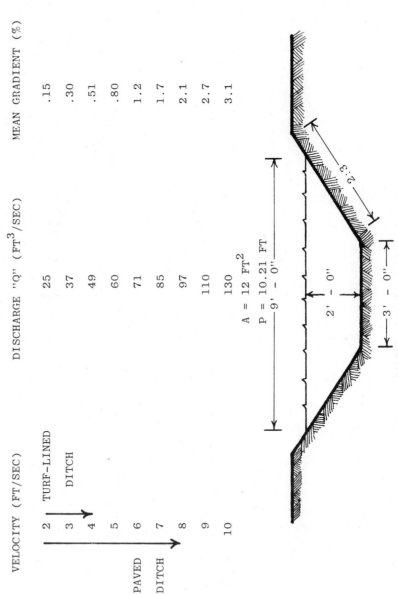

Figure 8.12. Trapezoidal ditch, 12.0 square feet.

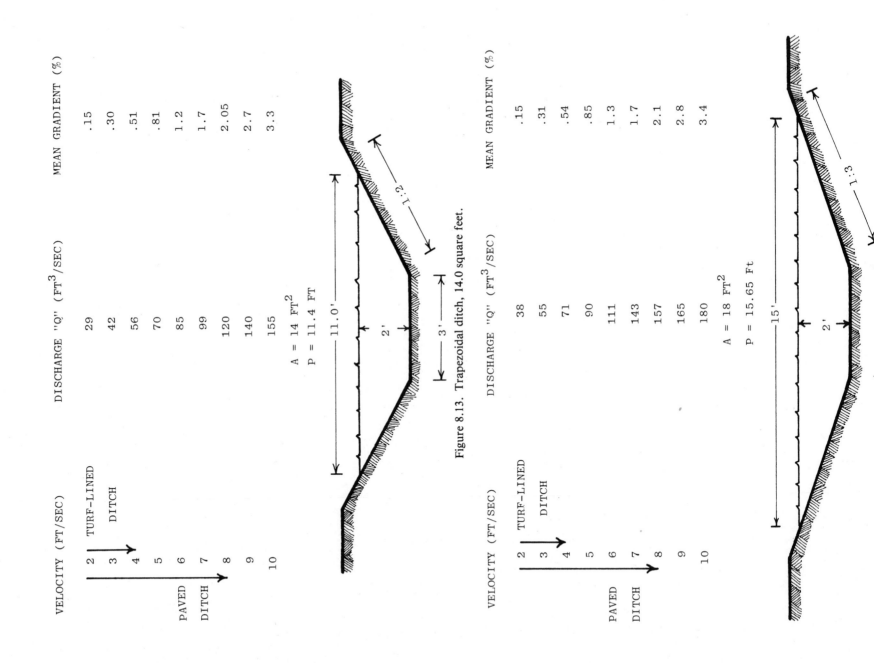

Figure 8.13. Trapezoidal ditch, 14.0 square feet.

Figure 8.14. Trapezoidal ditch, 18.0 square feet.

VELOCITY (FT/SEC)	DISCHARGE "Q" (FT^3/SEC)	MEAN GRADIENT (%)
TURF-LINED DITCH		
3 →	90	.19
4	135	.31
PAVED DITCH		
5	160	.495
6	185	.70
7	210	.98
8	260	1.3
9	280	1.7

A = 30 FT^2

P = 17.42 FT

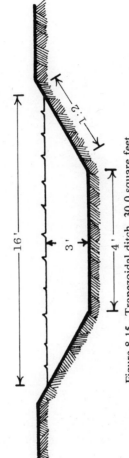

Figure 8.15. Trapezoidal ditch, 30.0 square feet.

VELOCITY (FT/SEC)	DISCHARGE "Q" (FT^3/SEC)	MEAN GRADIENT (%)
TURF-LINED DITCH		
3	130.0	.18
4 →	160.0	.32
PAVED DITCH		
5	200.0	.51
6	250.0	.72
7	290.0	.95

A = 39 FT^2

P = 22.97 FT

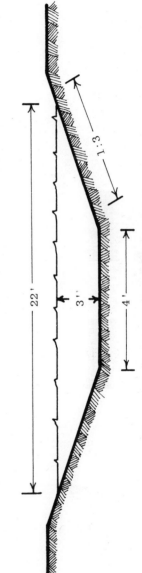

Figure 8.16. Trapezoidal ditch, 39.0 square feet.

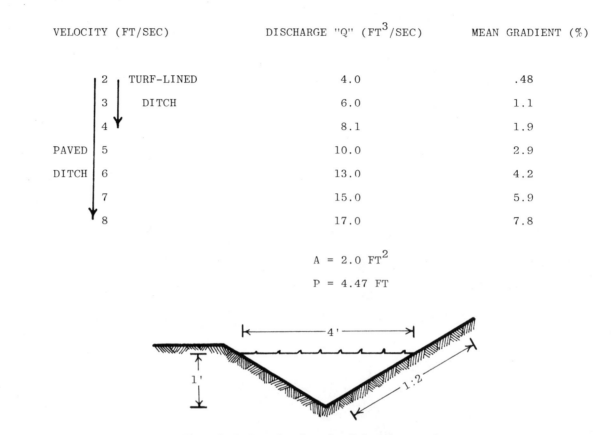

VELOCITY (FT/SEC)	DISCHARGE "Q" (FT^3/SEC)	MEAN GRADIENT (%)
2 TURF-LINED	4.0	.48
3 DITCH	6.0	1.1
4	8.1	1.9
PAVED 5	10.0	2.9
DITCH 6	13.0	4.2
7	15.0	5.9
8	17.0	7.8

$$A = 2.0 \text{ FT}^2$$

$$P = 4.47 \text{ FT}$$

Figure 8.17. Isosceles triangular ditch, 2.0 square feet.

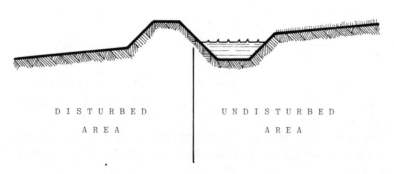

DISTURBED AREA   UNDISTURBED AREA

Figure 8.18. Dike and ditch diversion.

Vegetative Diversions

One of the more popular methods of creating surface flow diversions is with the use of berms. In many cases, topsoil must be removed in the mining process and the stockpile placed in such a way as to divert water from the disturbed areas. The diversion, however, should have a lower priority than the preservation of the topsoil material. Selection of overburden placement can play a role in creating a diversion when necessary. The proper method of stockpiling topsoil is presented in Figure 8.19.

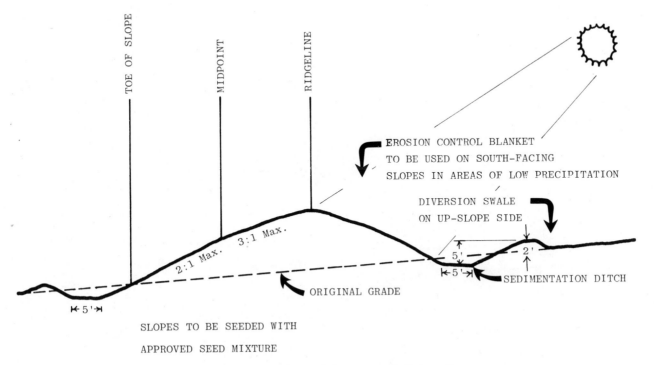

Figure 8.19. Proper technique to stockpile topsoil.

CONVEYANCE SYSTEMS

Mechanical Conveyance

Conveyance systems serve to move surface flow from one point to another. They are particularly useful when runoff cannot be adequately disposed of by conveyance across a slope. The object of using various conveyance systems is to move the runoff over a slope and into a safe outlet without subjecting the slope to damaging erosive forces. The location of disposal structures is important and consideration should be given to allowing the water to flow in the proper volume and velocity so as to prevent erosion. There are several devices that can be used, including:

A. Culverts
B. Slope drains
C. Relief culverts
D. Drop inlets

Culverts.   A Culvert can be defined as an enclosed channel that serves as a continuation of and a substitute for an open stream where the stream meets an artificial barrier such as a roadway.[3] The method of determining the size of the culvert needed is similar to that used to size ditches as described earlier.

There are several types of culverts, including reinforced

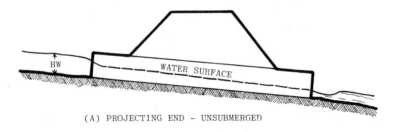

(A) PROJECTING END – UNSUBMERGED

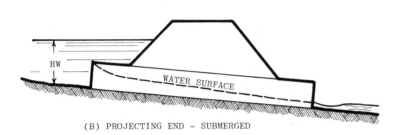

(B) PROJECTING END – SUBMERGED

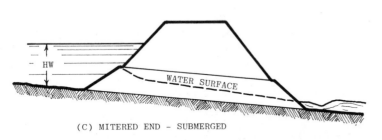

(C) MITERED END – SUBMERGED

Figure 8.20. Culverts flowing with inlet control (Adapted from American Iron and Steel Institute, *Handbook of Steel Drainage and Highway Construction Products,* 2d ed., New York: AISI, 1971, p. 22).

concrete pipe, corrugated metal, tile, cement–asbestos, cast–iron, plastic, and bituminous fiber. The two most commonly used culverts are the concrete and corrugated metal types.

There are two main types of culvert flow: *inlet control* and *outlet control.* Inlet control culverts have capacities that are affected only by entrance configuration and headwater depth.

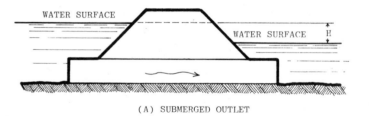

(A) SUBMERGED OUTLET

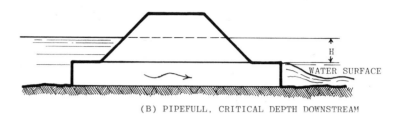

(B) PIPEFULL, CRITICAL DEPTH DOWNSTREAM

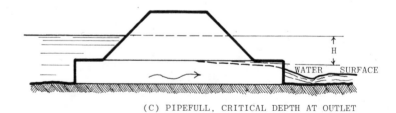

(C) PIPEFULL, CRITICAL DEPTH AT OUTLET

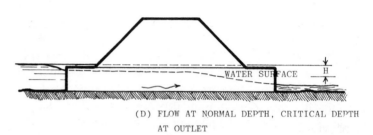

(D) FLOW AT NORMAL DEPTH, CRITICAL DEPTH AT OUTLET

Figure 8.21. Culverts flowing with outlet control (Adapted from American Iron and Steel Institute, *Handbook of Steel Drainage and Highway Construction Products,* 2d ed., New York: AISI, 1971, p. 23).

Table 8.2. Culvert Selection Chart.

DISCHARGE FT.³/SEC[a]	CULVERT STANDARD SIZES[b] (IN.)	MINIMUM COVER[c] (IN.)	MAX. COVER, 2⅔ x ½ IN. CORRUGATION SPECIFIED THICKNESS (IN.)						MAX. COVER, 3 x 1 IN. CORRUGATION SPECIFIED THICKNESS (IN.)					
			.052	.064	.079	.109	.138	.168	.052	.064	.079	.109	.138	.168
2.58	12	12	199	248	310									
4.51	15	12	159	199	248									
7.11	18	12	132	166	207									
10.46	21	12	113	142	178	249								
14.60	24	12	99	124	155	218								
19.60	27	12		111	138	193								
25.51	30	12		99	124	174								
40.23	36	12		83	103	145	186		76	95	121	167	214	263
59.15	42	12		71	88	124	160	195	65	81	102	143	185	225
82.59	48	12		62	77	109	140	171	57	71	91	125	161	197
110.87	54	12			66	93	120	147		63	80	111	143	175
144.28	60	12				79	102	125		57	72	100	129	156

[a] Calculated with formula $Q = 2.581 (d/12)^{2.5}$, where d = diameter of circular pipe in inches. (*Source:* American Iron and Steel Institute, *Handbook of Steel Drainage and Highway Construction Products,* 2d ed., 1971, p. 159).
[b] Circular corrugated steel pipe.
[c] From top of pipe to top of subgrade.

They always flow partially full and are usually steeply sloped. Since they are short tubes or orifices, they are critically sensitive to modifications in inlet geometry. If the inlet has been efficiently designed, full diameter flow can be achieved. Flared or rounded inlets are the most efficient.[4] Figure 8.20 illustrates the types of culverts that flow with inlet control.

With outlet control, headwater depth, tailwater depth, entrance configuration, and barrel characteristics all influence the culvert's drainage capacity. Culverts with outlet control may or may not flow full. The culvert acts as a long tube, with frictional resistance, invert slope, and tailwater depth generally producing full flow conditions. Inlet configuration and headwall design contribute little to the flow capacity. Figure 8.21 provides illustrations of various types of culverts with outlet control.[5]

Culverts should provide a stream or drainage channel with a direct entrance and a direct exit. Direct inlet and outlet is secured by one of three ways—by means of a channel change, a skewed alignment, or both. The ideal grade line of a culvert will produce neither silting nor scouring because of excessive velocity. At least 0.5 feet of slope in 100 feet of culvert will prevent sedimentation. A culvert should be long enough that the inlet and outlet do not become clogged with sediment or covered with a settling, spreading embankment. Headwalls or riprapped side walls should always be used in the more permanent structures. Outlets are potential erosion hazards and should be protected. Figure 8.22 illustrates a variety of outlets and the effects each creates on lateral scour. Culvert endwalls and wingwalls are illustrated in Figure 8.23. Use Table 8.2 for selecting the appropriate culvert.

Slope Drains. Slope drains, also called *chutes* or *downdrains,* are lined, artificial channels or conduits placed on a steep grade to rapidly lower the water level in a drainage sys-

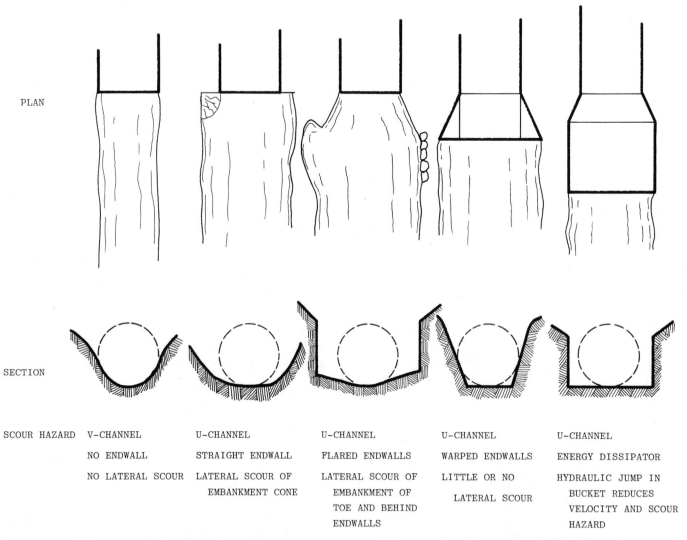

PLAN

SECTION

SCOUR HAZARD	V-CHANNEL	U-CHANNEL	U-CHANNEL	U-CHANNEL	U-CHANNEL
	NO ENDWALL	STRAIGHT ENDWALL	FLARED ENDWALLS	WARPED ENDWALLS	ENERGY DISSIPATOR
	NO LATERAL SCOUR	LATERAL SCOUR OF EMBANKMENT CONE	LATERAL SCOUR OF EMBANKMENT OF TOE AND BEHIND ENDWALLS	LITTLE OR NO LATERAL SCOUR	HYDRAULIC JUMP IN BUCKET REDUCES VELOCITY AND SCOUR HAZARD

Figure 8.22. Typical culvert outlets (Adapted from American Iron and Steel Institute, *Handbook of Steel Drainage and Highway Constitution Products,* 2d ed., New York: AISI, 1971, p. 177).

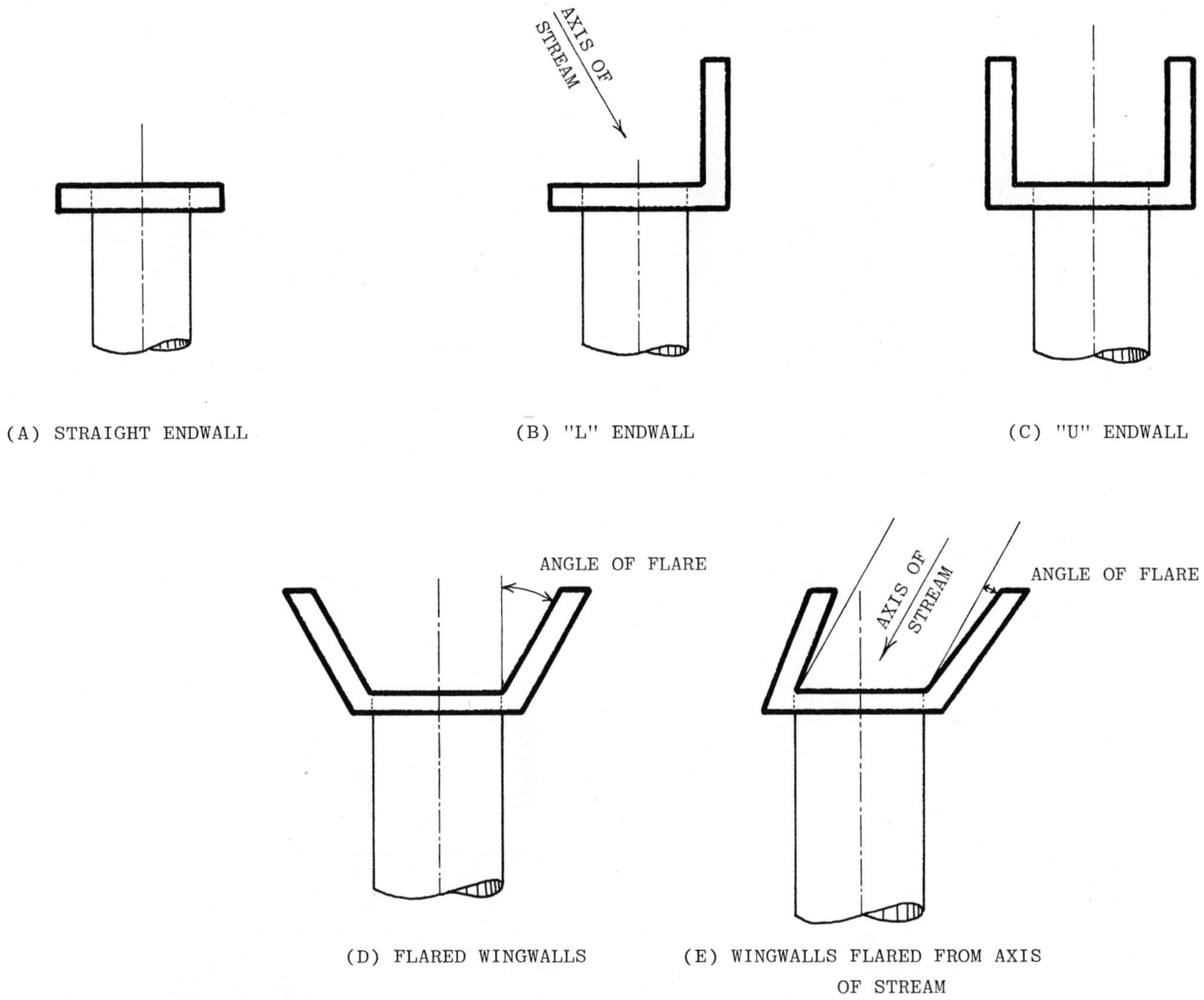
AXIS OF
STREAM
(A) STRAIGHT ENDWALL
(B) "L" ENDWALL
(C) "U" ENDWALL
ANGLE OF FLARE
AXIS OF
STREAM
ANGLE OF FLARE
(D) FLARED WINGWALLS
(E) WINGWALLS FLARED FROM AXIS OF STREAM

Figure 8.23. Culvert endwalls and wingwalls (From Skodje, Marvin, *Drainage,* vol. XIV, Action Guide Series of National Association of County Engineers, Washington, D.C.: Highway Users Federation, 1776 Massachusetts Ave., N. W., July 1972, p. 32).

tem. They are often placed on the fill slope of a road cut to carry water diverted from an interceptor dike down the face of the slope to a stabilized area. Slope drains can be constructed with a variety of techniques including the examples illustrated by Figure 8.24.

Relief Culvert.   A relief culvert is an enclosed conduit placed along a road at regular intervals with inlets in the upslope channel. Relief culverts serve to reduce the accumulation of waterflow volume within a roadside ditch. This, in turn, allows the surface water to flow across the landscape much as

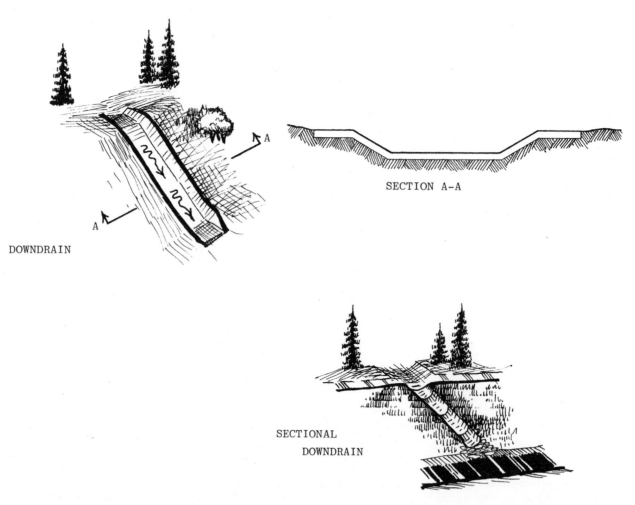

DOWNDRAIN

SECTION A–A

SECTIONAL
DOWNDRAIN

Figure 8.24. Downdrains (Adapted from Michigan Department of Natural Resources, *Michigan Soil Erosion and Sedimentation Control Guidebook,* Division of Land Resources Programs, Lansing, Mich.: 1980).

it would had the road not been built. Since roads serve as barriers to the natural sheet flow, the use of relief culverts in arid regions serve not only to reduce volume, but also to supply needed water to the vegetation downslope. Relief culverts, illustrated in Figure 8.25, should traverse the roadway at spacings indicated in Table 8.3.

Table 8.3. Relief Culvert Spacing.

GRADIENT OF ROADWAY	MINIMUM SPACING (LINEAR FEET)
1– 2%	1,000
2– 4%	800
4– 6%	600
6– 8%	400
8–10%	250

Adapted from Bureau of Land Management, *Oil and Gas-Surface Operating Standards for Oil and Gas Exploration and Development,* 2d ed., Washington, D.C.: U.S. Government Printing Office, 1978, p. 23.

Drop Inlets. A drop inlet is a type of structure that allows water to drop from a higher elevation to a lower outlet elevation smoothly without a freefall at the discharge area. This system should be employed where outlet stabilization is poor. This device will prevent excessive splash erosion caused by a freefall of runoff at the point of discharge. Both relief culverts and drop inlets are employed for long-term solutions. Other methods should be used for temporary situations. Drop inlets are illustrated in Figure 8.26.

Vegetative Conveyance

There are several vegetative methods that can be employed to convey water flow from one point to another in the rehabilitation process. Vegetative methods are generally preferred for temporary, short-term solutions to erosion problems. They are less expensive to implement and their natural decline corresponds in time with the establishment of a vegetative cover. They are also less obtrusive and tend to blend in well with the environment.

As mentioned earlier, grass-lined waterways or ditches serve as conveyance systems as well as diversions. These are easily constructed and are usually adequate. One additional method involves a device known as a level spreader (see Figure 8.27).

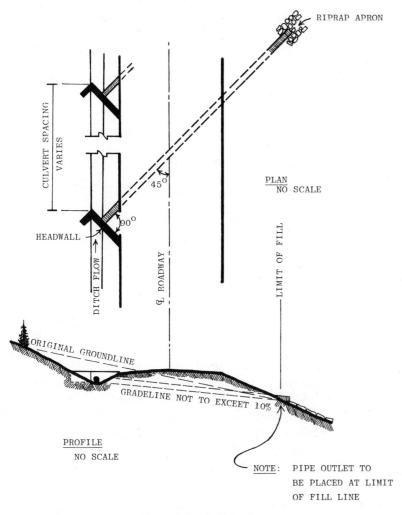

Figure 8.25. Relief culvert.

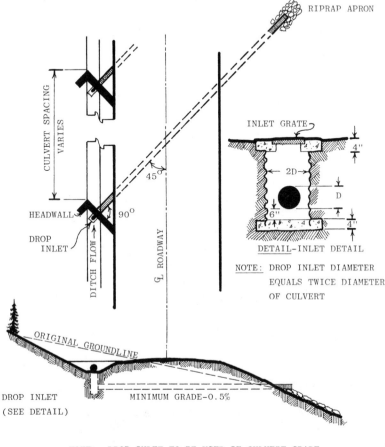

NOTE: DROP INLET TO BE USED IF CULVERT GRADE

FROM HEADWALL TO OUTLET IS IN EXCESS OF 10%

Figure 8.26. Relief culvert with drop inlet.

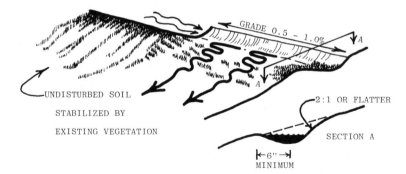

Figure 8.27. Level spreader (Adapted from Urban Land Institute, *Residential Erosion and Sediment Control,* Washington, D.C.: ULI, 1978, p. 44).

Level Spreader.   A level spreader is a device with an outlet constructed at zero grade across a slope to spread concentrated runoff so it may overflow at nonerosive velocities in the form of sheet flow over lower undisturbed areas that are stabilized by existing vegetation. It is generally used in transition zones located between nonstabilized or disturbed areas and stabilized, undisturbed areas.

STABILIZING AND DISSIPATING SYSTEMS

Mechanical Stabilizers and Dissipators

There are numerous methods that can be used to stabilize the soil or dissipate the energy of flowing water. Among the more popular are:

A. Benches or terraces
B. Retaining walls
C. Riprap

Benches and Terraces.   Benches are defined as the surface of an excavated area at the point between the material being mined and the original surface of the ground on which equipment can sit, move, or operate.[6] A terrace is an embankment or combination of an embankment and channel constructed across a slope to control erosion by diverting the water flow.[7] There are several types of terraces including *absorptive, bench,* and *drainage.*

The absorptive terrace is a ridge type of terrace used primarily for moisture conservation. Thus, it is constructed with a very gentle grade to allow moisture to seep into the soil. The bench is a terrace constructed approximately on the contour. It has a steep drop downslope but is gently sloped along the terrace. The drainage terrace is a broad, channel type used primarily to conduct water from the area at low velocity. It is used in areas with less absorptive soil and high rainfall.[8] Factors that contribute to the success of a terrace for erosion control include:

A. Soil type
B. Vegetal cover
C. Initial soil conditions
D. Precipitation rates
E. Terrace geometry
F. Gradient of terrace slopes
G. The number and spacing of terraces on a slope

Terraces should not be constructed that exceed 25 feet in width. They should have a freeboard of 30 to 42 inches and be carried along the slope at a consistent 5 percent grade to prevent silt accumulation in the beds. It would be wise to lay the terraces out with the aid of an instrument to ensure accuracy. Terraces are illustrated in Figure 8.28.

Retaining Walls. Retaining walls, as the name implies, retain the slopes in a steeply inclined position and work to prevent *sloughing* (sliding or collapse of the embankment). In rehabilitation, they are seldom employed but could certainly serve a vital need in situations where the soil is too steeply sloped for revegetation or stabilization. The retaining wall should be constructed with the following in mind:

A. The wall should slope inward toward the upslope side at a slight angle. This angle is called *batter* and should equal 1 inch for each foot of wall height (see Figure 8.29).
B. The wall should sit on a good base, either of compacted earth material, for short-term projects or on a stone or concrete foundation for long-term walls.
C. If constructed from stone, the larger stones should be placed on the bottom and the smaller stones on top.

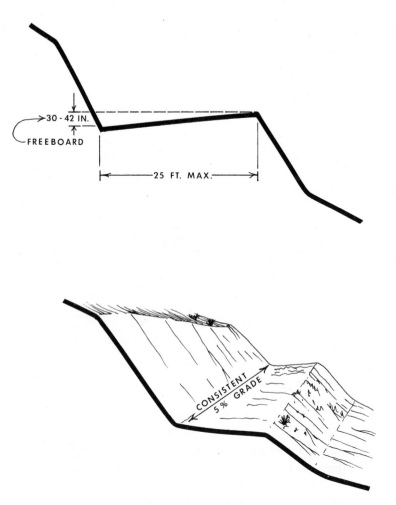

Figure 8.28. Drainage terrace.

D. Grading around the wall should provide a drainage swale upslope to reduce the hydraulic pressure from pushing against the wall.
E. Large, long-term walls that are needed to support large embankments should be designed by a landscape architect or civil engineer in order to ensure against failure.

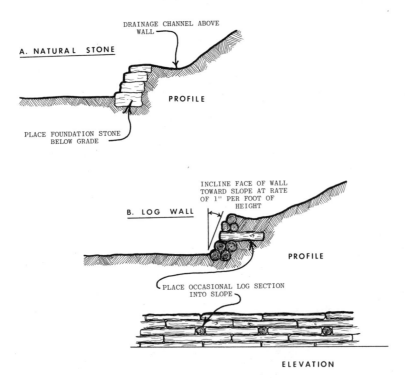

Figure 8.29. Typical retaining walls for temporary use.

The retaining walls illustrated in Figure 8.29 are small, short-term walls that can be constructed out of native materials for temporary stability. Materials such as stone or logs that are available in the project area are suggested.

Riprap. Riprap is a layer of broken rock, cobbles, or boulders that is placed on the land surface to protect the soil against the forces of moving water. It is normally used in areas where vegetation is not easily established and is particularly effective in areas where water is flowing at high velocities or in high concentrations. Its effectiveness is related to the fact that it allows water to infiltrate the soil and that the rocks dissipate the energy flow, especially at the drain outlets. It is especially effective on slopes, streams, and waterways.

Types of riprap. There are several types of riprap. However, only two seem appropriate to rehabilitation. These include *dumped riprap* and *wire-enclosed riprap*. Dumped riprap consists of stone or broken concrete that is dumped in place to form a well-graded mass with a minimum of voids. Dumped riprap must have a variety of sizes so that the smaller stones fill the gaps between the larger stones.

Wire-enclosed riprap consists of either mats or baskets fabricated from wire mesh and filled with stone, then connected together to be anchored to the slope. Both types are particularly valuable in areas where design flow conditions can cause erosion, in particular where soil erodibility is high, slopes are excessive, vegetation cover is low, or velocities too high for the soil to remain stable. Stones used for dumped riprap should be hard, durable, angular in shape, and resistant to weathering and water action. Rounded stones should not be used. Gradation requirements for riprap are listed in Table 8.4.

Slope preparation is critical to the success of riprap in an erosion control system. Slopes should be free of brush, trees, and stumps and should be graded to a smooth, uniform grade. Riprap to be used on streambanks or lakeshores should extend from two feet below the bed of a stream to the apparent high water line.

Stone used for wire-enclosed riprap should meet the same requirements as specified for dumped riprap. The fabric used

Table 8.4. Gradation Requirements for Riprap.

SIZE OF STONE (LB)	MAXIMUM % OF TOTAL WEIGHT SMALLER THAN GIVEN SIZE
100	100
60	80
25	50
2	10

Adapted from U.S. Department of Transportation, *Standard Specifications for Construction of Roads and Bridges on Federal Highway Projects*, no. 050–001–00145–4, Washington, D.C.: U.S. Government Printing Office, 1979, p. 241.

to enclose riprap should be constructed of galvanized welded wire fabric (2 × 4–12 ½ × 12 ½) of 4-foot widths. Ties and lacing should be galvanized, 12 gauge wire. Illustrations demonstrating the employment of riprap are designated as Figures 8.30 and 8.31.

Vegetative Stabilizers and Dissipators

Any vegetated soil surface acts as a stabilizing force against erosion. The method of establishing quick vegetative cover is determined by a variety of factors which will be discussed in the next section of this book.

The following is a comprehensive list of methods employed as vegetative stabilizers:

A. The establishment of seedlings
B. Hydroseeding
C. Drilling
D. Broadcasting
E. Mulching
F. Scarifying

Most of these will be covered in the next section. However, scarifying is related to surface manipulation and will be covered here.

Scarifying. Scarifying is any method employed that will roughen the texture of the surface in such a way as to lessen the impact of erosion. The main purpose of scarifying is to create

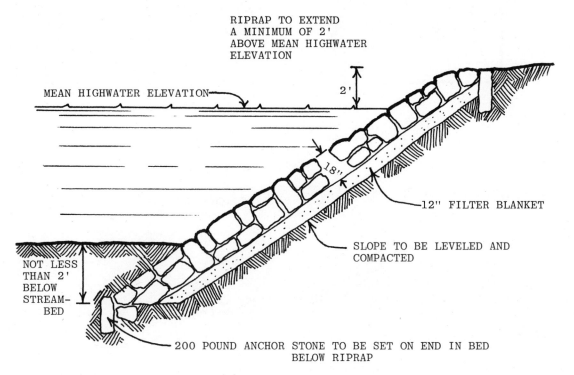

RIPRAP TO EXTEND A MINIMUM OF 2' ABOVE MEAN HIGHWATER ELEVATION

MEAN HIGHWATER ELEVATION

2'

18"

12" FILTER BLANKET

SLOPE TO BE LEVELED AND COMPACTED

NOT LESS THAN 2' BELOW STREAM-BED

200 POUND ANCHOR STONE TO BE SET ON END IN BED BELOW RIPRAP

Figure 8.30. Riprap along waterways.

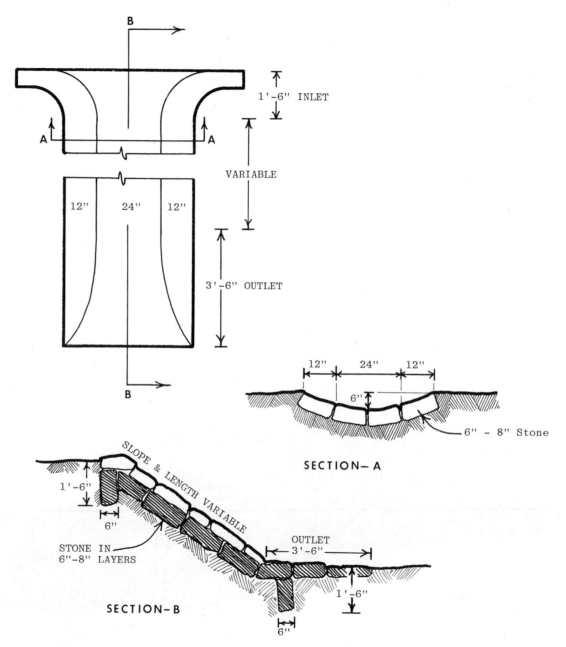

Figure 8.31. Riprap spillway.

resistance to moving water and increase the infiltration rates of the soil. In addition, in areas of low rainfall, roughened soil surfaces create microclimates that catch needed moisture, especially from blowing snow. Among the many ways to scarify the soil, the techniques most commonly used are tillage, basin-formers, gougers, and dozer treads.

Tillage. Tillage, or plowing, can be done by several types of equipment including plows, furrowers, offset discs, and chisels. Though standard farm implements, they are often redesigned to meet the needs of a particular rehabilitation project. All of them tend to turn the soil in such a way as to provide a coarser texture in the surface of the landscape. They all meet the objectives of providing resistance to moving water

and of increasing the rate of infiltration. Tillage is usually done prior to the planting bed preparation or to stabilize the soil until the proper time for planting.

Basin-former. The basin-former creates large depressions in the soil surface simulating the general effect of terracing. It is primarily used to create a favorable microclimate for a seed-bed on mine spoil slopes, especially in areas with low precipitation. The depressions collect runoff that would otherwise run down an uninterrupted slope, trap snow and topsoil that would normally blow away, and provide a collector for solar energy. They also act to prevent massive erosion, and provide shade and shelter for seed and seedlings.

The basin-former, illustrated in Figure 8.32, is a large blade

Figure 8.32. Basin-former.

mounted on the rear of an appropriately sized crawler tractor to create large depressions in the soil surface.

Gouger.   The gouger, as well as the basin-former, was designed by R. L. Hodder, senior research associate with the Montana Agriculture Experiment Station. The gouger (see Figure 8.33) is designed to be used much like the basin-former. The basins formed by the gouger are more numerous, smaller, and more suitable to certain types of drills used for planting.

Dozer treads.   One of the simplest methods of scarifying the surface is to make a final run with the dozer, moving up and down the slope as illustrated in Figure 8.34. This action slows runoff by creating grooves that are perpendicular to the flow. Treads running in the opposite direction can have a catastrophic effect.

RETENTION SYSTEMS

Mechanical Retention Systems

Any device constructed to retain water for a period of time in order to allow the flow to occur with controlled volume or velocity will serve to lessen erosive impacts. Such mechanical retention devices include check dams, sediment basins, and waterbars.

Check Dams.   Check dams are a series of obstructions placed in ditches or gullies that serve to lessen the effective gradient of the flow line. The dam impedes the water flow and slows the velocity immediately upstream, causing the suspended sediment to be deposited behind the dam as shown in Figure 8.35.

Check dams can be constructed in a variety of ways. Some dams are porous; others are not. Solid dams can be constructed out of concrete, sheet metal, or wet masonry. They

Figure 8.33. Gouger.

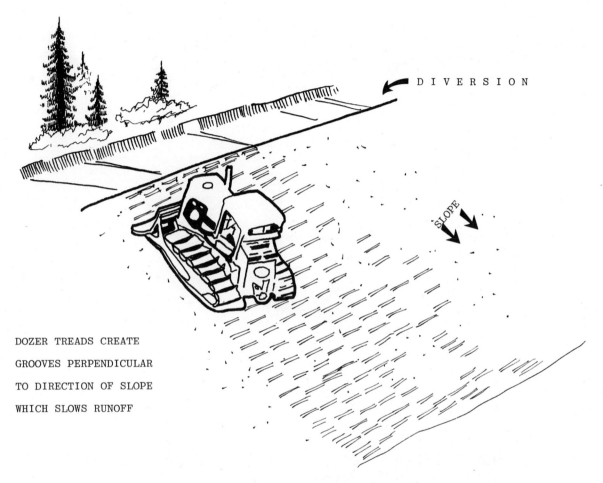

Figure 8.34. Slope scarification using dozer treads.

are relatively expensive when compared to the nonporous types, which are constructed out of rock, brush, or posts. Gray and Leisner provide guidelines for the spacing of check dams as related to gully gradient and dam height (see Figure 8.36).[9]

As shown in Figure 8.38, each dam should be constructed with an apron, a sill, and a freeboard allowance that permits overflow that will not touch the bank at either side of the gully.

Sediment Basins. Sediment basins are extremely effective and probably the most popular technique employed to correct surface disturbances by removing sediment as a resource out of place. They are also used on large construction sites. A

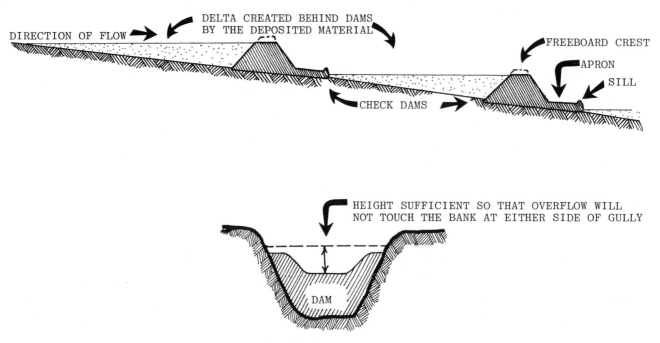

Figure 8.35. Check dams.

basin can be defined as a temporary or permanent water impoundment usually constructed by damming a waterway or drainage channel. The dam serves to stop the flow of water, allowing the sediment to settle to the bottom while the water flow is directed from the top, as seen in Figure 8.37.

Sediment basins should be constructed within the property limits at all flow outlets from a mining disturbance. Surface flow around the periphery of or directly through the disturbance is likely to contain a higher sediment load than it would on the undisturbed site. The water flowing out of the sediment basin is, in many instances, clearer than in the undisturbed state.

Permanent sediment basins will occasionally have to be dredged out in order to maintain their ability to receive the normal surface flow. The filtered inlet must also be maintained, and care should be taken to provide an energy dissipator at the outlet. If the need arises, a spillway may be incorporated into the design to safely handle occasional seasonal storm water.

Waterbars.   *Waterbar* and *waterbreak* are terms that are often used synonymously to refer to a shallow retention and diversion to direct water flow across a slope rather than downslope. It functions primarily in four ways, including:

A. The reduction of volume of flow
B. The reduction in the length of flow

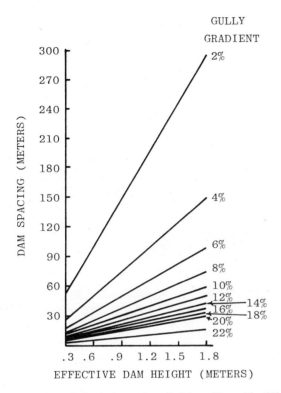

GULLY
GRADIENT

Figure 8.36. Spacing of check dams, installed in gullies with different gradients, as a function of effective dam height (From *Biotechnical Slope Protection and Erosion Control* by D. Gray and A. T. Leisner, copyright © 1982 by Van Nostrand Reinhold, reprinted by permission of publisher).

C. The reduction in the velocity of flow
D. The distribution of water into natural overland flow patterns

Waterbars are used primarily along linear disturbances such as roads or pipelines that are being rehabilitated, or in some cases, roads that are only used occasionally. There are basically two variables that affect design and location. These include spacing and geometric configuration. Generally spacing

should conform to Table 8.5 which identifies the allowable percentage of slope. Steeper slopes need greater quantities of diversion, thus a shorter distance between waterbars. Table 8.5 does not, however, take into consideration the various soil types nor the intensity of rainfall for a particular region. Therefore, the distances may have to be manipulated according to need.

The flow line along the waterbars should have a constant 2 percent grade for grassed surfaces with outlets distributed evenly down the natural slope. Waterbar construction should follow guidelines as shown in Figures 8.38 and 8.39.

CONCLUSIONS

The various erosion control systems described throughout this chapter are few compared to the many used in rehabilitation today. Each mine, region, soil type, or precipitation pattern will dictate how the problem is to be solved. The rehabilitation specialist should consider several criteria in choosing the system to be used. The first consideration is *longevity*. What will be the duration of the project or control needed? This will dictate the use of temporary, short-term devices as opposed to those that are more permanent.

Table 8.5.   Length Limits for Waterbar Spacing.

PERCENT SLOPE	MAXIMUM SLOPE LENGTH IN FEET
2	400
4–6	300
8	200
10	100
12	80
14–24	60

Source: Wyoming Soil Conservation Service, *Universal Soil Loss Equation,* Technical Note, n.d., p. 5.)

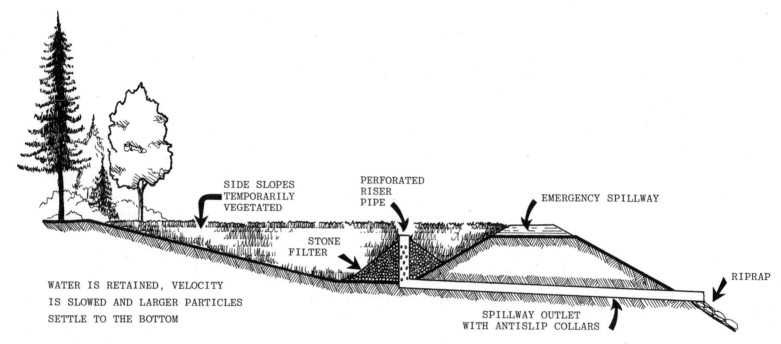

SIDE SLOPES
TEMPORARILY
VEGETATED

PERFORATED
RISER
PIPE

EMERGENCY SPILLWAY

STONE
FILTER

WATER IS RETAINED, VELOCITY
IS SLOWED AND LARGER PARTICLES
SETTLE TO THE BOTTOM

RIPRAP

SPILLWAY OUTLET
WITH ANTISLIP COLLARS

Figure 8.37. Profile through typical sediment basin.

Another consideration to be taken into account is the *source of construction materials*. In rehabilitation, as mentioned early in the chapter, slope stabilization is most needed from the time the final grading occurs until vegetation can become established. This means that temporary devices constructed out of natural materials indigenous to the site are in order and are usually preferred.

A third consideration is *cost*. One really should analyze the cost benefit of the various devices available and attempt to use those that are most cost efficient. The most expensive, long-lasting systems are often unnecessary.

The final consideration is choosing the proper erosion control system involves *labor*. Many systems can be constructed with "in-house" labor requiring no special skill. For example, check dams could be constructed out of rock material that is piled at various intervals in the bottom of a gully. Though the labor of only a single man in a front-end loader would be involved, the dams would solve enormous erosion problems.

REFERENCES

1. Michigan Department of Natural Resources, Division of Land Resource Programs, *Michigan Soil Erosion and Sedimentation Control Guidebook,* Lansing, Mich., 1980, p. 13.
2. Lanphair, Harlow C., and Fred Klatt, Jr., *Landscape Architecture Construction,* New York: Elsevier North Holland, Inc., 1980, p. 121.

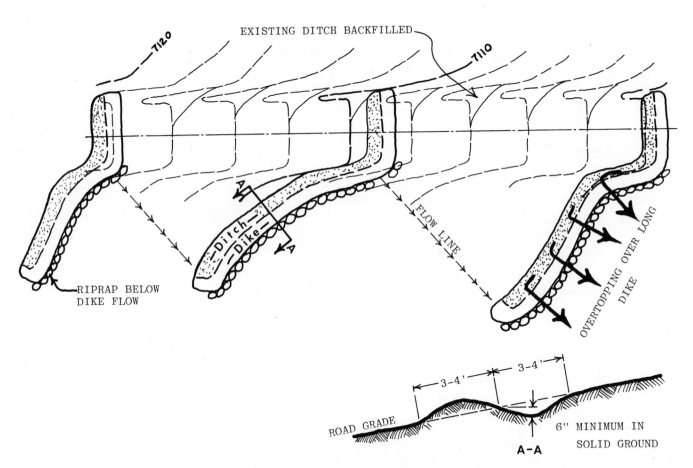

Figure 8.38. Waterbar construction—rehabilitated disturbances.

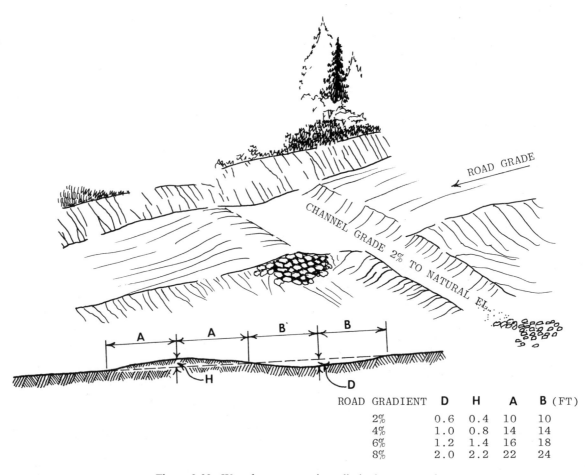

ROAD GRADIENT	D	H	A	B (FT)
2%	0.6	0.4	10	10
4%	1.0	0.8	14	14
6%	1.2	1.4	16	18
8%	2.0	2.2	22	24

Figure 8.39. Waterbar construction—limited access road.

3. American Iron and Steel Institute, *Handbook of Steel Drainage and Highway Construction Products,* 2d ed., New York, 1971, p. 79.

4. Ibid., p. 31.

5. Ibid., p. 21.

6. Environmental Protection Agency, *Erosion and Sediment Control,* vol. I, *Planning,* EPA Technology Transfer Seminar Publications, Washington, D.C.: Government Printing Office, 1976, p. 94.

7. Ibid., p. 101.

8. Ibid.

9. Gray, Donald H., and Andrew T. Leisner, *Biotechnical Slope Protection and Erosion Control,* New York: Van Nostrand Reinhold, 1982, p. 180.

PART IV
REHABILITATION:
REVEGETATION

9
Revegetation Problems

PLANT GROWTH FACTORS

Daubenmire, in his book *Plants and Environment,* indicates several factors that affect plant growth:[1]

A. Soils
B. Water
C. Temperature
D. Light
E. Atmosphere
F. Biotic relationships
G. Fire

Although it is beyond the scope of this chapter to reproduce the lengthy narrative describing the role of each factor in establishing healthy plant communities, the reader must realize that the intricate balance of a complex set of variables makes revegetative decisions difficult to comprehend.

Section 780.18 of the regulations promulgated under the Surface Mining Control and Reclamation Act of 1977 requires that each mining permit application contain a plan for revegetation activities. That plan should include:

A. Plant species to be used
B. Amount of seed or number of seedlings per acre
C. Planting and seeding methods
D. Mulching materials and methods
E. Fertilizers and lime, and application rates
F. Timing for implementation
G. Instructions for handling of topsoil
H. Tree and shrub stocking standards
I. Land use considerations

Planning the revegetation efforts in rehabilitation is complex at best. In most cases, the mining operation has altered the habitat in such a way that several of the growth factors have been affected.

Soils. Soils are critical for plant growth and survival. Daubenmire lists several aspects of soils that affect plant growth.[2] Among these are soil organisms, moisture and air, and solutes. Soil organisms include various bacteria, algae, nematodes, and so forth that work together to perform several roles. Their chief function is to cause the decay of organic matter, produce growth-stimulating substances, fix nitrogen, compete with higher plants for nutrients, mix soil, improve soil aeration, and improve aggregate structure.[3]

Soil contains pockets of space between the particles. This *pore space* contains varying proportions of air and water. Both are needed by plants, and if either is excessive, the other is deficient.[4]

Most nutrients needed by plants are taken in through the soil. Daubenmire states that these nutrients are taken through the roots by *soil solution*. Soil solution is the soil water that contains all the dissolved solids, liquids, and gases.[5]

Water. Available water is essential to plant growth. Water, available in many forms, includes that contained in the atmosphere and the soil. Plants obtain atmospheric water in many ways, including snow, rain, and humidity. Precipitation is available on a seasonal basis in most geographic locations. Knowledge of seasonal precipitation patterns is a vital key to revegetation planning since seeding should take place just prior to times of high precipitation.

Temperature. Plant species vary tremendously as to temperature tolerances. Daubenmire, however, points out that there is relatively little biological activity in plants whenever the environment is below 0°C or above 50°C. The temperature of the atmosphere and the soil is of major concern. Temperature changes are constantly occurring through radiation, convection, and conduction. Mining will often alter the natural color of the soil, which may increase or decrease the conduction. Microclimates that vary most with establishment of initial plant materials are temperatures that affect evaporation and permeation. Temperature variations result from several factors including color and composition of earth surfaces, porosity and water content of the soil, plant cover, snow cover, slope exposure, and topographic influences.[6]

Light. The energy necessary to sustain life on earth is derived from sunlight, directly by green plants and indirectly by other organisms.[7] Light varies according to several factors including *aspect,* or angle of slope in relationship to the position of the sun, and *stratification,* or the layering effect of overstory, midstory, and understory in an established, climax plant community.

In mining rehabilitation, the vegetation cover is likely to be monostands, low in diversity of species, and unlikely to be stratified until the plant community can become better established further down the successional track.

Atmosphere. The atmosphere contains a variety of nutrients in gaseous form that are necessary to the health of plant materials. Although the composition of nutrients in the atmosphere is often beyond the control of the rehabilitation specialist, problems that can be prevented sometimes do occur. Pollution suspended in the atmosphere will affect plant growth, particularly of susceptible species. One form of pollution that is often overlooked is air-borne sediment or dust. Dust around a mine area can clog the cells on the surface of the leaves that are responsible for gas exchange.

In part because gas exchange also occurs within the soil, it is important that the soil being revegetated be well aerated. Also, water vapor suspended in the atmosphere can be affected by wind and sun.

Biotic Factors. A symbiotic relationship exists among various organisms, whether they be plant or animal. The climax plant community, rich in diversity, is marked by species equilibrium in a symbiotic relationship. The populations of the various plants and animals in such an environment are held in check by the activities and locations of other organisms in the same community.

During rehabilitation, however, because the plant and animal communities start at a point very near the beginning of the successional processes, the community lacks diversity and stability. It becomes crucial for the rehabilitation specialist, therefore, to have a thorough knowledge of the plant community makeup.

Fire. The last growth factor listed by Daubenmire is fire. Fire selectively removes susceptible species and reduces competition. Fire has been used in rehabilitation to accomplish this very objective whenever undesirable, susceptible species invade and threaten the desired stand.

OPTIMUM AND LIMITING THRESHOLDS

It is important to note, after the review of the factors that affect plant growth, that living organisms have tolerances to these factors that are unique to each species. All species have optimum tolerances or thresholds. *Optimum* ranges are those that favor ultimate growth or health of a species. *Limiting* thresholds are those that allow the species to survive but do not, in most cases, proliferate growth. The outer range of limiting thresholds can cause species decline, as shown in Figure 9.1.

PLANT GROWTH REGIONS

Kuchler, Bailey, and others have been rather successful in dividing the United States into "ecoregions" and in giving a detailed description of the various growth factors involved in each area.[8] Their published information includes a description of landform, climate, vegetation, soils, and fauna, and serves as an initial resource for revegetative decisions. However, in describing the problems encountered in revegetation, for the scope of this book, we will examine the United States in two general segments—the East and the West with the 98th meridian generally serving as a boundary between the two.

LIMITING FACTORS—EAST

Chemical Properties

Problems encountered in revegetation processes in the East include pH, acid-induced toxicities, and nutrient deficiencies.

pH. The pH scale is logarithmic. The intensity of acidity or alkalinity changes tenfold for each unit change in pH. A pH of

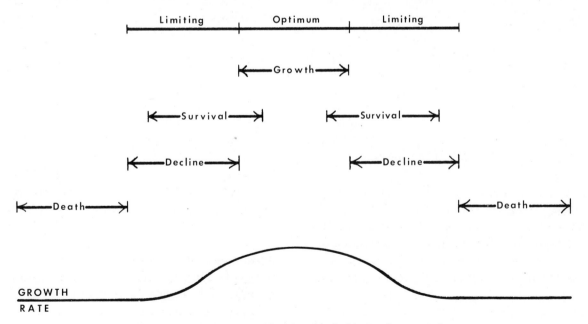

Figure 9.1. Optimum and limiting thresholds for plant growth.

4.0 is 10 times more Acidic than a pH of 5.0 and a pH of 3.0 is 100 times more Acidic than a pH of 5.0.[9] Vogel suggests that soil reaction (pH) is probably the most useful criterion for predicting the capacity of a minesoil to support vegetation. Not only is plant growth affected, but inferences can also be made about other growth qualities. The availability of some plant nutrients is limited in both extremely acid and strongly alkaline soils, but not in soils that are moderately acid to slightly alkaline.[10]

Minesoils are primarily acid in the East although one may occasionally encounter alkaline soils. Problems are most likely to occur whenever minesoils have a pH of 4.0 or lower—a common occurence in the East. The primary cause for extremely acid and toxic minesoils in the East is the oxidation of iron sulfides found in the coal and overburden strata.[11]

Acid-Induced Toxicities.

In addition to improper pH, there are other chemical problems that can limit revegetation of a particular site. These include an imbalance of elements, an excess of one element, or a high level of dissolved solids (salts).[12] Elements such as aluminum, iron, manganese, copper, nickel, and zinc become increasingly soluble as the pH decreases below 5.5. When the concentration of these elements exceeds certain levels, they become toxic to plants.[13] Vogel goes on to point out that this toxicity will fluctuate, regardless of pH, in different geologic materials. Plants that grow well in a soil with a pH of 4.5 may not survive in a different minesoil with the same pH.[14]

The elements found most often in concentrations toxic to plants in the East include aluminum and manganese. Aluminum toxicity reduces root growth while manganese toxicity results primarily in reduction of shoot growth. A recommended method for dealing with acid minesoils is to apply lime to raise the pH to 5.5 or higher. Toxic elements are precipitated out of soil solution whenever the pH is over 5.5.[15]

Nutrient Deficiencies.

Vogel states that minesoils are most often deficient in nitrogen and phosphorus. Nitrogen is deficient largely because of the absence or reduction of soils with an organic base, especially whenever topsoils have been removed. The deficiency may necessitate the addition of high-nitrogen fertilizer.[16]

There are three reasons for phosphorus deficiency in minesoils, including:

A. The overburden materials may contain only small amounts of phosphorus-bearing minerals.
B. The phosphorus compounds that do exist are insoluble in very acid and very alkaline materials.
C. There is no reservoir of organic phosphorus compounds.[17]

The rehabilitation specialist will likely have to recommend phosphorus fertilizer for phosphorus deficient minesoils.

Potassium deficiencies are less likely to occur in Eastern minesoils because of their availability in clay minerals, micas, and feldspars usually present in overburden materials.

Physical Properties

Problems encountered in revegetation processes in the East related to the physical properties of the soil include stoniness, particle-size distribution, bulk density, slope, erosion potential, color, and aspect.

Stoniness.

Stones and boulders can cause serious problems in a revegetation effort. They affect the types of equipment that can be employed and choice of plants used, especially trees.

Particle-Size Distribution.

Particle-size distribution refers to the amount and proportion of the various sizes of particles in the whole soil, including sand, silt, clay, and rock fragments.[18] This factor affects drainage and water-holding capacity, soil structure, bulk density, erodibility, cation exchange capacity, and workability of the soil. Coarse-textured soils dry out relatively quickly, especially at the surface where seed germination and root development take place. With fine-textured soils, such as found in clay materials, minesoils can be plastic when wet and very hard when dry.[19]

Bulk Density.   Bulk density is defined as the weight of a unit volume of dry soil, ordinarily expressed in grams per cubic centimeter.[20] Both soil particle and pore spaces are included within this volume. Loose and porous soils have low bulk density, whereas those soils that are highly compacted and high in clay content have high bulk density. The size and volume of pores within the soil structure are critical in that this space is where the soils hold the water and gases necessary for plant growth. Bulk density is a result of two primary factors:

A. The type of soils and geologic structure being mined
B. Excessive movement and compaction of heavy equipment

Slope and Erosion Potential.   The gradient of the slope can affect plant establishment. The loss of soil cover and seeds or seedlings through erosion is the main disadvantage of steep slopes (see Chapters 6, 7, and 8).

Color.   Soil color is a concern in revegetation efforts for two basic reasons. First, dark-colored soils absorb more heat from the sun's rays than light-colored varieties. Surface temperatures of dark-colored minesoils are lethal to seedlings, especially during the summer and on south- and west-facing slopes. Second, the color of minesoils can be an indicator of certain chemical characteristics. Vogel, for example, states that sandstone with gray interior color is unweathered and may be toxic to plants because it may contain unoxidized pyrite. He states further that black shales often are acid and toxic-forming and should be buried under nontoxic material or topsoil.[21]

Aspect.   Aspect is the direction that a slope faces in relationship to the sun. South- and west-facing slopes, which tend to be hotter and evaporate more quickly, should be revegetated with plants needing sunlight. Mulching would prove to be more valuable on southern and western slopes. In contrast, northern and eastern slopes, because they are cooler and evaporate relatively more slowly, should be revegetated with plants needing less sunlight and precipitation.[22]

Biological Properties

The biological properties that play a role in revegetation efforts include microorganisms and soil fauna. Both are essential for the survival and growth of many plant species and the reestablishment of natural ecosystems.

Microorganisms.   Vogel indicates that minesoils are not completely sterile in that they contain bacteria, fungi, and *actinomycetes,* a bacterial organism of the genus *Actinomyces.* It is the most numerous microorganism in the soil and is primarily responsible for the decomposition of organic matter.[23] These organisms are relatively inactive in soils with pH under 5.0 and, according to Vogel, are few in number in unvegetated minesoil when compared to those in agricultural and forested soils.[24] In most cases, as the vegetation cover becomes established, microorganisms increase in population and activity. Occasionally, they must be added artificially. These facts point out the need for conserving topsoil as a major source of necessary microorganisms. It is the most practical way to ensure their presence for the reestablishment of vegetation.

Soil Fauna.   Soil fauna includes such organisms as worms, beetles, and insects that dwell in the soil and that are responsible for consuming and altering organic matter such as plant litter, and burying or mixing it with the soil.[25] Minesoils, which are relatively devoid of soil fauna, are not likely to be populated until vegetation becomes reestablished. Vogel states that natural reestablishment of soil fauna populations is relatively slow and may even take several years since these organisms are not very mobile. Immediate replacement of topsoil is probably the most promising means of reestablishing these organisms on mined sites.[26]

LIMITING FACTORS—WEST

Chemical Properties

Problems of pH, salinity, and nutrient deficiencies affect revegetation efforts in the West.

pH. Soils in the West are less likely to be acidic than those in the East, although the problems encountered with acid minesoils in the East are also prevalent in acid soils in the West. Minesoils in the West will often have pH values in excess of 8.0. High pH values are likely to naturally occur in arid areas with rainfall below 20 inches per year. The reason is a lack of extensive leaching which leaves the base status of the parent rock material intact. If the thin topsoil layer has been preserved in the mining process, it is likely that species adapted to alkaline soils will perform well in most areas in the West.

Salinity. The geologic structure west of the 100th meridian is composed of large amounts of calcium, magnesium, potassium, and sodium. The concentration of these elements is particularly high in overburden material because of the continual leaching of soluble salts and sodium through the surface soil and their accumulation at greater depths. Saline and *sodic* soils (those containing sufficient sodium to interfere with the growth of most crop plants) are most likely to occur in valleys, depressions, poorly drained areas, and areas having a high water table.

Cook, Hyde, and Sims state that rehabilitation of saline areas is usually achieved by leaching soluble salts from the root zone. They add that the salinity of the soil can be reduced by approximately half, depending on the texture of the soil, with six acre-inches of water.[27] The method for determining the saline–sodic composition within the soil is by the electrical conductivity of a soil saturation extract. Plant responses can be predicted by using the guidelines in Table 9.1.

Cook and his coauthors suggest that salinity problems caused by poor drainage or a high water table can be corrected with drainage pipes.[28] Salts can also be leached, as mentioned earlier, with the use of copious amounts of water—a limited resource in those areas where this problem is likely to occur. Salts also move upward through the soil through capillarity and accumulate in spite of leaching efforts in some cases. The most promising solution to the salinity problem is the use of salt-tolerant plants. Among those species that are commonly used in the West for saline conditions are Fourwing saltbush (*Atriplex canescens*), Inland saltgrass (*Distichlis spicata*), Tall wheatgrass (*Agropyron elongatum*), Russian wildrye (*Elymus junceus*), Alkali sacaton (*Sporobolus airoides*), Greasewood (*Sarcobatus vermiculatus*), and Winterfat (*Ceratoides lanata*).[29]

Nutrient Deficiencies. As in the East, it is difficult to address the topic of nutrient deficiencies on a nonsite-specific basis. The soils in the West are highly variable, and nutrient levels are equally variable. The use of fertilizers in the West has given mixed results. Any application of fertilizer on mined land should be based on the results of intensive soil testing. Cook, Hyde, and Sims indicate that fertilizers consisting of nitrogen, phosphorus, and potassium, alone and in combination, applied at the time of planting when topsoil is replaced have only modestly benefited seedling establishment.[30] The

Table 9.1. Plant Responses for Saline-sodic Soils.

0–2 mmhos/cc	Salinity effects usually negligible
2–4 mmhos/cc	Yield of very salt-sensitive plants restricted
4–8 mmhos/cc	Yield of salt-sensitive plants restricted
8–16 mmhos/cc	Only a few salt-tolerant plants yield well
> 16 mmhos/cc	Yield of most species unsatisfactory

Source: Cook, Wayne C., Robert M. Hyde, and Phillip L. Sims, *Revegetation Guidelines for Surface Mined Areas,* Science Series no. 16, Fort Collins, Colo.: Colorado State University, 1974.

greatest benefit to be derived from applications of fertilizer occurs after the vegetation becomes established.[31]

Physical Properties

Physical problems frequently encountered in the West include lack of topsoil, improper soil texture, and difficult slope and aspect conditions.

Lack of Topsoil.

Because of the arid nature of the lands in the West, there has been a general lack of topsoil development. Although its value in revegetation efforts has already been pointed out, it is worth repeating that all efforts should be made to preserve this resource. Artificially produced topsoil is expensive and generally lacks many of the life-supporting attributes of natural topsoil.

In some cases, the subsoils can serve as a plant growth medium if they are not saline and if they have the proper texture. Topsoil should have a minimum available moisture capacity of 7 percent by weight and an organic matter content that ranges from 3 to 20 percent.[32] The rehabilitation specialist will wish to have a growth medium of at least 18 inches. The top 6 inches of this medium should be topsoil. The lower 12 inches should be composed of subsoil with adequate texture to promote storage of water to field capacity that is received during seasons of high precipitation.[33] The subsoil should be composed of material known as *selected overburden*. The selected overburden should be identified and stockpiled for use in the rehabilitation of seedbeds.

Improper Soil Texture.

Most of the soils in the West are fine textured and composed of clayey material. These soils are impermeable to water, which inhibits the storage of precipitation and gases and the leaching of salts, as mentioned earlier. This condition is further complicated by the low proportions of organic material needed to provide the bulk-density discussed earlier in the chapter.

Slopes.

Slopes in the West range from extremely flat to extremely steep. Both conditions present problems similar to those in the East. To a certain degree, slopes can be manipulated during the surface-grooming stage to provide proper drainage and an adequate seedbed for revegetation.

Aspect.

Aspect, discussed in depth in our description of the problems encountered in the East, is highly critical for arid and semiarid regions in the West where the angle of the slope in relationship to the sun makes the difference whether an area is successfully revegetated or not. In many areas of the West, the natural vegetative composition on a south-facing slope is entirely different from the composition on the north. In higher elevations where snowfall is the major source of precipitation, a major portion of the moisture leaves the site on the south-facing slope through evaporation. However, on north-facing slopes, the evaporation is much slower, and the precipitation is more likely to enter the soil and be available for an extended period of time.

Biological Properties

Among the most prominent biological problems that one encounters in the West are a lack of moisture, a lack of organic matter, the uncontrolled grazing and browzing of seedlings.

Lack of Moisture.

Most authorities agree that adequate moisture is the factor that contributes most to successful rehabilitation of lands disturbed by mining, drilling, and exploration for minerals in the western states. Moisture conservation practices should take place on all rehabilitation projects. Cook and his coauthors state that the foothills and mountainous areas in Colorado, Utah, and Wyoming receive most of their precipitation from snow. This is supplemented by occasional spring and summer rainfall. They state further that the northern Great Plains region of eastern Wyoming and Montana, and North Dakota receives most of its annual precipitation as spring and summer showers, while the desert Southwest in New Mexico, Colorado, Arizona, and Utah receives much of its precipitation as late-summer and fall rain.[34]

Reclamation of areas in the West is difficult not only because of low precipitation but because of the erratic and unpredictable nature of rain and snowfall. Thus most areas of low precipitation will have natural plant regeneration taking place only every 5 to 7 years when 2 or more successive moisture years take place.[35]

Lack of Organic Matter.   The problem of inadequate organic matter is easy to understand because of the facts presented earlier regarding the lack of vegetative cover in arid and semiarid lands. When plant life is somewhat sparse, the amount of forest or plant litter and other types of biological debris is likely to be low. Organic material is a major source of nitrogen which can be artificially added to the planting media. However, the other attributes of good topsoil, the presence of microorganisms and improved soil texture, are usually lacking without a natural organic base for the seedbed. The practice of burning slash piles from logging operations in areas in close proximity to rehabilitation projects is certainly archaic and should be discouraged if the material can be economically used. Its value in the reestablishment of a viable ecosystem is perhaps beyond measure.

Uncontrolled Grazing and Browzing of Seedlings.   In areas where the density of the human population is somewhat low and that of wildlife populations relatively high, there is likely to be a condition that some rehabilitation experts call the "green grass syndrone." This is likely to occur whenever the revegetated minesoils are abundant in vegetation cover when compared to the surrounding landscapes. Deer, elk, and antelope may find the rehabilitation project irresistable and consume months of hard work geared to the establishment of a balanced ecosystem. In some areas, it has been suggested

that the wildlife be fenced out until an adequate stand of cover can be established.

CONCLUSION

In making rehabilitation decisions, one is faced with an array of difficult problems and barriers that must be solved. These vary greatly from one geographic location to another. The general problems listed and described in this chapter are hardly inclusive of all the problems that may be unique to a particular site. It is crucial, however, that the rehabilitation specialist be intimately familiar with the makeup of the ecosystem of the area. One must have a knowledge of the various successional stages and the vegetal composition in each. All the various growth factors must be examined to determine which have been affected by the mining operation and altered to the degree that will inhibit revegetation efforts. Experts in soils, wildlife, hydrology, vegetation, and so forth should be consulted whenever necessary.

REFERENCES

1. Daubenmire, R. F., *Plants and Environment,* 2d ed., New York: John Wiley and Sons, 1959.
2. Ibid., p. 4.
3. Ibid., p. 30.
4. Ibid., p. 36.
5. Ibid., p. 37.
6. Ibid., p. 158.
7. Ibid., p. 214.
8. Bailey, Robert G., *Description of the Ecoregions of the United States,* Ogden, Utah: Intermountain Region, USDA Forest Service, 1980.
9. Vogel, *A Guide for Revegetating Coal Minesoils,* p. 11.
10. Ibid.
11. Ibid., p. 12.
12. Ibid., p. 13.
13. Ibid.
14. Ibid.
15. Ibid.

16. Ibid.
17. Ibid., pp. 13, 14.
18. Ibid., p. 15.
19. Ibid.
20. Ibid.
21. Ibid., p. 16.
22. Ibid., p. 17.
23. Brady, Nyle C., *The Nature and Properties of Soils,* 8th ed., New York: Macmillan Company, 1974, p. 127.
24. Vogel, *A Guide for Revegetating Coal Minesoils,* p. 17.
25. Ibid.
26. Ibid.
27. Cook, Wayne C., Robert M. Hyde, and Phillip L. Sims, *Revegetation Guidelines for Surface Mined Areas,* Science Series no. 16, Fort Collins, Colo.: Colorado State University, 1974, p. 36.
28. Ibid.
29. Ibid., p. 37.
30. Ibid., p. 15.
31. Thornburg, Ashley A., *Plant Materials for Use on Surface-Mined Lands in Arid and Semi-Arid Regions,* Washington, D.C.: USDA Soil Conservation Service, 1982, p. 8.
32. Cook, Hyde, and Sims, *Revegetation Guidelines,* p. 14.
33. Ibid.
34. Ibid., p. 2.
35. Ibid.

10

Revegetation Species Selection

INTRODUCTION

To properly manage the landscape and predict the possible consequences of rehabilitation decisions, one must be able to determine whether land can be returned to its premined condition or to suitable postmining use. The landscape's ability to accept revegetation attempts, which is by far the major determining factor of success, can be strengthened through the analysis and use of the physiographic zone involved. In general, physiographic zones are characterized by distinctive regions of landforms, climate, soils, vegetation, and, in some cases, human activities. By understanding these processes and relationships, decisions on plant selection for rehabilitation can be analyzed before costly mistakes are made.

BROAD VEGETATION SYSTEMS

In a classification based largely on appearance, the United States' main vegetation communities consist of tundra, forests, grasslands, and desert shrub. These distributions are to a large extent controlled environmentally and chiefly climatically. These communities are, therefore, organized colonies composed of varying sizes and species whose members have evolved in similar environment. It is the rehabilitation specialist's responsibility to be intimately familiar with the biological make-up of each broad vegetation system in which the rehabilitation project is found.

PHYSIOGRAPHIC ZONES

Classification of these zones regionalizes the data into manageable proportions and provides a framework of analysis for extrapolation of knowledge from one area for application in the management of revegetation in another area. To make revegetation decisions on a national, state, and local level requires a classification that is objective (based on observed properties), covers the entire country, and is hierarchical, allowing for both broad levels of generalization and specific information.

There have been various approaches to analyzing physiographic zones. One of the most comprehensive large-scale approaches appears in Robert G. Bailey's analysis of the ecoregions of the United States.[1] The term *ecoregion,* originally proposed by J. M. Crowley, is conceptually similar to the term *physiographic zones* used throughout this chapter. A hierarchy of ecoregions ranging from a broad category based on climatic similarity to a highly specific level based on a single soil type is presented in Table 10.1.

SPECIES SELECTION

The rehabilitation of surface mined lands presents difficult ecological and economic problems. The extent of success in past rehabilitation programs has been extremely varied, and efforts are being made to improve the effectiveness of

Table 10.1.   A Hierarchy of Ecosystems.

NAME	DEFINED AS INCLUDING
Domain	Subcontinental area of related climates
Division	Single regional type at Koppen's Type (Trewartha, 2d ed.)
Province	Broad vegetation region with the same type or types on zonal soils
Section	Climatic climax at the level of Kuchler's potential vegetation types (Kuchler, p. 116)
District	Part of a section having uniform geomorphology at the level of Hammond's land-surface form regions (Hammond, map 4)
Landtype association	Group of neighboring landtypes with recurring pattern of landforms, lithology, soils, and vegetation assoc.
Landtype	Group of neighboring phases with similar soil series or families with similar plant communities at the level of Daubenmire's habitat type (Daubenmire, p. 300)
Landtype phase	Group of neighboring sites belonging to the same soil series with closely related habitat types
Site	Single soil type or phase and single habitat type or phase

Source: Bailey, Robert G., *Description of the Ecoregions of the U.S.*, Ogden, Utah: Intermountain Region, USDA Forest Service, 1980.

rehabilitation programs. Revegetation is the single most critical key to a successful rehabilitation program.

The most critical element in a revegetation process is the selection of appropriate plant species. If plant species that are not adapted to the site conditions are used, the revegetation effort will undoubtedly fail. The selection of adaptable species that will provide the desired short-term and long-term results requires thorough analysis and careful consideration. All plant growth factors discussed in the last chapter must be examined.

Plant species native to the rehabilitation area have been widely recommended as desirable species for revegetation. The concept of utilizing native species for revegetation would seem appropriate considering the fact that native vegetation is an expression of both local soil and climate.[2] In recent years, introduced species have received considerable attention in mined-land rehabilitation and have become widely used for revegetation. Although introduced species have shown desirable short-term characteristics, questions arise concerning the ecological impacts on plant communities dominated by aggressive introduced species.

There are several factors to consider when selecting species suitable for revegetation including postmining land use, physiographic geography, site-specific information, and plant growth requirements.

Postmining Land Use

Postmining land use should have a significant influence on species selection. The species used in revegetating a site should be capable of accommodating the desired use. Planning for rehabilitation must include consideration of the proposed land use plan and the mining operation plan. Because of their interrelationships, these plans should be developed simultaneously prior to disturbance of the site as part of a comprehensive program. Postmining land uses may vary considerably, depending on location and surrounding environmental conditions. Typical uses may include forestry, grazing, cropping, wildlife habitat management, recreation, or construction. Each of these uses would most likely require a different revegetation plan with the species selected accordingly.

In the arid and semiarid West, postmining land uses are often severely limited by the physiographic characteristics of the area, particularly the amount and distribution of precipitation. In most cases, rehabilitation plans are developed to return the site back to its premining natural use. This typically includes grazing and/or wildlife habitat enhancement.

Different plant species and seeding rates may be used depending on the primary objective. For example, if wildlife habitat enhancement is the primary objective, plant species should be selected that will provide a variety of cover and potential food sources. Consideration should be given to creating habitat "edges" that will tend to promote increased wildlife activity.[3] On the other hand, if commercial grazing is the primary objective, total production and species palatability is important. Plant species that are aggressive, highly productive, and palatable are generally considered desirable. Often, introduced species are favored over native species because of their aggressive growth and high palatability. Both a wildlife habitat and domestic pastures can be created successfully if a carefully integrated revegetation and management plan is developed. Careful selection of plant species suitable for both uses is necessary.

Physiographic Geography

The use of the concept *physiographic regions* is important when selecting plant species for revegetation. Physiographic regions, described earlier, should be used to detail homogeneous areas. They provide important general information necessary for understanding plant ecosystems and for selecting suitable species. However, caution should be exercised to avoid selecting plant species based primarily on regional physiographic information. Physiographic regions should serve primarily as a starting point for species selection. Specific physical characteristics will vary with each site. Therefore, species should be chosen utilizing an appropriate combination of regional physiographic and site-specific information.

Site-Specific Information

Detailed information specific to the rehabilitation site is essential for selecting suitable species. Information concerning climatic, edaphic, topographic and biotic conditions of the site is required. Baseline data concerning these characteristics should be obtained prior to mining operations. Identification of premining plant communities and species can provide valuable information for the revegetation process. However, it must be remembered that site conditions are to be altered. Therefore, it is essential that postmining data be collected concerning site conditions in order to evaluate the degree of alteration. Soil chemical and physical properties, such as pH, texture, depth, organic matter, and soil nutrients, are often adversely affected by mining operations. Drainage patterns and microclimates are also altered. Therefore, it is important that plant species be selected that are adaptable to the new conditions. Native communities often contain numerous species that can be utilized successfully.

In some cases where severe changes occur in site conditions, particularly soil conditions, properly tested introduced species may be required. This points out the importance of postmining rehabilitation practices such as grading, topsoiling, and seedbed preparation. Mulches, soil amendments, and seeding methods can also play an important part in the successful establishment of the species seeded.

Plant Growth Requirements

Germination and growth requirements are obviously important considerations for revegetation species. Accurate information is necessary if appropriate species are to be selected. Plant species requirements must be compatable with postmining site conditions. As mentioned before, native plant communities often contain a large number of adaptable species. A relatively large amount of information is available from public and private sources concerning species performance on various mined sites. Future research studies will undoubtedly continue to provide more information on plant species.

A problem often encountered with native species is an inadequate seed source. In some instances, seed must be gathered by hand in the wild, which is extremely time consuming and costly. Genetic variation can be a problem if foreign sources are used and can result in a significant variation of plant growth characteristics. Furthermore, careful attention must be given to appropriate seed treatments and germination requirements to achieve successful establishment.

CREATING COMMUNITY STABILITY

Community stability can be interpreted as a stage of dynamic equilibrium that persists over at least several decades in terrestrial plant communities and can be recognized by a relatively constant species composition and structure.[4] Stable communities are generally self-perpetuating and possess the ability to withstand considerable environmental stress without a dramatic change in floristic composition or community structure. However, limited compositional and structural variations are a normal phenomenon in a stable community.[5] Typically, in prairie and grassland ecosystems, mature stable communities are associated with a high species diversity. High species diversity is generally desirable in grassland rehabilitation. Food chains differ considerably between stable and unstable communities. Food chains in unstable communities are usually less complex. As a result, unstable communities are more sensitive to environmental disturbances. A disturbance at one trophic level is quickly felt at all other levels.[6]

Another general characteristic of stable communities is the decrease in total production as compared to unstable communities. This is because the biomass in stable communities accumulates in a few individuals of many species, whereas in unstable communities, the biomass accumulates in a large number of individuals of a very few species.[7]

Community stability should be an important consideration when selecting species for revegetation. If reestablishment of a community similar to that existing before any disturbance is desired, high species diversity should be sought for grassland ecosystems. High species diversity should result in a more rapid development of a stable community, provided well-adapted species are used. It is also important that interspecies competition be evaluated when determining seeding rates to achieve a more diverse plant community.

SEED MIX CONSIDERATIONS

Seed mix formulation is typically accomplished using two basic approaches including the *general seed mix* and the *specific seed mix*.

General Seed Mix

The general approach, which is the most widely used in revegetation practices, involves the development of one seed mix containing a large amount of seed of numerous species adapted to the overall conditions of the site. This approach assumes that through natural successional processes, plant communities containing the species best adapted to varying microclimatic conditions will develop. Although this assumption may be valid, community development is slow and initial seed costs are high. Furthermore, this approach results in an inefficient use of native seeds which may be difficult to acquire. One advantage of this approach is that less detailed site analyses are required than in the specific approach, and the development of the seed mix is simplified. Also, inaccurate assumptions concerning site conditions and species adaptability are less critical owing to the large number of species scattered throughout the site.

Specific Seed Mix

The specific approach requires a detailed site analysis that identifies microclimatic variations of the site such as soil characteristics, slope aspect, drainage patterns, and so forth. Specific seed mixes are then tailored to these different microclimatic conditions. This approach tends to accelerate the successional process through careful selection of several species that are best adapted to each microclimatic condition. The result is a more rapid development of a stable community and an increased seed development. Although a more detailed site analysis and careful selection of plant species are required, this approach could provide improved success in revegetation efforts.

In both approaches, seed mixtures should contain a variety of adaptable species. A combination of warm and cool season species should be utilized to increase diversity and seasonal adaptability. A combination of bunchgrass and stoloniferous types is desirable under most circumstances. Native forbs and shrubs should also be included. Certain legume species that promote soil fertility can also be beneficial. Seeding rates should receive careful attention and reflect the relative competitiveness of each species to promote increased species diversity. Seeding should be done prior to the period of greatest expected precipitation. Adequate topsoil, seedbed preparation, soil amendments, fertilization, irrigation, and mulches are all important factors to consider.

NATIVE VERSUS INTRODUCED SPECIES

Recently, considerable discussion has occurred concerning the extensive use of introduced species in the revegetation of disturbed sites. There is very little consensus regarding the use of highly aggressive introduced species. The U.S. Office of Surface Mining regulations require that all disturbed land, except water areas and the surface area of roads that are approved as part of the postmining land use, shall be seeded or planted to achieve a permanent vegetative cover of the same seasonal variety for the area of disturbed land.[9]

According to Weiner, introduced species are also allowed after appropriate field trials have demonstrated that the introduced species are desirable and necessary to achieve the approved postmining land use. Introduced species can also be used when they are proved to be necessary to achieve a quick, temporary, and stabilizing cover that aids in controlling erosion.[9]

It has become common practice for introduced species to be included and in many cases represent a large percentage of the seed mix. Presently, considerable interest is being given to the characteristics of native versus introduced species in the plant community. Although insufficient long-term data are available for revegetated sites, general characteristics have been observed in reestablished communities. Considerable research is presently being conducted in areas of the United States where surface mining is prevalent.[10] What follows is a general summary of commonly observed characteristics of native and introduced species on rehabilitated sites of the western grasslands.

Establishment

The primary reasons introduced species have been widely used in seed mixes for revegetation is because of their rapid establishment and aggressive growth characteristics. A primary objective in revegetation is to quickly establish vegetative cover to stabilize the soil. This purpose is promoted by the desirable characteristics demonstrated by many introduced species. On the other hand, native species have often shown slower initial establishment and growth than certain introduced species. Several factors may be involved in explaining the problems associated with the establishment of native species, including incompatability with existing soil conditions, inadequate consideration of germination requirements, poor seedbed preparation, inappropriate planting time, and inferior seed quality. However, often the biggest problem affecting native species establishment is the strong competition from introduced species. In such a situation, native species have difficulty establishing themselves and growing. A recent study at Colstrip, Montana, shows that if competitive introduced species are eliminated from the seed mix and only native species used, an excellent rate of establishment and site stabilization can be achieved.[11]

Species Diversity

High species diversity is typically characteristic of undisturbed native grassland ecosystems. However, species diversity is usually quite low in plant communities dominated by highly aggressive introduced species.[12] In these communities, species composition consists primarily of many individuals of a relatively few species. Low species diversity is often characteristic of a relatively unstable community that may be more sensitive to environmental disturbances. Plant communities composed of predominately native species commonly have a more diverse species composition. In these communities, floristic composition and biomass are shared by a large number of different species, which often results in a more stable plant community. Increased species diversity also provides a wider range of wildlife habitats. A recent study at Colstrip showed an acceptable level of species diversity in sites utilizing exclusively native species.[13]

Productivity

Past studies have shown that utilization of introduced species can increase productivity considerably as compared to native stands of vegetation.[14] Recent studies at Colstrip have indicated that total production may decline in plant communities consisting of introduced species as the community matures.[15] Future data will be needed on the long-term productivity of plant communities dominated by a relatively few introduced species. More diverse, native plant communities typically have resulted in lower levels of productivity. Lower productivity is commonly associated with increased species diversity and stability.[16] However, the Colstrip study of native species showed that high levels of productivity can be achieved on diverse native stands.[17] Favorable production stability in light of climatic fluctuation was also exhibited. Results of recent studies at Colstrip suggest that although more diverse plant communities on mine spoils may not offer as much in terms of initial- or peak-year productivity, these communities may be superior with respect to long-term stability and productivity.[18]

Management

Although significantly higher production levels may be achieved by utilizing introduced species, more intense management will also be required to maintain this high productivity. On the other hand, well-adapted native species survive with little or no maintenance.[19] Overgrazing should be avoided on all stands although overgrazing on stands containing a large percentage of introduced species with low species diversity may be more likely unless careful management is utilized. Therefore, higher productivity levels commonly associated with aggressive introduced species will probably require more intensive management practices to maintain production levels.

CONCLUSIONS

Many factors must be considered when selecting species for use in revegetation of disturbed sites. Proposed land use, physiographic geography, site-specific conditions, and plant requirements are important considerations. Furthermore, basic ecological principles should be understood and utilized in developing a revegetation plan. Revegetation of grassland ecosystems in the arid and semiarid regions of the Western United States present difficult problems owing to severe environmental limitations, particularly the rate and distribution of precipitation. The following is a list of general considerations for revegetation of a wide variety of plant communities:

A. High species diversity is desirable to achieve long-term community stability.
B. Annual cover crops should be considered to provide a more suitable environment for long-lived species establishment under adverse conditions.
C. Native species generally possess greater tolerance to severe environmental stress than do introduced species.
D. Use of highly aggressive introduced species will generally require increased management efforts as compared to native communities to maintain high levels of productivity.
E. Seed mixes including species and rates should reflect the physical characteristics of the site including microclimatic variations and native vegetation to promote more efficient use of native seeds and to reestablish as quickly as possible a plant community similar to that which existed before the disturbance.
F. Species selected for revegetation must reflect the proposed use of the land.
G. Native species can produce a diverse plant community with good establishment and site stabilization characteristics as well as acceptable levels of productivity, provided competition from aggressive introduced species is eliminated.

REFERENCES

1. Bailey, *Ecoregions of the United States.*
2. Cook, Hyde, and Sims, *Revegetation Guidelines.*
3. U.S. Department of the Interior, Fish and Wildlife Service, *Mined Land Reclamation for Fish and Wildlife,* Washington, D.C.: Government Printing Office, 1978.
4. Mueller-Dombois and Ellenberg, *Vegetation Ecology.*
5. Ibid.
6. Smith, Robert L., *Ecology and Field Biology,* 2d ed., New York: Harper and Row, 1974.
7. Miller, G. T., Jr., *Living in the Environment,* 2d ed., Belmont, Calif.: Wadsworth Publishing Co., 1979.
8. Weiner, Daniel Philip, *Reclaiming the West: The Coal Industry and Surface-Mined Lands,* New York: Inform, Inc., 1980.
9. Ibid.
10. DePuit, E. J., *Research on Revegetation of Surface Mined Lands at Colstrip, Montana: Progress Report, 1975–1977,* Research Report no. 127, Bozeman, Mont.: Montana Agricultural Experiment Station, Montana State University, 1978.
11. DePuit, E. J. *Establishment of Diverse Native Plant Communities on Coal Surface-Mined Lands in Montana as Influenced by Seeding Methods, Mixture and Rate,* Research Report no. 163, Bozeman, Mont.: Montana Agricultural Experiment Station, Montana State University, 1980.
12. DePuit, Research Report no. 127.
13. DePuit, Research Report no. 163.
14. Currie, Pat O., "Revegetating Mined Land for Grazing," *Journal of Soil and Water Conservation,* July–August 1981, pp. 213–215.
15. DePuit, Research Report no. 127.
16. Smith, *Ecology and Field Biology.*
17. DePuit, Research Report no. 127.
18. Ibid.
19. Environmental Protection Agency, *Evaluation of the Environmental Effects of Western Surface Coal Mining,* vol. I, Washington, D.C.: Government Printing Office, 1979.

11
Seeding and Mulching Methods

INTRODUCTION

Revegetation is the initial concern for most professionals involved in rehabilitation of surface mined land. Revegetation is primarily responsible for slope stabilization and for returning the land to an acceptable state of ecological stability. The revegetation process involves the following steps:

A. Grading and leveling
B. Seedbed preparation
C. Seeding methods
D. Mulching
E. Management

GRADING AND LEVELING

After the mineral has been excavated from the mine surface, the site is seldom in a satisfactory state for revegetation efforts. It is usually necessary that the spoil piles be graded and leveled to properly provide a rooting medium. The revegetation efforts are often imperiled by the haphazard thought given to this important step. Success may well depend on the operator's knowledge as to when and how to grade and level a site prior to seedbed preparation.

One of the greatest mistakes made in grading and leveling is to create a compacted surface. This can be prevented by limiting the operation to times when the soil is neither wet nor muddy. The weight of the earth-moving equipment on wet soils will likely create a hard, impervious surface. This could likely occur on clay or silt soil material even when dry. If the structure of the soil is such that compaction is likely, alternative types of equipment may need to be employed to execute this important phase of the revegetation process. Vogel points out that abandoned, dated mine sites may be better left alone, rather than graded and leveled.[1] He identifies the hazard in this case as the likelihood that toxic or acid elements within the soil that would have probably leached downward would be placed once again within reach of the root zone by grading or leveling.

Regardless of the type of soils being seeded or the type of equipment used, the surface should not be graded or leveled to a fine, smooth surface. A less erodible surface should be created with numerous microclimatic zones from a textured or an undulating surface grade. In addition, coarse spoil material of acceptable quality should be stockpiled in reserve to be used for the layer below the topsoil to increase permeability and lessen the dangers of sheet erosion. This selected overburden, as described in earlier chapters, can occasionally be found on the surface between the topsoil and the deepest zone penetrated by roots.

One of the final steps to be taken when grading and leveling is the utilization of implements to loosen or break up the compaction caused by heavy equipment. Such implements commonly include chisels and rippers. The rehabilitation specialist would be well advised to have the soil tested prior to directing the grading and leveling operation to insure a greater measure of success in the seeding process.

SEEDBED PREPARATION

The suitable seedbed should provide numerous microsites for the favorable establishment of seedlings. The seedbed should provide the biological and mechanical qualities of any natural, undisturbed site. The biological qualities are supplied through the proper use of topsoiling techniques. The mechanical qualities are supplied by providing a subsoil with the proper texture, pH, and permeability. Herein lies the dilemma, however. The process of putting on the topsoil following the grading and leveling operation will often create compaction. Compaction can be relieved by using rippers or chisels as suggested earlier, but this mixes the topsoil with the subgrade, which reduces the quality of this valuable resource. Therefore, it is suggested that the chiseling take place on the subgrade prior to the placement of topsoil and the compaction of the topsoil be reduced by the utilization of a disc-harrow prior to seeding. Other types of implements can also be employed, but the physical condition of the land surface and the size of the site should be considered in making decisions as to the size and type of equipment that can effectively be used. For steep slopes, "tracking in" may be employed whereby the operator runs a tracked vehicle up and down the slope to provide numerous depressions that create small microsites and prevent sheet erosion.

SEEDING METHODS

The most efficient method of establishing plant materials on a site has proved to be seeding. The object of seeding is to uniformly distribute the seed in high enough quantities under the proper cultural conditions to insure a high degree of germination and root establishment. There are commonly two general methods of distributing seed: broadcasting and drilling. Each method has advantages and disadvantages.

Broadcasting

Broadcasting is any method that distributes the seed directly onto the surface of the soil without soil coverage. Equipment commonly used includes the "whirlwind" fan (also known as air blast seeders), hydroseeders, aircraft, and hand seeders. The *fan seeder* blows the seed out and away from the seeder in a circular pattern. The operation must be followed by a spring-toothed harrow, small disc, or other implement that can cover the seed to an appropriate depth.

Hydroseeders are a type of broadcasting equipment that applies seed which is mixed with water. Seeds can also be mixed with fertilizer and mulch to provide them with a "head-start" in rooting. This is a common practice in the East, especially with sites containing steep slopes and highwalls common to the Appalachian region.

Hydroseeders are not as successful in arid regions. There must be adequate precipitation to keep the seed moist for two to three weeks until the roots are established on the seedlings. The areas in the West most appropriate for the use of hydroseeders would be higher, mountainous areas that have frequent afternoon showers.

Aircraft can be used most efficiently on large acreages and in areas where mud or other adverse surface conditions prevent the use of conventional equipment. Helicopters are more popular than fixed-wing aircraft because of their versatility. If aircraft are to be used, landing areas must be close and use of ground-support equipment employed.

Handseeders are frequently used in areas with extremely rough terrain or on small parcels that cannot be serviced with larger equipment.

The advantages of broadcasting are related mostly to the type of terrain that must be seeded. Drills frequently cannot function properly on rough or steep terrain or on sites containing rocks and stones on the surface. The main disadvantage to the use of broadcasting for seeding is the need to increase seeding rates to levels often twice those of drilling.

Drilling

A *drill* is an implement that drops seed into a small furrow cut by a disc. If the terrain allows, drilling is preferred to broadcasting because it distributes the seed more uniformly while placing the seed under the proper soil depth. Implements will vary in design according to the type of seed being planted or the type of site in which the operation will occur. Cook, et al. indicate that the following types of drills are currently being used for rehabilitation:

A. Special grassland drills: designed to handle small seeded grasses
B. "Nisbet" single- or double-disc drill with depth bands: designed to be used on sandy or sandy loam soils
C. Rangeland single-disc, deep-furrow drill or the John Deere Van Brunt single-disc, semideep furrow drill: designed to be used for clay loam soils that have been previously tilled or summer fallowed
D. "Nobel" drill: designed for use on compacted soils, or rocky, gravelly soils and along cuts and fills with gentle slopes
E. Rangeland drills equipped with special seeder attachments: used for small seed or seed with hairy coats[2]

Cook, et al. also point out that all drills used in rehabilitation should have separate containers for small and large seed and should possess agitators to prevent the seed from lodging in the boxes.[3]

Seeding Rates

Drilling. The seeding operation for drilling involves two factors: the drill row spacing and the number of pure live seed to be planted per row (the term *pure live seed* refers to the number of seeds of a particular variety that is likely to germinate). Drill rows are normally 6 to 7 inches apart unless a deep-furrow drill is employed. These require a spacing of 12 to 14 inches apart to prevent seed from being buried too deep by the adjacent furrow opener. Spacings wider than these invite weed invasion between rows.

The quantity of viable seed is generally expressed in pounds per acre since the actual number of seed per unit of soil surface area must be considered. Therefore, when planting small-seeded species, fewer pounds per acre are required because of the greater number of seeds per pound compared to large-seeded species. The number of seeds per acre is also based on several other factors. The type of equipment being used to distribute the seed will often dictate the seeding rate. Generally, twice as much seed is required when broadcasting than is required when drilling. Aspect will often dictate seeding rates. Cook et al. state that 15 pounds per acre of crested wheatgrass are required for slopes with south and west exposures, whereas only 7 to 10 pounds per acre are required on north and east slopes.[4]

When drilling grass seed on favorable sites, there should be 20 to 25 pure live seeds planted per square foot. If forbs are added to the seeding mixture, about 3 to 5 seeds per square foot should be planted. Browse, when added to the mixture, should be planted at 1 to 2 seeds per square foot. When the forbs and browse are added, the quantity of grass seed should be reduced accordingly.[5]

Planting rates should be increased from 50 to 100 percent on critical sites such as west and south exposures. Since seeding rates are dependent on the quality of seed, the rates are expressed as pure live seed (PLS).

Pure Live Seed. Good, high-quality seed that has been properly tested and tagged should be used to help ensure the successful establishment of plant cover. The quality of seed is determined by information found on the seed tag. Two of the values listed on the tag that are used to compute pure live seed include seed purity and germination percentages. PLS is calculated by multiplying the seed purity times the germination percentage and dividing by 100. If the tag on the seed, for example, indicates that the seed contains 95 percent purity and 80 percent germination, the percent PLS would 76: (95 × 80) ÷ 100 = 76 percent. In other words, of 100 pounds of bulk seed, only 76 pounds would actually germinate.

Sample Problems

A. If 325 bulk pounds of seed were ordered that had ratings of 95 percent for germination and 90 percent for purity, how many pounds of actual PLS could be used for revegetation?

$$.95 \times .90 \times 325 = 278 \text{ PLS}$$

B. In the same circumstances as above, how much bulk seed is required to equal one pound of PLS?

$$1.0 \div (.90 \times .95) = 1.17 \text{ pounds bulk/pound PLS}$$

C. Assume 17 PLS is needed per acre. The seed has an 85 percent purity designation and a 92 percent germination rate. How much bulk seed is required to seed 8 acres?

$$\% \text{ PLS} = .85 \times .92 = 78.2\%$$

$$1 \text{ pound PLS} = 1.0 \div .782 = 1.28 \text{ pounds bulk}$$

$$1.28 \times 17 \times 8 = 174.08 \text{ pounds bulk seed}$$

D. How many acres could be planted with 200 pounds of seed with 87 percent purity and 85 percent germination assuming the site needed 15 pounds PLS per acre?

$$\% \text{ PLS} = .85 \times .87 = 73.95 \text{ percent per pound}$$

$$73.95 \text{ percent of 200 pounds} = 147.9$$

$$147.9 \div 15 = 9.86 \text{ acres}$$

Season for Seeding. The time of the year that seeding occurs is critical to revegetation success, especially in arid regions of the country. The primary rule to follow is that seeding should take place during the season just prior to the time of year that receives the most dependable precipitation. For example, the seeding should take place by the middle of April for areas with spring and summer precipitation seasons.

In the East, most precipitation patterns favor early spring seeding for cool season species, whereas early to mid-spring is the most appropriate time to sow perennial and some annual warm season species. Most annual species should be seeded from mid-spring to early summer.

Problems unique to the West are sometimes difficult to overcome because of low precipitation. The time for planting in many areas is limited to a few weeks during the year. In the mountainous areas where most of the precipitation is received in the form of snow, fall seeding should take place just after the first killing frost. The seed should lay dormant and then sprout whenever the environmental conditions are ideal in the spring. If the planting were to be delayed until spring, by the time the ground dries enough for equipment use, the seeding would take place beyond the normal precipitation season. Late summer seeding should take place in those areas where the major precipitation season is during the fall. This is likely to be the case in some of the areas of the Southwest. Late summer and early fall seeding is usually recommended for cool season grasses and legumes if the soil moisture is favorable.

MULCHING

The natural surface of the land in an undisturbed state is covered with a layer of organic debris made up mostly of leaves and twigs. This layer serves as an excellent source of organic matter which is broken down by microorganisms to release minerals into the soil where they become available to plants. In addition to the nutrients, this layer of natural mulch serves to reduce loss of soil moisture through evaporation and to minimize erosion potential. In the revegetation of surface mines, it is common to add an artificial mulch to the soil to serve the same purposes.

The use of mulch involves four basic methods.

A. The use of rocks as mulch
B. The manipulation of the soil surface
C. Chemicals in the form of soil binders and tackifiers
D. Organic mulches and other biodegradable materials

Rock Mulches

Rock mulches (riprap) are found to be highly effective in erosion control and their use has already been described in Chapter 8. Because of the weight and density of rock mulch, it has been found that a one-inch deep layer of crushed gravel 1½ inches to 2 inches in diameter has been more effective in erosion control than 2 tons of straw per acre.[6] The use of rock for mulch encourages the invasion of adopted indigenous species. It is not recommended that this mulch be used in disturbed areas for which planting of introduced species has been proposed. It is likely to be impractical, as well, on large sites. One should remember that rocks offer no biological advantage in supplying nutrients for the plants. They are only used to stabilize slopes and prevent erosion.

Soil Manipulation

The purpose of soil manipulation is to impede runoff, increase infiltration, and provide a microsite advantageous for germination and rooting. To provide an effective surface, it has been found that in gouging the earth's surface, the dimensions of the furrow should be at least 10 inches deep, 18 inches wide, and 24 inches long. Dozer basins, which are enlargements of gouging depressions, are generally 2 feet deep, 3½ feet wide, and 15 feet long. The dozer basins should be spaced 30 feet apart to allow additional treatments to occur between.

Chemicals

Binders. Chemicals can be used as either a soil binder or a tackifier. A tackifier is used with a seed/fertilizer treatment, whereas a soil binder is used without. The main purpose of the soil binder is the control of erosion. Chemicals used as binders include polyvinyl acetate homopolymers, vinyl acrylic copolymers (PVA), liquid latex, copolymers of methacrylates and acrylates, and styrene butadiene (SBR).[7] All of these binders are a mixture of high molecular weight polymeric particles dispersed in a continuous aqueous phase and are the basic ingredients in paint and glue.[8] Current commercial names of these chemicals are Aerospray 70, Crust 500, Curasol AK, Enviro, MGS, Stickum, Terra Kote, Soil Bond, and Soil Seal.[9] No recommendation of one product over another is implied. Most offer good initial erosion protection.

There are disadvantages in using these chemicals. Most require a curing time to form a crust prior to their effectiveness. Until the chemicals have been properly cured, their use can be drastically diminished by rain or low temperatures. In addition, some of the crusts formed by the binders may shed most of the moisture that would normally permeate into the ground. This is particularly a problem in areas with low natural precipitation. Finally, the seedlings sometimes have difficulty breaking through the crust.

Tackifiers. Tackifiers may be added to either the top of a mulch or to a hydromulch slurry to tack the mulch to the ground. This generally stabilizes the soil from the effects of wind and water. Tackifiers may be organic or inorganic.

Organic tackifiers. Organic tackifiers include products such as Ecology Controls M-Binder, Kelgum, Terra Tack I, II, and

III, Bio Binder, Petroset SB, Verdyol Super, Conwed Fiber, and Silva Fiber. Many of these are normally added to a slurry (a liquid-like mix used in hydromulching). The author does not recommend one product over another.

Inorganic tackifiers. Those tackifiers that are inorganic in nature include asphalt, SBR, and Super Slurper. None carries the author's recommendation, and the effectiveness of each type on a site-specific basis may, through necessity, only be determined through testing. State highway departments have proved to be excellent sources for tests conducted for certain climates and on specific soils that may be unique to the rehabilitation specialist's geographical area.

Because wood fiber adheres well to slopes, its addition to tackifiers is suggested by many manufacturers for additional resistance to erosion. Long narrow wood fibers are preferred over finely ground products. The most commonly used wood includes fibers from aspen, alder, and hemlock. Hemlock lasts longer but is more difficult to obtain. Nonvirgin wood fibers, such as those derived from paper, have proved to be ineffective, having little or no tackifying effect and readily washing away from moderate rainfall. When they are used as a hydromulch, it is recommended that the seeding operation take place in two separate applications. The seed and fertilizer should be placed in the first application, with the mulch (fiber) and tackifier added in the second.

Asphalt tackifiers. Asphalt emulsion is a tackifier used almost exclusively with straw. The dark color it produces can assist in increasing soil temperatures in cool climates—a possible disadvantage in hot climates. Because of the oil base and labor costs involved in cleaning up overspray, this mulch tends to be more expensive.

Organic Mulches and Other Biodegradable Materials

Organic mulches are usually composed of residues from agricultural crops or industrial products. These include such products as straw, hay, wood fiber, woodchips, bark, fabrics, jute, excelsior, woven paper, and plastic fibers. Their use is characterized by low-purchase cost and easy application. Occasionally, nitrogen should be added to facilitate the decomposition process.

Jute, excelsior, paper, plastics, and fabrics are weed-free and can be installed in any season. They are usually purchased in rolls or mats, which may be difficult to install on rocky soils. The mats are anchored to the soil by wire staples, which increases the cost of installation. It is necessary to maintain the mats because of the occasional tears that may occur. Of these products, excelsior and jute have proved to have better features and higher rates of both biological and erosion control than plastic mats, which only control erosion.

Woodchips and bark are generally a timber mill residue. They compare with straw and wood fiber but are still slightly surpassed in performance by straw. Maximum effectiveness is obtained when partially worked into the soil and with a layer 1 inch deep on the surface. Slopes steeper than 2 to 1 and south- or west-facing generally require a heavier application. The greater size of woodchips and bark compared to straw and wood fiber requires a longer decomposition time; visible chunks have been noted two years after treatment. The biggest disadvantage of these mulches is the equipment required for application. Fine dust particles bother workers, whereas large chips, rocks, twigs, and trash jam the augers and gears in the equipment.

The most commonly used mulches are straw and hay because of their availability and relatively low cost. The most serious problem connected with their use is wind during application. Because of the light weight of both straw and hay, a net or tackifier is often necessary. The seeds usually contained in the harvested crop of straw and hay can be either beneficial or detrimental. A clean grain straw should be used to avoid potential invasion from weed seeds. Wild grass hay is excellent for use in areas that are to be revegetated by native plant species, provided the hay can be gathered when the seeds are mature. If introduced plants are to be planted, wild grass hay may be a source of competition.

The greater the quantity of hay or straw used, the better erosion is controlled. However, one should determine the upper threshold since too much can be harmful. A thick layer of straw mulch may smother seedlings by blocking out light and water. It may also become a fire hazard.

Methods of Applying Mulches

Mulches are generally applied by one of the following methods:

    A. Rolling and anchoring
    B. Manual application
    C. Blowing
    D. Hydromulching
    E. Crimping and punching

Rolling and Anchoring. Rolled mats of jute, excelsior, fabric, and plastic meshes, anchored with wire staples, are the most expensive method of application owing to high installation costs and continued maintenance labor costs. Mats should only be used in critical areas needing immediate attention and areas inaccessible to machinery.

Manual Application. Manual application usually consists of spreading hay or straw with a pitchfork or by hand. It is also used in some cases for bark or rock and is slow, inefficient, and very expensive. It is only recommended in areas that are rough and rocky or in areas that are inaccessible to machinery.

Blowing. Mulch spreaders and blowers can handle distances up to 85 feet at rates of 15 tons per hour. Both straw and bark can be blown but the latter is not as popular as a result of the problems normally associated with bark spreading. It is a dry process and often spreads bothersome dust during application. An injection of water into the airstream that blows the mulch can be used to overcome the problem. This process is also limited by the effects of the wind.

Hydromulching. Hydromulching, also called *hydraulic mulching,* is a mulch applied in a water slurry that may also contain seed, fertilizer, erosion control compounds, growth regulators, and soil amendments. The most important aspect of hydromulching is that it tends to adhere to the soil on steep slopes while holding the seed in place during heavy rain and wind. Hydromulches have strict particle size requirements so the particles may be easily pumped through ½ inch nozzles, and at the same time not be so buoyant as to remain in suspension during moderate agitation. One disadvantage of hydromulch is that premature germination is likely to occur, leading to the ultimate loss of the entire crop because of adequate moisture in the mulch but insufficient soil moisture content. Therefore, its use is limited in arid regions.

Advantages of hydromulching include minimal labor costs, easy steep-slope coverage, easy application, few overspray problems, and easy cleanup with water. The best results in hydromulching can be obtained first by broadcasting seed onto the bare ground and then by applying a hydromulch in a separate treatment.

Crimping and Punching. Mulches can also be anchored by punching, crimping, or by slot mulching. In all three methods the mulch is anchored by soil. Equipment used to "punch" the mulch into the ground include a *mulch tiller,* a *modified sheepsfoot roller,* and a *weighted agricultural disc.* After the mulch is spread onto the surface, the operator will go over the area with one of the machines which leaves the straw protruding above the ground surface, creating "whisker dams."

MANAGEMENT

The time frame for the period between the planting of seeds to the appearance of an adequate stand of vegetation is critical and requires management attention if the whole revegetation program is to be successful. Through necessity, a site may be seeded at a time of the year not considered conducive to successful germination. Artificial forms of precipitation may have to be added to insure germination during critical times. An invasion of weeds may threaten the revegetation process. Therefore, the operator must maintain control of the seedling environment until such time when the seedlings are able to withstand stress.

Irrigation.   Surface mine sites are usually large and linear. Their boundary configurations create a difficult pattern in which to establish an irrigation system. As mentioned earlier, the areas east of the 100th meridian usually get enough precipitation that revegetation is easy to introduce, provided all the other growth factors are satisfactory. In the West, however, precipitation patterns are not so accommodating. There is a potential need for irrigation, were it only available. Unfortunately, water is not readily available and must be used sparingly. The rehabilitation specialist should check water-rights laws in the state prior to developing an irrigation plan. If the water is available and is needed, then it should be used, especially when attempts are made to seed during dry seasons. Its use should certainly expand the planting season.

Weed Control.   Unwanted weeds and grasses create severe competition with planted species and cause high mortality that could result in crop failures. Occasionally, weeds are welcome in that they provide cover and begin the natural succession processes. The rehabilitation specialist must assess the relative values of weeds and planted species in terms of forage value, erosion control, and cover.

Summer Fallow.   Summer fallow is designed to control weeds during the summer growing season prior to fall planting. It preserves soil moisture that would otherwise be used by annual weeds and grasses and also prevents weeds from going to seed, thereby reducing the likelihood of thick stands of weeds competing with newly emerged seedlings. Summer fallowing is accomplished in two ways: by tillage and with chemicals.

Tillage is generally costly on steep or rocky slopes. Under these conditions, selective herbicides are recommended. Summer fallowing with tillage involves frequent plowing during the growing season to prevent the invasion of weeds. It is necessary mostly when land shaping is completed in the fall or spring but when seeding does not take place until the following fall.

The use of herbicides.   Cook et al. state that the application of preemergence and/or postemergence herbicides as a summer fallowing practice gives significantly better stands of seeded vegetation than can be obtained from untreated areas where the seed is drilled directly into the growth of weeds.[10] The preemergence herbicide *Siduron* (Tupersan) should be applied in the fall at a rate of 5 pounds of active ingredient per acre or in the early spring mixed with .75 pounds of active ingredient of Paraquat per acre to control most annual grasses until the following fall.[11] A postemergence herbicide, such as *2,4-D* at 1.5 pounds of acid equivalent per acre may need to be added during the latter part of June to control the late germination of annual broadleaf plants.[12] Table 11.1 lists herbicides that are used for control of weeds prior to seeding or for summer fallowing purposes.

Mowing.   It normally takes from 3 to 5 years after seeding for a seeded stand to become established. A stand is said to be *closed* if it is thick enough to keep weedy species out. It will remain closed if the stand receives proper maintenance care. A satisfactory stand contains at least four plants per square foot. Cook points out that to maintain optimum vigor, plants must have sufficient photosynthetic tissue to manufacture food for plant sustenance and to replenish carbohydrate reserves.[13]

Table 11.1.   Herbicides Recommended for Control of Weeds Prior to Seeding or for Summer Fallow Purposes.

TRADE NAMES	TYPE	KIND	APPLICATION AND SEEDING	USES
Siduron (Tupersan)	Preemergence	Selective	Immediately after	Annual grass weeds
Paraquat	Postemergence	Contact foliage	Immediately after	Broadleaf and grass weeds
Fenac	Preemergence	Temporary soil sterilant	After 3 or 4 months	Broadleaf and grass weeds
Atrazine	Preemergence and early postemergence	Temporary soil sterilant	After 2 or 3 months	Broadleaf and grass weeds
Simazine	Preemergence	Temporary soil sterilant	After 4 to 5 months	Broadleaf and grass weeds
Monuron (Telvar)	Somewhat selective preemergence	Temporary soil sterilant	After 6 to 8 months	Annual grasses and broadleaf weeds
Amitrole	Postemergence	Contact foliage	Almost immediately after	Broadleaf and grass weeds
Lorox	Pre- and post-emergence	Selective	After 1 to 2 months	Annual broadleaf and grass weeds

Source: Cook, Wayne C., et al., *Revegetation Guidelines for Surface Mined Areas,* Science Series no. 16, Fort Collins, Co.: Colorado State University, 1974.

Plants depend entirely upon reserve foods stored in the roots and crowns for new spring growth. They utilize from 45 to 75 percent of the total reserve food to produce the first 15 to 20 percent of the current year's growth, after which there is a gradual replenishment of reserve food.[14] Maximum reserves during the annual life cycle cannot occur until the plant approaches maturity or produces seed.

Proper management, therefore, dictates that plants should not be mowed too low or too frequently during early growth. Plants should not be mowed lower than a four inch stubble height, and mowing should not be done until plants have formed seed heads or are fully mature.[15]

Use of Fire.   Most fires harm plant life. However, if burning can be carried out in a prescribed manner, the harmful effects can be minimized and used as a management tool. A crop should never be burned before it reaches full maturity. Fires that burn on terrain greater than 30 percent create so much heat at the surface that crowns of grasses are destroyed[16] Since fire destroys most shrubby species, it should not be used to manicure or remove old growth on seeded mine spoils.

Grazing.   New, tender seedlings are quite palatable to livestock and wildlife. However, uncontrolled grazing can play havoc with the revegetation program. It is suggested, therefore, that livestock be withheld following seeding until the plants become established—a period of 3 to 5 years depending on the site and species planted. It commonly takes 5 years for shrubby species to become established and 3 years for grasses and forbs.[17] Big game, which is much more difficult to control, may need to be fenced out of the area during critical times.

REFERENCES

1. Vogel, *A Guide for Revegetating Coal Minesoils*, p. 123.
2. Cook, Hyde, and Sims, *Revegetation Guidelines*, p. 5.
3. Ibid.
4. Ibid., p. 9.
5. Ibid.
6. Meech, Constance P., "Mulches and Their Use in Rehabilitation," *Rehabilitation of Mined-Land Disturbances in the Western U.S.*, ed. Dennis L. Law, 1st Annual KSU Symposium, Manhattan, Kans.: Department of Landscape Architecture, Kansas State University, 1982, p. 154.
7. Ibid., p. 155.
8. Ibid.
9. Ibid.
10. Cook, Hyde, and Sims, *Revegetation Guidelines*, p. 19.
11. Ibid.
12. Ibid.
13. Ibid., p. 24.
14. Ibid.
15. Ibid.
16. Ibid.
17. Ibid.

PART V
THE REHABILITATION
PLAN

12
Determining the Rehabilitation
Potential of Mined Lands

INTRODUCTION

Approximately one-third of the nation's lands are under the stewardship of the federal government. The Departments of Interior and Agriculture and other surface management agencies have the responsibility of managing the land in such a way as to ensure the highest level of productivity. Federal land is capable, in most cases, of supporting multiple land uses. With the push to extract minerals, especially those that are energy-related, the agencies responsible for managing the land are under constant pressure from various interested parties, such as mining and petroleum companies and ranchers with grazing leases, to ensure maximum production. Added to this are the pressures from various environmental groups that oppose the destruction of the land.

Both public and private lands should be safeguarded from the crimes committed in the past on private lands by the mining companies, as described in earlier chapters. The abuses threatened the social and environmental fabric of our nation.

Many lands are extremely sensitive to interference by mining operations. As previously mentioned, the environment is composed of a series of intricately balanced natural systems. In some cases, the systems are threatened by mining in such a way as to create irrevocable damage. One purpose of planning is to identify the landscape's potential for being rehabilitated.

CATEGORIES OF LANDS THAT SHOULD NOT BE DISTURBED

Lands with Vulnerable Cultural Resources

Mining operations can affect human life in a variety of ways. Chapter 3 addressed the cultural impacts of mining in detail. The planning processes should identify those cultural resources that will be affected. Once the resources are identified, methods can be decided on to mitigate the negative aspects of mining. Among the normally sensitive cultural resources that should be included in the planning are:

A. Economics
B. Health and safety
C. Aesthetics

The Surface Mining Control and Reclamation Act of 1977 states that the protection of the public health, safety, and general welfare of citizens affected by mining operations shall be a function of the various compliance agencies of state and federal governments. In many instances, environmental damage is directly related to social or cultural impacts. The effects of any irreversible alteration in the economic stability of a region will persist for generations. Polluted environments will affect the health and welfare of the human population, sometimes miles from the source.

The Surface Mining Control and Reclamation Act of 1977 addresses both environmental and social issues in its requirements. The act, however, only affects the mining of coal. The mining of other minerals should come under similar safeguards. The various state laws should be studied and necessary requirements implemented into the planning procedures. The Environmental Protection Performance Standards (Section 515) of the act is provided in Appendix A.

Lands with Fragile Environmental Features

Potential environmental impacts were outlined in Chapters 4 and 5 with special emphasis on the geological and biological elements. Procedures described in this chapter are intended primarily to identify those properties within the environment that are sensitive. Again, the Surface Mining Control and Reclamation Act of 1977 deals primarily with those concerns.

PROCESSES FOR PLANNING

The processes used to determine the rehabilitation potential of mined lands consist of the following:

A. Identification of major surface disturbances
B. Identification of planning objectives
C. Development of a resource data pool
D. Development of mapping techniques
E. Mapping resources
F. Determination of environmental and visual sensitivity
G. The establishment of priorities

Identification of Major Surface Disturbances

The aim of this process is a comparison or overlay of the various surface disturbances with the zones within the landscape that have been identified as sensitive. The following steps should be followed to determine the extent of surface disturbances:

A. Develop a base map that has the following features:
  1. Topographic features with a contour interval not exceeding 20 feet
  2. Property and ownership boundaries
  3. An appropriate scale, which will vary from site to site and with the extent of information to be recorded
  4. Improvements such as buildings, roads, and so forth
B. Conduct office reconnaissance, in which the rehabilitation specialist identifies disturbances, improvements, or features found through remote sensing or aerial photographs and adds them to the base map.
C. Conduct field reconnaissance, during which the rehabilitation specialist will visit the site to add detail and verify information on the base map as needed.

Identification of Planning Objectives

After the extent of surface disturbances has been identified, the rehabilitation specialist is better equipped to determine postmining land uses. If this process takes place prior to mining, the mining plan can direct the operation in such a way as to facilitate the development of a postmining land use plan to be implemented as soon as the mineral is removed. The Surface Mining Control and Reclamation Act of 1977 states, "Mining and reclamation operations shall require the operation as a minimum to restore the land affected to a condition capable of supporting the uses which it was capable of supporting prior to any mining, or higher or better uses of which there is reasonable likelihood, so long as such use or uses do not present any actual or probable hazard to public health or safety or pose any actual or probable threat of water diminution or pollution, and the permit applicants' declared proposed land use following reclamation is not deemed to be impractical or unreasonable, inconsistent with applicable land use policies and plans, involves unreasonable delay in implementation, or is violative of Federal, State, or local law; . . .''

Developing a Resource Data Pool

The rehabilitation specialist must have a basis on which to make prudent decisions. In all cases, various elements that comprise the natural systems described throughout this book must be identified. The planner must not, however, burden himself with unnecessary data. Only those forms of information relevant to the particular site or circumstance need to be acquired. At a minimum, however, it is suggested that information be gathered on the following:

A. Slopes
B. Soils/geology
C. Vegetation
D. Water resources
E. Wildlife
F. Visual resources

It must be emphasized that this list does not take into account unique problems that may be site specific. Each site is different and requires its own set of resource evaluations.

Development of Mapping Techniques

A variety of methods could be used to map the various resources outlined above. With the development of computer graphics technology, the need for superior graphic skill has diminished. The rehabilitation planner must decide what technique to use based on the size of the project, the amount of information to be collected, the complexities involved, the degree of detail involved, and the capabilities of the personnel implementing the method. For the purposes of this book,

however, an overlay process will be suggested. It can be implemented for most projects. In each case, the sensitive aspects of each resource should be rendered with a dark tone and the less sensitive with a light tone.

Mapping Resources

Slopes.   Slopes are critical to facility planning and for the stabilization of soils during rehabilitation. Flat slopes lend themselves to most types of construction but may have drainage problems. Steep slopes are more difficult for construction projects, have higher potential for erosion, and thus, are more difficult to rehabilitate.

Slopes should be expressed as a percentage. For example, a 6 percent slope would have a 6 foot drop for every 100 feet of slope length. Slope percentages can be computed from any topographic map. In most cases, a USGS, 7.5 minute topographic map will suffice.

In developing a slope analysis, the rehabilitation specialist should take into consideration the types of equipment or vehicles that will be used in the mining area and the standard slopes that can properly facilitate the equipment's use. It would be wise to also consider the various conditions that exist relative to soil types, vegetation, and geology that affect erosion and sedimentation during the exploration and production of the mine.

The slope analysis should provide information to demonstrate what surface disturbances that are ready for rehabilitation have a high potential for erosion. It should also provide information that can be used as a guide for rehabilitation standards and specifications.

Slopes can be mapped by using a ''tic'' chart developed by computing the maximum slope in a slope range and determining the distances between topographic lines. The ''tic'' chart is illustrated in Figure 12.1 and was developed from a 7.5 minute USGS map with a 40-foot contour interval. The slope ranges are 0–6%, 7–25%, 26–33%, and over 33%. A map developed

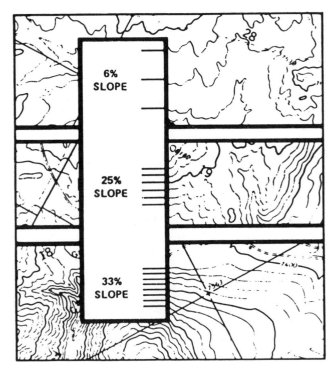

Figure 12.1. Slope tic chart (From Bureau of Land Management).

by the author for the Tip Top Oil and Gas Field in Wyoming is illustrated in Figure 12.2.

Soils/Geology. Data on soils and other geotechnical resource information are critical to the resource inventory. Soils and surficial geology constitute the medium in which construction, rehabilitation, and maintenance occur. Soils and surficial geology, in consort with other site factors, determine whether a site is suitable, moderately suitable, or unsuitable for specific uses. Soil and other site characteristics describe the potentials and limitations of each site and therefore enable accurate site-specific planning and engineering design for development, rehabilitation, and maintenance.

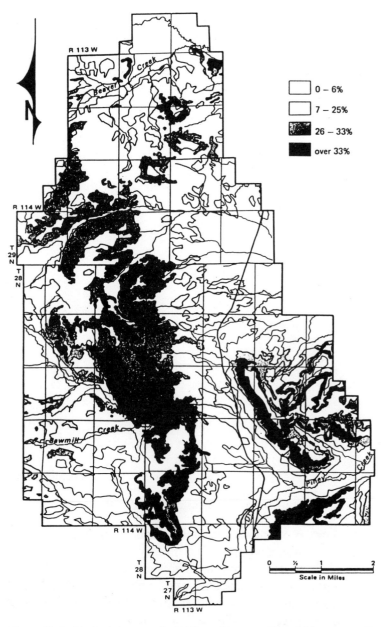

Figure 12.2. Typical slope analysis (From Bureau of Land Management).

Soil and surficial geology is primarily used to understand soil suitability for planning, locating, and developing facilities within the mine. It is also used to identify problem areas critical to safety and the environment. In such cases, more testing and additional engineering are required.

Soils data should be used to classify soil mapping units by their erosion susceptibility and revegetation potential. The same data may also be used to prescribe specific construction and revegetation practices for each soil mapping unit.

There are basically three data sources from which to develop soil mapping units. They include:

A. Geologic hazard survey
B. Agronomic soil survey
C. Engineering soil survey

Geologic hazard survey. The geologic hazard survey will provide the following information:

A. Erosion and sedimentation susceptibility
B. Potential aquifer recharge zones
C. Potential borrow areas
D. Potential slope instability
E. Other hazards as may be apparent

During the geologic hazard analysis, areas should be identified and mapped as follows:

A. High erosion using drainage density analysis
B. Potential instability
C. Soils of fine particulate where erosion will create severe sedimentation problems and potential stream pollution
D. Good borrow sites if they appear to be few in number and, therefore, a valuable resource
E. Potential aquifer recharge zones

Agronomic soil survey. The best available soil inventory is a completed level II soil survey. It contains data needed to accomplish the rehabilitation specialist's objectives. The Soil Conservation Service (SCS) may not have a published county soil survey but may have a completed but unpublished survey or a partial survey that might include the mining area. Upon request, the SCS will usually make that information available. Any level II survey should still be randomly checked in the field by a qualified soils specialist to ensure the accuracy of soil boundaries.

A secondary source is a level III soil survey. A follow-up field-directed survey should be conducted to verify the soil association and soil complex boundaries. If used, the soil association should be subdivided by soil series for more finite soil descriptions.

Another equally good source is a field-directed survey conducted by a qualified soil specialist or consultant. Should the survey be contracted, it would still be necessary to oversee and randomly check it to ensure its accuracy. In a field-directed survey, data gathering is limited to specific soil factors affecting the objectives of the soil survey.

Engineering soil survey. In addition to the agronomic inventory, an engineering soil survey should be conducted concurrently. It is essential that the following data, particularly with regard to the "C" horizon and substrate or regolith material, be accurately determined:

A. Unified classification.
B. Gradation analysis.
C. Atterburg limits.
D. Depth to bedrock.
E. Depth to seasonal high water table.
F. Any additional data that are essential for planning, future construction, engineering, rehabilitating, or maintaining a particular site for a specific use. This primarily pertains to those sites that have been iden-

tified as areas requiring additional testing and engineering development.

Information and data can be transferred to charts to ease in interpretation and assessment through the use of forms illustrated in Figures 12.3 to 12.5. For the purposes of rehabilitation, values for items A–F above should be assigned and mapped according to major criteria, including establishment of vegetation potential and erosion susceptibility. Linscott suggests that values should be mapped according to the matrix illustrated in Figure 12.6.[1]

There is a strong likelihood that these values cannot be assigned until the vegetative analysis is completed. The correlation between soils and vegetation is extremely close, and in some cases, the soils and vegetation inventories are made simultaneously.

Vegetation. Vegetal cover is highly site specific and demands thorough site investigation by plant specialists. Premining vegetation provides valuable information but may not indicate the potential that a site has for plant reestablishment. Several reasons may account for this, including:

A. Premining land use may have been altered to such a degree that existing plant communities are not stabilized, climax situations.
B. Improper maintenance or overgrazing may create the impression that the potential for revegetation is lower than it is in reality.
C. The soils and geologic structure of the premining site may be so drastically altered by the mining process that the plant specialist gets a false sense of security regarding the potential a site has for revegetation.

For these reasons, it is essential that the planning process gather information on the history of the ways land was used, agronomic procedures, mining processes, and typical vegetative succession for the immediate area. Climatic data as well as maintenance procedures are also considered critical.

Most of the above is highly specific from site to site, and it is difficult to prescribe a procedure for the purposes of this book. Nevertheless, sensitivity categories should be developed as follows:

A. Low vegetative potential—severe sensitivity
B. Moderately low vegetative potential—moderately severe sensitivity
C. Moderately high vegetative potential—moderately low sensitivity
D. High vegetative potential—low sensitivity

Premining vegetation analysis should reveal the percentage of cover and of grasses. Percent cover is an indication of how well the site will support vegetation. Percent grasses, or any plant type with a fibrous root structure, will indicate how well those species that resist erosion will reestablish.

Water Resources. The water resources analysis should provide data that will assist in developing proper rehabilitation guidelines for sedimentation control until the area reaches slope and vegetation stabilization. Critical zones include riparian habitats which are determined by landform; all springs, ponds, and wells; and potential aquifer recharge zones. Those intermittent and perennial streams without riparian habitat should be mapped as moderate zones.

Wildlife. The major objective in mapping wildlife resources is to identify and regulate those zones where the existence or welfare of wildlife may be seriously impaired by the mining operation. Wildlife needs food, cover, and territory, all of which can be destroyed by mining. Rehabilitation efforts should be geared toward reestablishment of native vegetation losses. When vegetation has been mapped, critical wildlife areas call attention to those zones where wildlife and vegetation are essentially interdependent. In addition to land surface considerations, riparian systems with critical fish and wildlife species must be protected and/or rehabilitated as quickly as possible.

MAPPING UNIT LOG

SOIL CHARACTERISTICS

SOILS SPECIALISTS:

PAGE: _____
DATE: _____

| SOIL MAPPING UNIT | DEPTH TO | | DEPTH FROM SURFACE | CLASSIFICATION | | REACTION(PH) | COLOR | AVAILABLE WATER HOLDING CAPACITY | SODIUM ABSORBTION RATIO | PERMEABILITY | COARSE FRACTION GREATER THAN 3" | PERCENTAGE LESS THAN 3" PASSING SIEVE | | | | LIQUID LIMIT | PLASTICITY INDEX | OTHER |
	BEDROCK	SEASONAL HIGH WATERTABLE		USDA TEXTURE	UNIFIED							NO. 4 (4.7 MM)	NO. 10 (2.0 MM)	NO. 40 (.42 MM)	NO. 200 (.074 MM)			

The soil and site data found on the Mapping Unit Log is defined as the minimum data necessary to rate the erosion susceptibility and revegetation potential of each soil mapping unit, to interpret use suitabilities, and to recommend specific construction and revegetation materials and practices.

Since this process must be applied statewide, it must be flexible enough to be used for a wide range of site situations, numerable combinations or permutations of various site and soil characteristics. For instance, slope ranges and the effect of slope will depend upon such factors as precipitation and soil type. Therefore, it is emphasized that decisions concerning methods and criteria for measuring and surveying site and soil characteristics be at district levels. For the same reasons, the interpretations for planning and implementation must also be at the local level.

Figure 12.3. Mapping unit log—soil characteristics (From Bureau of Land Management).

			MAPPING UNIT LOG												
AVERAGE ANNUAL PRECIPITATION:			SITE CHARACTERISTICS										PAGE		
PREDOMINANT WIND DIRECTION:													DATE		
SOIL MAPPING UNIT	SITE CHARACTERISTICS					GEOLOGIC HAZARD ANALYSIS						EROSION FACTOR		REVEGETATION FACTOR	
	ASPECT	SLOPE RANGE	% COVER	% GRASSES	OTHER	EROSION SUSCEPTIBILITY	POTENTIAL SLOPE INSTABILITY	SEDIMENTATION SUSCEPTIBILITY	POTENTIAL AQUIFER RECHARGE	POTENTIAL BORROW	OTHER	RATING	LIMITING FACTORS	RATING	LIMITING FACTORS

Figure 12.4. Mapping unit log—site characteristics (From Bureau of Land Management).

MAPPING UNIT LOG

SOIL/SITE SUITABILITIES

PAGE: _____

SOIL MAPPING UNIT	LOCATIONS				ROADS				PIPELINES			
	FACTOR	ENGINEERING LIMITATIONS	REVEGETATION LIMITATIONS	REFERENCE	FACTOR	ENGINEERING LIMITATIONS	REVEGETATION LIMITATIONS	REFERENCE	FACTOR	ENGINEERING LIMITATIONS	REVEGETATION LIMITATIONS	REFERENCE

Figure 12.5. Mapping unit log—soil/site suitabilities (From Bureau of Land Management).

ESTABLISHMENT OF
VEGETATION

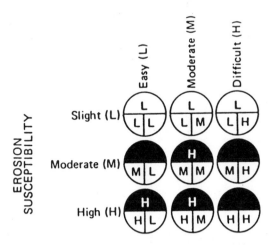

NOTE: Establishment of vegetation is defined as the natural or inherent potential for a site to establish vegetative cover. Use SCS range site data as a source.

Each of these symbols is associated with a soil mapping unit and, therefore, needs only to be translated as having a low (L-white), moderate (M-gray), or high (H-black) soil sensitivity.

Figure 12.6. Rehabilitation priority matrix (From Bureau of Land Management).

The most valuable resource for wildlife data is usually the advice and data collected from wildlife biologists. State park and wildlife departments usually have staff biologists who can provide assistance. Zones not considered to be critical include situations where exploration and/or mining are likely not to have a negative impact on habitats of special concern. Considered to be moderately sensitive are those situations where exploration or mining may negatively affect wildlife species or habitats of special concern on a temporary basis. All riparian zones, critical big-game winter ranges, migratory corridors, fawning grounds, sensitive species habitats, and special wildlife management areas should be considered as moderate for mapping purposes. Areas considered to be critical include those situations where exploration and/or mining can produce a permanent and irreversible negative impact on a wildlife species or habitat of special concern.

Visual Resources. Visual quality is a relatively new environmental concern. The resource is generally computed by considering distance zones and scenic quality. Distance zones are critical because of the impact distance has on quality. An unpleasant scene is less critical whenever it lies far away. Pleasant scenes, on the other hand, are more meaningful when the viewer has easy visual access.

Distance zones. Distance zones are mapped by first determining the location of travel routes within the site. Foreground, midground, and seldom-seen zones are then identified. The distance from travel routes to these zone limits will, of course, vary from site to site. Generally, however, foreground zones are all areas that can be seen from each travel route up to a quarter of a mile. Midground zones are all areas that can be seen between a quarter mile and 3 to 5 miles. Seldom-seen zones are all portions of the area that cannot be seen from primary travel routes.

Scenic quality. The criterion of scenic quality is extremely subjective and will vary from one individual to another. Efforts have been made to establish evaluation criteria that will standardize the output. The criteria and methodology suggested here were developed by the author and others in work conducted for the Bureau of Land Management in Wyoming.[2] Criteria used to evaluate scenery include the following:

A. Landform
B. Vegetation
C. Water
D. Color
E. Adjacent scenery
F. Scarcity
G. Disturbance

Figure 12.7 provides a chart one could use to establish scenic values. Figure 12.8 provides the rating criteria.

scenic quality inventory & evaluation chart

rating criteria & score

low = 0–11
moderate = 12–18
high = 19–37

key factors			
landform	Low, rolling hills, foothills or flat valley bottoms. Interesting detail landscape features few or lacking. **1**	Steep canyons, mesas, buttes, cinder cones and drumlins; or interesting erosional patterns or variety in size and shape of landforms; or detail features present and interesting though not dominant or exceptional. **3**	High vertical relief as expressed in prominent cliffs, spires or massive rock outcrops, or severe surface variation or highly eroded formations including major badlands or dune systems; or detail features dominant and exceptionally striking and intriguing such as glaciers. **5**
vegetation	Little or no variety or contrast in vegetation. **1**	Some variety of vegetation, but only one or two major types. **3**	A variety of vegetative types as expressed in interesting forms, textures, and patterns. **5**
water	Absent, or present, but not noticeable. **0**	Flowing, or still, but not dominant in the landscape. **3**	Clear and clean appearing, still, cascading white water, any of which are a dominant factor in the landscape. **5**
color	Subtle color variations, contrast or interest; generally mute tones. **1**	Some intensity or variety in colors and contrast of the soil, rock and vegetation, but not a dominant scenic element. **3**	Rich color combinations, variety or vivid color; or pleasing contrasts in the soil, rock, vegetation, water or snow fields. **5**
adjacent scenery	Adjacent scenery has little or no influence on overall visual quality. **0**	Adjacent scenery moderately enhances overall visual quality. **3**	Adjacent scenery greatly enhances visual quality. **5**
scarcity	Interesting within its setting, but fairly common within the region. **1**	Distinctive, though somewhat similar to others within the region. **2**	One of a kind; or unusually memorable, or very rare within region. Consistent chance for exceptional wildlife or wildflower viewing, etc. **6**
disturbance	Modifications are so extensive that scenic qualities are for the most part nullified or substantially reduced. **-4**	Scenic quality is somewhat depreciated by inharmonious intrusions, but not so extensive that the scenic qualities are entirely negated or modifications add little or no visual variety to the area. **0**	Free from aesthetically undesirable or discordant sights and influences; or modifications add favorably to visual variety. **5**

Rate for scenery under the most critical conditions (i.e., highest user period or season of use, sidelight, proper atmospheric conditions, etc.).

Values for each rating criterion are maximum and minimum scores only. It is also possible to assign scores within these ranges.

Figure 12.7. Scenic quality inventory and evaluation chart (From Bureau of Land Management).

scenic quality rating criteria:

landform
Topography becomes more interesting as it gets steeper or more massive, or more severely or universally sculptured. Outstanding landforms may be monumental as the Grand Canyon, the Sawtooth Mountain Range in Idaho, and the Wrangell Mountain Range in Alaska, or they may be exceedingly artistic and subtle as certain badlands, pinnacles, arches and other extraordinary formations.

vegetation
Give primary consideration to the variety of patterns, forms, and textures created by plant life. Consider short-lived displays when they are known to be recurring or spectacular. Consider also smaller scale vegetational features which add striking and intriguing detail elements to the landscape; e.g., gnarled or windbeaten trees, Joshua trees, etc.

water
Water is that ingredient which adds movement or serenity to a scene. The degree to which water dominates the scene is the primary consideration in selecting the rating score.

color
Consider the overall color(s) of the basic components of the landscape (i.e., soil, rock, vegetation, etc.) as it appear during seasons or periods of high use. Key factors to use when rating "color" are variety, contrast and harmony.

adjacent scenery
Consider the degree to which scenery outside the scenery unit being rated enhances the overall impression of the scenery within the rating unit. The distance which adjacent scenery will influence scenery within the rating unit will normally range from 0–5 miles, depending upon verticality of topography, vegetative cover and other such factors. This factor is generally applied to units which would normally rate very low in score, but the influence of the adjacent unit would enhance the visual quality and raise the score.

scarcity
This factor provides an opportunity to give added importance to one or all of the scenic features that appear to be relatively unique or rare within one physiographic region. There may also be cases where a separate evaluation of each of the key factors does not give a true picture of the overall scenic quality of an area. Often it is a number of not so spectacular elements in the proper combination that produces the most pleasing and memorable scenery. The scarcity factor can be used to recognize this type of area and give it the added emphasis it needs.

disturbances
Consider the impact of change on the visual quality of the characteristic landscape. Cultural modifications in the landform/water, vegetation and addition of structures should be considered and may detract from the scenery in the form of a negative intrusion or actually compliment or improve the scenery quality of a unit. Be careful not to confuse interest with scenery quality. Rate accordingly.

Figure 12.8. Scenic quality rating criteria (From Bureau of Land Management).

Developing the visual resources map.   A map of the site area should be used as a base with the sensitivity zones delineated accordingly. The zones are determined by utilizing the matrix illustrated by Figure 12.9, which compares distance zones with scenic quality.

Environmental Sensitivity

All the resource overlays, including slopes, soils, vegetation, water resources, wildlife, and visual resources should be cross-referenced to graphically portray a range of sensitivity levels for each resource. The purpose of the *environmental sensitivity composite* is to bring each of the overlays together into a single drawing which will illustrate all the ranges of sensitivity within the area. This drawing is particularly valuable in assessing environmental problems prior to the beginning of the mining operation. If a proposed development spills into a sensitive area, the rehabilitation specialist is able to quickly assess the nature of potential problems and propose development guidelines that will enhance future rehabilitation.

The composite can be made in several ways. If the overlays are fairly simple in detail, then a cursory linking of like tones into cells would probably suffice, especially since only three tones are required. Representing low, moderate, and high sensitivity, the three tones also indicate the area's rehabilitation priorities. If the mapped resources offer a complex variety of gray tones, then each small cell may have to be given a numerical value and then linked accordingly. A computer could also be used for determining values.

DETERMINING THE REHABILITATION POTENTIAL

The series of overlays now provide a basis by which one can determine how easily a site lends itself to rehabilitation efforts. Specific resources peculiar to a site generally make a description quite difficult as to how one would use the data to make land use decisions. However, the map can be used to assist in determining stockpile locations, road alignment, potentially hazardous slopes, potential erosion hazards, sensitive wildlife habitats, and so forth. It is imperative that the rehabilitation specialist remember two important guidelines.

First, the rehabilitation specialist is under an obligation to become intimately acquainted with the site and the various natural systems that make up its environment. He should also have an understanding of the intricate interrelationships that exist there. This enables the specialist to focus on the effects one aspect of the site will have on another. Second, the rehabilitation specialist must rely on other professional specialists. The author knows that whatever one's training happens to be, it is likely to focus on a narrow portion of the complex nature of rehabilitation. The rehabilitation specialist that attempts to make decisions based only on his own knowledge or experience is flirting with disaster.

REFERENCES

1. Law, Dennis L., Lester L. Linscott, and Richard L. Hopkins, *Oil and Gas Field Rehab,* Cheyenne, Wyo.: Bureau of Land Management, 1981, p. 24.
2. Ibid., pp. 37, 38.

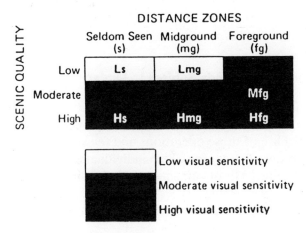

Figure 12.9. Visual sensitivity matrix (From Bureau of Land Management).

13
The Rehabilitation Plan

INTRODUCTION

An outline of the requirements set forth by the Surface Mining Reclamation and Control Act of 1977, Section 508, will serve as a basis for discussing rehabilitation plans. State laws are also pertinent, and each rehabilitation specialist should work closely with officials of state regulatory agencies since their requirements are sometimes much more stringent. The specialist should be as familiar with these laws as are the personnel used by state and federal agencies to monitor compliance. It is much better for the mining company to make every effort to comply with legal standards and requirements and maintain a basis for discussion than to attempt to get around them in some way. Poor working relationships can prove to be costly over the long run, and noncompliance generally results in stiff fines and bureaucratic delays.

FEDERAL PLAN REQUIREMENTS

As a part of the application for a permit to mine, a reclamation plan is required. The mining company must be able to define, in adequate detail, its ability to reclaim the mining area.

The rehabilitation plan should address the following subjects:

A. Identification of lands subject to mining
B. Premining site conditions
C. Proposed postmining land uses
D. Description of how postmining land use is to be accomplished
E. Engineering techniques to be used in mining and rehabilitation
F. Minimizing future disturbances on mining sites
G. Estimated timetables
H. Compliance with nonfederal regulations
I. Compliance with air and water quality laws
J. Physical, environmental, and climatological constraints
K. Interests and options on contiguous sites
L. Results of test borings
M. Protection of water resources

Identification of Lands Subject to Mining

The rehabilitation plan should include a statement identifying the lands subject to surface coal mining operations over the estimated life of those operations and the size, sequence, and timing of the subareas for which individual permits for mining will be sought.[1] The document should contain graphic illustrations of land holdings, types of leases, duration of leases, names of property owners, legal descriptions, and all improvements, including such items as roads, drilling rigs, and so forth.

Premining Site Conditions

The rehabilitation plan should include a statement of the condition of the land covered by the permit prior to any mining including the following:

A. Uses existing at the time of the application, and if the land has a history of previous mining, the uses that preceded the former operation.
B. The capability of the land prior to any mining to support a variety of uses, with consideration given to soil and foundation characteristics, topography, and vegetation cover, and, if applicable, a soil survey prepared pursuant to the location of prime agricultural lands.
C. Productivity of the land prior to mining, including an appropriate classification as prime farm lands, as well as the average yield of food, fiber, forage, or wood products from such lands obtained under high levels of management.[2]

Drawings of maps showing the locations of previously excavated underground mines and surface soils would be appropriate and should be furnished with the narrative.

Proposed Postmining Land Use

The rehabilitation plan should state the use that is proposed for the land following rehabilitation and should discuss the capacity of the rehabilitated land to support a variety of alternative uses and the relationship of such uses to existing land use policies and plans. The plan should also record the comments of any owners of surface land rights and of state and local government or agency officials who would have to in-

itiate, implement, approve, or authorize the proposed use of the land following rehabilitation.[3]

Description of how Postmining Land Use Is to Be Accomplished

The rehabilitation plan should include narrative and illustrations that describe how the proposed postmining land use is to be achieved. All necessary support activities should also be included.[4] This section, in addition to the required narrative, should also include drawings and diagrams to assist the reader in understanding the intentions of the mine operator.

Engineering Techniques

The rehabilitation plan should describe the engineering techniques to be used for both mining and rehabilitation. It should also set forth the types and uses of the various equipment to be employed in the project. The description of the engineering techniques should include the following:

A. A plan for the control of surface water drainage and water accumulation.
B. A plan, where appropriate, for backfilling, soil stabilization, and compacting, grading and appropriate revegetation.
C. A plan for soil reconstruction, replacement, and stabilization according to performance standards delineated in Section 515 (Appendix A).
D. A per-acre cost estimate for the rehabilitation of food, forage, and forest lands including a statement as to how the mining company plans to comply with Section 515.

Minimizing Future Disturbances

The rehabilitation plan should explain how the mine operator intends to maximize the utilization and conservation of the solid fuel resource being recovered so that future disturbances to the land can be minimized.[5] If at all possible, the mining operation should completely recover the mineral deposit. This would help guarantee that the land would not, at some future date, be once again disturbed.

Estimated Timetables

The regulatory agency requires, as part of the rehabilitation plan, a detailed timetable for the accomplishment of each major step.[6] This assists the regulatory agency in its efforts to monitor compliance of the various activities scheduled to take place. Steps considered to be "major" will likely vary from site to site. The timetable also serves as a cursory review of the rehabilitation procedures to be employed.

Compliance with Nonfederal Regulations

The rehabilitation plan must give an account of how the mining operator plans to comply with surface owner plans and applicable state and local land use plans and programs.[7] The underlying concern here is how the mining operation will interfere with the growth and development of the community in which the operation is located. In addition to the environmental dimensions of a typical mining operation, there are various social aspects that must be considered.

Compliance with Air and Water Quality Laws

The rehabilitation plan must recount the steps to be taken to comply with applicable air and water quality laws and regulations. In addition, any of the applicable health and safety standards of Section 515 or of state and local regulatory agencies must be considered and addressed in the plan.[8]

Physical, Environmental, and Climatological Constraints

Consideration should be given to developing the rehabilitation plan in a manner consistent with local physical, environmental, and climatological conditions.[9] This requirement, more than any other in the rehabilitation plan, ensures that the actions taken by the operator are site specific and meet the needs of a particular set of environmental constraints. Decisions cannot be made on a statewide or regional basis wherever revegetation is concerned. Those conditions peculiar to the site must be the only ones used. The various resources used to determine the rehabilitation potential of a site, as spelled out in Chapter 12, should be used as a minimum standard.

Interests in and Options on Contiguous Sites

The rehabilitation plan should include statements on all lands, interests in lands, or options on such interests held by the operator. The narrative should include pending bids on interests in lands by the operator, which are contiguous to the area to be mined by the permit.[10] This requirement ensures that consideration will be given to the total venture since a permit may be granted that, in actuality, only covers a portion of the land that the mining operator plans to eventually utilize.

Results of Test Borings

It is likely that the mining operator has taken test borings over the site to be mined in an effort to determine subsurface data. The rehabilitation plan should include the results of test borings with any other appropriate or equivalent information and data. Information should include the location of subsurface water and an analysis of the chemical properties of the test material, including the acid-forming properties of the mineral and overburden.[11] Federal requirements state than only information that pertains to the analysis of the chemical and physical properties of the coal shall be kept confidential and not made a matter of public record. This does not include information regarding mineral or elemental contents that are potentially toxic to the environment.[12]

Protection of Water Resources

Finally, the rehabilitation plan should include a detailed description of the measures to be taken during the mining and rehabilitation process to ensure the protection of the following from any adverse effects:

A. The quality of surface and ground water systems, both on- and off-site
B. The rights of present users to such water
C. The quantity of surface and ground water systems, both on- and off-site, or alternative sources of water where protection of the present quantity of water cannot be ensured

CONCLUSIONS

The conclusion of this chapter will have to suffice as a conclusion to the book. Following this final chapter are two appendixes. Appendix A is a copy of Secton 515 of the Surface Mining Control and Reclamation Act of 1977, describing the environmental protection performance standards. Appendix B is a list of suggested plant materials commonly used in the East and the West for rehabilitation purposes. The list is simply for reference. The rehabilitation specialist may or may not have success with certain species on the list for a number of reasons. Although some experimentation is sometimes required, local authorities should provide assistance to those practicing in areas in which they are unfamiliar.

Finally, a quote from the prophet Isaiah:

The earth mourns and withers,
The world languishes and withers;
The heavens languish together with the earth,
The earth lies polluted under its inhabitants,
For they have transgressed the laws,
Violated the statutes,
Broken the everlasting covenant.
Therefore, a curse devours the earth, and its inhabitants
   suffer for their guilt;
Therefore, the inhabitants of the earth are scorched,
And few men are left.

Isaiah 24:4–6

REFERENCES

1. Surface Mining Control and Reclamation Act of 1977, Public Law 95–87, 91 Stat. 478.
2. Ibid.
3. Ibid.
4. Ibid.
5. Ibid., 91 Stat. 479.
6. Ibid.
7. Ibid.
8. Ibid.
9. Ibid.
10. Ibid.
11. Ibid.
12. Ibid.

Glossary

Alluvial—Pertaining to or composed of any sediment deposited by flowing water.

Alluvium—Gravel, sand, silt, clay, or similar detrital material deposited or moved by running water.

ANFO (Ammonium Nitrate Fuel Oil)—A powdered explosive material used in blasting or loosening overburdens for easier removal.

Aquifer—A water-bearing bed or stratum (layer) of permeable rock, sand, or gravel capable of yielding adequate quantities of water.

Barrier—The material required near an outcrop that acts as a natural barrier to water drainage, while supporting and preventing spoils from slipping down the slope.

Bench—A shelf or ledge on which mining activities occur; commonly used in contour strip mining. Synonymous terms include *terrace, rimcutting,* and *workbench.*

Biomass—The total dry weight of all living organisms that can be supported at each trophic level in a food chain.

Biome—A major ecological community type.

Briny Water—Water saturated or strongly impregnated with common salt.

Bituminous—Resembling, containing, or impregnated with an asphalt material.

Blasting Round—A group of holes drilled in rock to receive explosives.

Channelization Equilibrium—A condition in which the forces giving rise to channel development are the same in magnitude as the forces resisting initial channel development.

Climate—The statistical collective of an area's weather conditions during a relatively long interval of time (usually several decades).

Climax Ecosystem (Climax Community)—A relatively stable stage of ecological succession; a mature ecosystem with a diverse array of species and ecological niches, capable of using energy and cycling critical chemicals more efficiently than simpler, immature ecosystems.

Climax Species—Species that dominate an ecosystem, usually at a mature stage of ecological succession.

Compaction—The packing of loose surface materials into a hard, heavy surface.

Competition—Two or more species in the same ecosystem attempting to use the same scarce resources.

Contour—An imaginary line along the earth's surface connecting the points of equal elevation.

Detachment—The removal of transportable fragments of soil material from a soil mass by an eroding agent, usually falling raindrops, running water, or wind. Through detachment, soil particles or aggregates are made ready for transport (soil erosion).

Diversity—Physical or biological complexity of a system, which in many cases leads to ecosystem stability.

Drainage Density—The cumulative length of channel segments in a unit area, usually expressed in miles per square mile.

Ecological Succession—Change in the structure and function of an ecosystem; replacement of one type of community or organism with a different community over a period of time (see primary succession, secondary succession).

Ecosystem—Self-sustaining and self-regulating community of organisms interacting with one another and with their environment.

Emission Factor—An empirically derived mathematical relationship between pollutant emission rate and some characteristic of the source such as volume, area, mass, or process output.

Environment—Aggregate of external conditions that influence the life of an individual organism or population.

Ephemeral Stream—A stream with surface water flow only after a storm and lasting a very short time.

Erosion—The wearing away of the land surface by running water, wind, ice, or other geological agents, including such processes as gravitation creep; the detachment and movement of soil or rock fragments by water, wind, ice, or gravity.

Evapotranspiration—Loss of water from the soil both by evaporation and by transpiration from the plants growing thereon.

Food Chain—Sequence of transfers of energy in the form of food from organisms in one trophic level to those in another when one organism eats or decomposes another.

Food Web—Complex, interlocking series of food chains.

Ground Water—That part of subsurface water that completely saturates the rocks and is under hydrostatic pressure.

Grubbing—An operation for removing stumps and roots.

Habitat—Place where an organism or community of organisms naturally lives or grows.

Head-of-the-Hollow (also Valley Fill)—A basic mining method by which overburden material from adjacent contour or mountain-top mines is placed in compacted layers in narrow, steep-sided hollows so that surface drainage is possible.

Highwall—The face of an exposed wall created by the removal of a down-sloped surface.

Impermeable—Not permitting water to pass through under the head differences ordinarily found in ground water. Applied to strata such as clays and shales.

Indigenous—Occurring naturally; native.

Inlet—An opening for intake in a pipe or culvert.

Jettie—A structure extended into a drainage or stream to influence the current.

Leaching—(1) The removal of soluble salts or metals from the accompanying materials by the use of a suitable solvent, (2) process of decomposition under natural agencies of an outcrop. Surface waters penetrating downward may dissolve some or all of the mineral in their path, thus carrying it away from the surface zone.

Net Primary Productivity—Rate at which plants produce usable food or chemical energy (usable biomass). Obtained by subtracting the rate of respiration from the gross primary productivity.

Oil Shale—Geologic formations that contain a solid hydrocarbon called kerogen, which when heated yields combustible gases, shale oil, and a waste product called spent or retorted shale.

Orphan Lands—Disturbed surfaces resulting from surface mines that were inadequately rehabilitated by the operator and for which he no longer has any fixed responsibility. It usually refers to lands mined before the passage of comprehensive rehabilitation laws.

Outlet—A means of exit from a pipe or culvert.

Overburden—The surface waste of worthless rock overlying a flat or moderately inclined economic deposit that must be removed to expose underlying material deposits.

Parting—The material that separates two seams of mineral deposits.

Perennial Stream—A stream that flows continuously during all the calendar year as a result of ground water discharge or surface runoff.

Permeability—(1) The quality of a soil horizon that enables water or air to move through it, (2) The property or capacity of a porous rock sediment or soil for transmitting a fluid without impairment of the structure of the medium; a measure of the relative ease of fluid flow under unequal pressure.

Phytotoxic—Capable of harming plant life.

Pollutant—Any gasious, chemical, or organic waste that contaminates air, soil, atmosphere, or water by the discharge of noxious substances.

Primary Succession—Ecological succession that begins on an area where there is no viable soil to act as a growth medium or an area that has not been previously occupied by a community of organisms.

Railroad Spur—Not a main line, but a short side track used primarily to service an industrial resource.

Runoff—A portion of precipitation that appears in surface streams. It is the same as streamflow unaffected by artificial diversions, storage, or other works of man, in or on the stream.

Saline-Sodic Soil—A soil containing sufficient exchangeable sodium to interfere with the growth of most crop plants and containing appreciable quantities of soluble salts. The soil must have an exchangeable sodium percentage greater than 12 to qualify as saline-sodic.

Seam—A band of mineral deposits found at various depths, angles, and thicknesses.

Secondary Succession—Ecological succession that begins on an area with a viable soil source and which, in previous times, had been occupied by a community or organism.

Sewage Effluent—Waste material discharged into the environment especially as a pollutant. The discharged waste is a product of human feces and organic residues.

Slump—Downard movement of soils on a slope.

Soil Toxicity—A characteristic of certain materials located in the A and B horizons making them harmful to plant growth.

Spoil—The overburden or noncoal material removed to gain access to the coal or mineral material in surface mining and stacked at the surface of a mine either in conical heaps or in layered deposits.

Species Diversity—Ratio between the number of species in a community and the number of individuals in each species.

Stability—Persistence of the structure of a system, (such as an ecosystem, community, or organism) over time.

Strip Mine—Refers to a procedure of mining that entails the complete removal of all material from over the product to be mined in a series of rows or strips; also, referred to as an open cut, open pit, or surface mine.

Surface Mining—A broad term used to describe the process of removing the earth's surface to uncover mineral deposits.

Surface Water—Waters on the surface of the earth, including water in streams, lakes, ponds, ice, snow, glaciers, etc.

TDS—Total dissolved solids.

Tilth—The physical condition of soil as related to its ease of tillage, fitness as a seedbed, and its impedance to seedling emergence and root penetration.

Topography—The exact physical features and configuration of a place or region; the detailed and accurate description of the slope in a place or region.

Topsoiling—The process of replacing the topsoil of a mined site in order to return it to productivity.

Traverse—A route or way across or over.

Undercut—To cut away material from the underside of an object.

Water-Holding Capacity—The ability of a soil to hold water in its pore spaces, where water is available for plants.

Weathering—All physical and chemical changes produced in rocks, at or near the earth's surface, by atmospheric agents.

Weir—A dam in a stream to raise the water level, divert its flow, or measure its volume of flow.

Zero-Order Watershed—The smallest area that supports the creation of a channel high in the drainage network.

Appendix A

SURFACE MINING CONTROL AND RECLAMATION ACT OF 1977 PORTIONS OF SECTION 515 ENVIRONMENTAL PROTECTION PERFORMANCE STANDARDS

General performance standards shall be applicable to all surface coal mining and reclamation operations and shall require the operation as a minimum to:

(1) conduct surface coal mining operations so as to maximize the utilization and conservation of the solid fuel resource being recovered so that reaffecting the land in the future through surface coal mining can be minimized;

(2) restore the land affected to a condition capable of supporting the uses which it was capable of supporting prior to any mining, or higher or better uses of which there is reasonable likelihood, so long as such use or uses do not present any actual or probable hazard to public health or safety or pose any actual or probable threat of water diminution or pollution, and the permit applicants' declared proposed land use following reclamation is not deemed to be impractical or unreasonable, inconsistent with applicable land use policies and plans, involves unreasonable delay in implementation, or is violative of Federal, State, or local law;

(3) except as provided in subsection (c) with respect to all surface coal mining operations backfill, compact (where advisable to insure stability or to prevent leaching of toxic materials), and grade in order to restore the approximate original contour of the land with all highwalls, spoil piles, and depressions eliminated (unless small depressions are needed in order to retain moisture to assist revegetation or as otherwise authorized pursuant to this Act): *Provided, however,* That in surface coal mining which is carried out at the same location over a substantial period of time where the operation transects the coal deposit, and the thickness of the coal deposits relative to the volume of the overburden is large and where the operator demonstrates that the overburden and other spoil and waste materials at a particular point in the permit area or otherwise available from the entire permit area [are] insufficient, giving due consideration to volumetric expansion, to restore the approximate original contour, the operator, at a minimum, shall backfill, grade, and compact (where advisable) using all available overburden and other spoil and waste materials to attain the lowest practicable grade but not more than the angle of repose, to provide adequate drainage and to cover all acid-forming and other toxic materials, in order to achieve an ecologically sound land use compatible with the surrounding region: *And provided further,* That in surface coal mining where the volume of overburden is large relative to the thickness of the coal deposit, and where the operator demonstrates that due to volumetric expansion the amount of overburden and other spoil and waste materials removed in the course of the mining operation is more than sufficient to restore the approximate original contour, the operator shall after restoring the approximate contour, backfill, grade, and compact (where advisable) the excess overburden and other spoil and waste materials to attain the lowest grade but not more than the angle of repose, and to cover all acid-forming and other toxic materials, in order to achieve an ecologically sound land use compatible with the surrounding region and that such overburden or spoil shall be shaped and graded in such a way as to prevent slides, erosion, and water pollution and is revegetated in accordance with the requirements of the Act;

(4) stabilize and protect all surface areas including spoil piles affected by the surface coal mining and reclamation operation to effectively control erosion and attendant air and water pollution;

(5) remove the topsoil from the land in a separate layer, replace it on the backfill area, or if not utilized immediately, segregate it in a separate pile from other spoil and when the topsoil is not replaced on a backfill area within a time short enough to avoid deterioration of the topsoil, maintain a successful cover by quick growing plant or other means thereafter so that the topsoil is preserved from wind and water erosion, remains free of any contamination by other acid or toxic material, and is in a usable condition for sustaining vegetation when restored during reclamation, except if topsoil is of insufficient quantity or of poor quality for sustaining vegetation, or if other strata can be shown to be more suitable for vegetation requirements, then the operator shall remove, segregate, and preserve in a like manner such other which is best able to support vegetation;

(6) restore the topsoil or the best available subsoil which is best able to support vegetation;

(7) for all prime farm lands as identified in section 507 (b)(16) to be mined and reclaimed, specifications for soil removal, storage, replacement, and reconstruction shall be established by the Secretary of Agriculture, and the operator shall, as a minimum, be required to—

(A) segregate the A horizon of the natural soil, except where it can be shown that other available soil materials will create a final soil having a greater productive capacity; and if not utilized immediately, stockpile this material separately from other spoil, and provide needed protection from wind and water erosion or contamination by other acid or toxic material;

(B) segregate the B horizon of the natural soil, or underlying C horizons or other strata, or a combination of such horizons or other strata that are shown to be both texturally and chemically suitable for plant growth and that can be shown to be equally or more favorable for plant growth than the B horizon, in sufficient quantities to create in the regraded final soil a root zone of comparable depth and quality to that which existed in the natural soil; and if not utilized immediately, stockpile this material separately from other soil, and provide needed protection from wind and water erosion or contamination by other acid or toxic material;

(C) replace and regrade the root zone material described in (B) above with proper compaction and uniform depth over the regraded spoil material; and

(D) redistribute and grade in a uniform manner the surface soil horizon described in subparagraph (A);

(8) create, if authorized in the approved mining and reclamation plan and permit, permanent impoundments of water on mining sites as part of reclamation activities only when it is adequately demonstrated that—

(A) the size of the impoundment is adequate for its intended purposes;

(B) the impoundment dam construction will be so designed as to achieve necessary stability with an adequate margin of safety compatible with that of structures constructed under Public Law 83–566 (16 U.S.C. 1006);

(C) the quality of impounded water will be suitable on a permanent basis for its intended use and that discharges from the impoundment will not degrade the water quality below water quality standards established pursuant to applicable Federal and State law in the receiving stream;

(D) the level of water will be reasonably stable;

(E) final grading will provide adequate safety and access for proposed water users; and

(F) such water impoundments will not result in the diminution of the quality or quantity of water utilized by adjacent or surrounding landowners for agricultural, industrial, recreational, or domestic uses;

(9) conduct any augering operation associated with surface mining in a manner to maximize recoverability of mineral reserves remaining after the operation and reclamation are complete; and seal all auger holes with an impervious and noncombustible material in order to prevent drainage except where the regulatory authority determines that the resulting impoundment of water in such auger holes may create a hazard to the environment or the public health or safety; *Provided,* That the permitting authority may prohibit augering if necessary to maximize the utilization, recoverability or conservation of the solid fuel resources or to protect against adverse water quality impacts;

(10) minimize the disturbances to the prevailing hydrologic balance at the mine site and in associated offsite areas and to the quality and quantity of water in surface and ground water systems both during and after surface coal mining operations and during reclamation by—

(A) avoiding acid or other toxic mine drainage by such measures as, but not limited to—

(i) preventing or removing water from contact with toxic producing deposits;

(ii) treating drainage to reduce toxic content which adversely affects downstream water upon being released to water courses;

(iii) casing, sealing, or otherwise managing boreholes, shafts, and wells and keep acid or other toxic drainage from entering ground and surface waters;

(B)(i) conducting surface coal mining operations so as to prevent, to the extent possible using the best technology currently available, additional contributions of suspended solids to streamflow, or runoff outside the permit area, but in no event shall contributions be in excess of requirements set by applicable State or Federal law;

(ii) constructing any siltation structures pursuant to subparagraph (B)(i) of this subsection prior to commencement of surface coal mining operations, such structures to be certified by a qualified registered engineer to be constructed as designed and as approved in the reclamation plan;

(C) cleaning out and removing temporary or large settling ponds or other siltation structures from drainways after disturbed areas are revegetated and stabilized; and depositing the silt and debris at a site and in a manner approved by the regulatory authority;

(D) restoring recharge capacity of the mined area to approximate premining conditions;

(E) avoiding channel deepening or enlargement in operations requiring the discharge of water from mines;

(F) preserving throughout the mining and reclamation process the essential hydrologic functions of alluvial valley floors in the arid and semiarid areas of the country; and

(G) such other actions as the regulatory authority may prescribe;

(11) with respect to surface disposal of mine wastes, tailings, coal processing wastes, and other wastes in areas other than the mine working or excavations, stabilize all waste piles in designated areas through construction in compacted layers including the use of incombustible and impervious materials if necessary and assure the final contour of the waste pile will be compatible with natural surroundings and that the site can and will be stabilized and revegetated according to the provisions of this Act;

(12) refrain from surface coal mining within five hundred feet from active and abandoned underground mines in order to prevent breakthroughs and to protect health or safety of miners: *Provided,* That the regulatory authority shall permit an operator to mine near, through or partially through an abandoned underground mine or closer to an active underground mine if (A) the nature, timing, and sequencing of the approximate coincidence of specific surface mine activities with specific underground mine activities are jointly approved by the regulatory authorities concerned with surface mine regulation and the health and safety of underground miners, and (B) such operations will result in improved resource recovery, abatement of water pollution, or elimination of hazards to the health and safety of the public;

(13) design, locate, construct, operate, maintain, enlarge, modify, and remove or abandon, in accordance with the standards and criteria developed pursuant to subsection (f) of this section, all existing and new coal mine waste piles consisting of mine wastes, tailings, coal processing wastes, or other liquid and solid wastes, and used either temporarily or permanently as dams or embankments;

(14) insure that all debris, acid-forming materials, toxic materials, or materials consisting of a fire hazard are treated or buried and compacted or otherwise disposed of in a manner designed to prevent contamination of ground or surface waters and that contengency plans are developed to prevent sustained combustion;

(15) insure that explosives are used only in accordance with existing State and Federal law and the regulations promulgated by the regulatory authority, which shall include provisions to—

(A) provide adequate advance written notice to local governments and residents who might be affected by the use of such explosives by publication of the planned blasting schedule in a newspaper of general circulation in the locality and by mailing a copy of the proposed blasting schedule to every resident living within one-half mile of the proposed blasting site and by providing daily notice to resident/occupiers in such areas prior to any blasting;

(B) maintain for a period of at least three years and make available for public inspection upon request a log detailing the location of the blasts, the pattern and depth of the drill holes, the amount of explosives used per hole, and the order and length of delay in the blasts;

(C) limit the type of explosives and detonating equipment, the size, the timing and frequency of blasts based upon the physical conditions of the site so as to prevent (i) injury to persons, (ii) damage to public and private property outside the permit area, (iii) adverse impacts on any underground mine, and (iv) change in the course, channel, or availability of ground or surface water outside the permit area;

(D) require that all blasting operations be conducted by trained and competent persons as certified by the regulatory authority;

(E) provide that upon the request of a resident or owner of a man-made dwelling or structure within one-half mile of any portion of the permitted area the applicant or permittee shall conduct a pre-blasting survey of such structures and submit the survey to the regulatory authority and a copy to the resident or owner making the request. The area of the survey shall be decided by the regulatory authority and shall include such provisions as the Secretary shall promulgate.

(16) insure that all reclamation efforts proceed in an environmentally sound manner and as contemporaneously as practicable with the surface coal mining operations: *Provided, however,* That where the applicant proposes to combine surface mining operations with underground mining operations to assure maximum practical recovery of the mineral resources, the regulatory authority may grant a variance for specific areas within the reclamation plan from the requirement that reclamation efforts proceed as contemporaneously as practicable to permit underground mining operations prior to reclamation:

(A) if the regulatory authority finds in writing that:

(i) the applicant has presented, as part of the permit application, specific, feasible plans for the proposed underground mining operations;

(ii) the proposed underground mining operations are necessary or desirable to assure maximum practical recovery of the mineral resource and will avoid multiple disturbance of the surface;

(iii) the applicant has satisfactorily demonstrated that the plan for the underground mining operations conforms to requirements for underground mining in the jurisdiction and that permits necessary for the underground mining operations have been issued by the appropriate authority;

(iv) the areas proposed for the variance have been shown by the applicant to be necessary for the implementing of the proposed underground mining operations;

(v) no substantial adverse environmental damage, either on-site or off-site, will result from the delay in completion of reclamation as required by this Act;

(vi) provisions for the off-site storage of spoil will comply with section 515 (b)(22);

(B) if the Secretary has promulgated specific regulations to govern the granting of such variances in accordance with the provisions of this subsection and section 501, and has imposed such additional requirements as he deems necessary;

(C) if variances granted under the provisions of this subsection are to be reviewed by the regulatory authority not more than three years from the date of issuance of the permit; and

(D) if liability under the bond filed by the applicant with the regulatory authority pursuant to section 509 (b) shall be for the duration of the underground mining operations and until the requirements of sections 515 (b) and 519 have been fully complied with.

(17) insure that the construction, maintenance, and postmining conditions of access roads into and across the site of operations will control or prevent erosion and siltation, pollution of water, damage to fish or wildlife or their habitat, or public or private property;

(18) refrain from the construction of roads or other access ways up a stream bed or drainage channel or in such proximity to such channel so as to seriously alter the normal flow of water;

(19) establish on the regraded areas, and all other lands affected, a diverse, effective, and permanent vegetative cover of the same seasonal variety native to the area of land to be affected and capable of self-regeneration and plant succession at least equal in extent of cover to the natural vegetation of the area; except, that introduced species may be used in the revegetation process where desirable and necessary to achieve the approved postmining land use plan;

(20) assume the responsibility for successful revegetation, as required by paragraph (19) above, for a period of five full years after the last year of augmented seeding, fertilizing, irrigation, or other work in order to assure compliance with paragraph (19) above, except in those areas or regions of the country where the annual average precipitation is twenty-six inches or less, then the operator's assumption of responsibility and liability will extend for a period of ten full years after the last year of augmented seeding, fertilizing, irrigation, or other work: *Provided,* That when the regulatory authority approves a long-term intensive agricultural postmining

land use, the applicable five- or ten-year period of responsibility for revegetation shall commence at the date of initial planting for such long-term intensive agricultural postmining land use: *Provided further,* That when the regulatory authority issues a written finding approving a long-term, intensive, agricultural postmining land use as part of the mining and reclamation plan, the authority may grant exception to the provisions of paragraph (19) above;

(21) protect offsite areas from slides or damage occurring during the surface coal mining and reclamation operations, and not deposit spoil material or locate any part of the operations or waste accumulation outside the permit area;

(22) place all excess spoil material resulting from coal surface mining and reclamation activities in such a manner that—

(A) spoil is transported and placed in a controlled manner in position for concurrent compaction and in such a way to assure mass stability and to prevent mass movement;

(B) the areas of disposal are within the bonded permit areas and all organic matter shall be removed immediately prior to spoil placement;

(C) appropriate surface and internal drainage systems and diversion ditches are used as to prevent spoil erosion and movement;

(D) the disposal area does not contain springs, natural water courses or wet weather seeps unless lateral drains are constructed from the wet areas to the main underdrains in such a manner that filtration of the water into the spoil pile will be prevented;

(E) if placed on a slope, the spoil is placed upon the most moderate slope among those upon which, in the judgement of the regulatory authority, the spoil could be placed in compliance with all the requirements of the Act, and shall be placed, where possible, upon, or above, a natural terrace, bench, or berm, if such placement provides additional stability and prevents mass movement;

(F) where the toe of the spoil rests on a downslope, a rock toe buttress, of sufficient size to prevent mass movement, is constructed;

(G) the final configuration is compatible with the natural drainage pattern and surroundings and suitable for intended uses;

(H) design of the spoil disposal area is certified by a qualified registered professional engineer in conformance with professional standards; and

(I) all other provisions of this Act are met.

(23) meet such other criteria as are necessary to achieve reclamation in accordance with the purposes of this Act, taking into consideration the physical, climatological, and other characteristics of the site; and

(24) to the extent possible using the best technology currently available, minimize disturbances and adverse impacts of the operation on fish, wildlife, and related environmental values, and achieve enhancement of such resources where practicable;

(25) provide for an undisturbed natural barrier beginning at the elevation of the lowest coal seam to be mined and extending from the outslope for such distance as the regulatory authority shall determine shall be retained in place as a barrier to slides and erosion.

(C)(1) Each State program may and each Federal program shall include procedures pursuant to which the regulatory authority may permit surface mining operations for the purposes set forth in paragraph (3) of this subsection.

(2) Where an applicant meets the requirements of paragraphs (3) and (4) of this subsection a permit without regard to the requirement to restore to approximate original contour set forth in subsection 515 (b)(3) or 515 (d)(2) and (3) of this section may be granted for the surface mining of coal where the mining operation will remove an entire coal seam or seams running through the upper fraction of a mountain, ridge, or hill (except as provided in subsection (c)(4)(A) hereof) by removing all of the overburden and creating a level plateau or a gently rolling contour with no highwalls remaining, and capable of supporting postmining uses in accord with the requirements of this subsection.

(3) In cases where an industrial, commercial, agricultural, residential or public facility (including recreational facilities) use is proposed for the postmining use of the affected land, the regulatory authority may grant a permit for a surface mining operation of the nature described in subsection (c)(2) where—

(A) after consultation with the appropriate land use planning agencies, if any, the proposed postmining land use is deemed to constitute an equal or better economic or public use of the affected land, as compared with premining use;

(B) the applicant presents specific plans for the proposed postmining land use and appropriate assurances that such use will be—

(i) compatible with adjacent land uses;

(ii) obtainable according to data regarding expected need and market;

(iii) assured of investment in necessary public facilities;

(iv) supported by commitments from public agencies where appropriate;

(v) practicable with respect to private financial capability for completion of the proposed use;

(vi) planned pursuant to a schedule attached to the reclamation plan so as to integrate the mining operation and reclamation with the postmining land use; and

(vii) designed by a registered engineer in conformance with professional standards established to assure the stability, drainage, and configuration necessary for the intended use of the site;

(C) the proposed use would be consistent with adjacent land uses, and existing State and local land use plans and programs;

(D) the regulatory authority provides the governing body of the unit of general-purpose government in which the land is located and any State or Federal agency which the regulatory agency, in its discretion, determines to have an interest in the proposed use, an opportunity of not more than sixty days to review and comment on the proposed use;

(E) all other requirements of this Act will be met.

(4) In granting any permit pursuant to this subsection the regulatory authority shall require that—

(A) the toe of the lowest coal seam and the overburden associated with it are retained in place as a barrier to slides and erosion;

(B) the reclaimed area is stable;

(C) the resulting plateau or rolling contour drains inward from the outslopes except at specified points;

(D) no damage will be done to natural watercourses;

(E) spoil will be placed on the mountaintop bench as is necessary to achieve the planned postmining land use: *Provided,* That all excess spoil material not retained on the mountaintop shall be placed in accordance with the provisions of subsection (b)(22) of this section;

(F) insure stability of the spoil retained on the mountaintop and meet the other requirements of this Act;

(5) The regulatory authority shall promulgate specific regulations to govern the granting of permits in accord with the provisions of this subsection, and may impose such additional requirements as he deems to be necessary.

(6) All permits granted under the provisions of this subsection shall be reviewed not more than three years from the date of issuance of the permit, unless the applicant affirmatively demonstrates that the proposed development is proceeding in accordance with the terms of the approved schedule and reclamation plan.

(d) The following performance standards shall be applicable to steep-slope surface coal mining and shall be in addition to those general performance standards required by this section: *Provided, however,* That the provisions of this subsection (d) shall not apply to those situations in which an operator is mining on flat or gently rolling terrain, on which an occasional steep slope is encountered through which the mining operation is to proceed, leaving a plain or predominantly flat area or where an operator is in compliance with provisions of subsection (c) hereof:

(1) Insure that when performing surface coal mining on steep slopes, no debris, abandoned or disabled equipment, spoil material, or waste mineral matter be placed on the downslope below the bench or mining cut: *Provided,* That spoil material in excess of that required for the reconstruction of the approximate original contour under the provisions of paragraph 515 (b)(3) or 515 (d)(2) shall be permanently stored pursuant to section 515 (b)(22).

(2) Complete backfilling with spoil material shall be required to cover completely the highwall and return the site to the appropriate original contour, which material will maintain stability following mining and reclamation.

(3) The operator may not disturb land above the top of the highwall unless the regulatory authority finds that such disturbance will facilitate compliance with the environmental protection standards of this section: *Provided, however,* That the land disturbed above the highwall shall be limited to that amount necessary to facilitate said compliance.

(4) For the purposes of this subsection (d), the term "steep slope" is any slope above twenty degrees or such lesser slope as may be defined by the regulatory authority after consideration of soil, climate, and other characteristics of a region or State.

(E)(1) Each state program may and each Federal program shall include procedures pursuant to which the regulatory authority may permit variances for the purposes set forth in paragraph (3) of this subsection, provided that the watershed control of the area is improved; and further provided complete backfilling with spoil material shall be required to cover completely the highwall, which material will maintain stability following mining and reclamation.

(2) Where an applicant meets the requirements of paragraphs (3) and (4) of this subsection a variance from the requirement to restore

to approximate original contour set forth in subsection 515 (d)(2) of this section may be granted for the surface mining of coal where the owner of the surface knowingly requests in writing, as a part of the permit application that such a variance be granted so as to render the land, after reclamation, suitable for an industrial, commercial, residential, or public use (including recreational facilities) in accord with the further provisions of paragraphs (3) and (4) of this subsection.

(3)(A) After consultation with the appropriate land use planning agencies, if any, the potential use of the affected land is deemed to constitute an equal or better economic or public use;

(B) is designed and certified by a qualified registered professional engineer in conformance with professional standards established to assure the stability, drainage, and configuration necessary for the intended use of the site; and

(C) after approval of the appropriate state environmental agencies, the watershed of the affected land is deemed to be improved.

(4) In granting a variance pursuant to this subsection the regulatory authority shall require that only such amount of spoil will be placed off the mine bench as is necessary to achieve the planned postmining land use, insure stability of the spoil retained on the bench, meet all other requirements of this Act, and all spoil placement off the mine bench must comply with subsection 515(b)(22).

(5) The regulatory authority shall promulgate specific regulations to govern the granting of variances in accord with the provisions of this subsection, and may impose such additional requirements as he deems to be necessary.

(6) All exceptions granted under the provisions of this subsection shall be reviewed not more than three years from the date of issuance of the permit, unless the permittee affirmatively demonstrates that the proposed development is proceeding in accordance with the terms of the reclamation plan.

(f) The Secretary, with the written concurrence of the Chief of Engineers, shall establish within one hundred and thirty-five days from the date of enactment, standards and criteria regulating the design, location, construction, operation, maintenance, enlargement, modification, removal, and abandonment of new and existing coal mine waste piles referred to in section 515 (b)(13) and section 516 (b)(5). Such standards and criteria shall conform to the standards and criteria used by the Chief of Engineers to insure that flood control structures are safe and effectively perform their intended function. In addition to engineering and other technical specifications the standards and criteria developed pursuant to this subsection must include provisions for: review and approval of plans and specifications prior to construction, enlargement, modification, removal, or abandonment; performance of periodic inspections during construction; issuance of certificates of approval upon completion of construction; performance of periodic safety inspections; and issuance of notices for required remedial or maintenance work.

Appendix B

PLANT MATERIALS USED FOR REHABILITATION

Plant Species for Revegetating Coal Surface-Mined Lands in the Eastern United States (From: Vogel, Willis G., *A Guide For Revegetating Coal Minesoils In The Eastern United States*, USDA Northeastern Forest Experiment Station, 1981)

SCIENTIFIC NAME	COMMON NAME
GRASSES	
Agropyron smithii	Western wheatgrass
Agrostis gigantea	Redtop
Andropogon gerardi	Big bluestem
Arrhenatherum elatius	Tall oatgrass
Avena sativa	Oats
Bothriochloa caucasica	Caucasian bluestem
Bouteloua curtipendula	Sideoats grama
Brachiaria ramosa	Browntop millet
Bromus inermis	Smooth brome
Buchloe dactyloides	Buffalograss
Cynodon dactylon	Bermudagrass
Dactylis glomerata	Orchardgrass
Echinochloa crusgalli var. *frumentacea*	Japanese millet
Elymus canadensis	Canada wildrye
Eragrostis curvula	Weeping lovegrass
Eragrostis trichodes	Sand lovegrass
Festuca arundinacea Selection Ky-31	Tall fescue 'Kentucky-31'
Festuca rubra	Red fescue
Lolium multiflorum	Annual ryegrass
Lolium perenne	Perennial ryegrass

SCIENTIFIC NAME	COMMON NAME
Panicum clandestinum	Deertongue
Panicum miliaceum	Broomcorn millet
Panicum virgatum	Switchgrass
Paspalum dilatatum	Dallisgrass
Pennisetum americanum	Pearl millet
Phalaris arundinacea	Reed canarygrass
Phleum pratense	Timothy
Poa compressa	Canada bluegrass
Poa pratensis	Kentucky bluegrass
Schizachyrium scoparium	Little bluestem
Secale cereale	Rye
Setaria italica	Foxtail millet
Sorghastrum nutans	Indiangrass
Sorghum bicolor	Sorghum
Sorghum sudanense	Sudangrass
Tripsacum dactyloides	Eastern gamagrass
Triticum aestivum	Winter wheat
FORBS—LEGUMES	
Astragalus cicer	Cicer milkvetch
Cassia fasciculata	Partridge pea
Coronilla varia	Crownvetch
Desmanthus illinoensis	Illinois bundleflower

SCIENTIFIC NAME	COMMON NAME
Glycine max	Soybean
Lathyrus sylvestris	Flatpea
Lespedeza cuneata	Sericea lespedeza
Lespedeza daurica var. *schimadai*	Prostrate lespedeza
Lespedeza stipulacea	Korean lespedeza
Lespedeza striata	Common lespedeza
Lespedeza striata var. Kobe	Kobe lespedeza
Lotus corniculatus	Birdsfoot trefoil
Medicago sativa	Alfalfa
Melilotus alba	White sweetclover
Melilotus officinalis	Yellow sweetclover
Trifolium ambiguum	Kura clover
Trifolium hybridum	Alsike clover
Trifolium incarnatum	Crimson clover
Trifolium medium	Zigzag clover
Trifolium pratense	Red clover
Trifolium repens	White clover
Trifolium repens 'ladino'	Ladino clover
Vicia grandiflora	Bigflower vetch
Vicia villosa	Hairy vetch
Vigna unguiculata	Black-eyed cowpea

FORBS—NONLEGUMES

Fagopyrum esculentum	Buckwheat
Helianthus annuus	Common sunflower
Helianthus maximiliani	Maximilian sunflower
Polygonum cuspidatum	Japanese fleeceflower

TREES—CONIFERS

Juniperus scopulorum	Rocky Mountain juniper
Juniperus virginiana	Eastern redcedar
Larix decidua	European larch
Larix leptolepis	Japanese larch
Picea abies	Norway spruce
Picea glauca	White spruce
Picea rubens	Red spruce
Pinus banksiana	Jack pine

SCIENTIFIC NAME	COMMON NAME
Pinus echinata	Shortleaf pine
Pinus elliottii	Slash pine
Pinus nigra	Austrian pine
Pinus palustris	Longleaf pine
Pinus ponderosa	Ponderosa pine
Pinus resinosa	Red pine
Pinus rigida	Pitch pine
Pinus rigida x. *P. taeda* (*P. xrigitaeda*)	Pitch x loblolly hybrid
Pinus strobus	Eastern white pine
Pinus sylvestris	Scotch pine
Pinus taeda	Loblolly pine
Pinus virginiana	Virginia pine
Pseudotsuga menziesii	Douglas fir
Taxodium distichum	Baldcypress

TREES—HARDWOODS

Acer rubrum	Red maple
Acer saccharinum	Silver maple
Acer saccharum	Sugar maple
Alnus glutinosa	European black alder
Betula lenta	Sweet birch
Betula nigra	River birch
Betula papyrifera	Paper birch
Betula pendula	European white birch
Betula populifolia	Gray birch
Carya spp.	Hickory
Carya illinoensis	Pecan
Castanea mollissima	Chinese chestnut
Catalpa spp.	Catalpa
Celtis occidentalis	Hackberry
Cornus florida	Flowering dogwood
Elaeagnus angustifolia	Russian olive
Fraxinus americana	White ash
Fraxinus pennsylvanica	Green ash
Juglans nigra	Black walnut
Liquidambar styraciflua	Sweetgum
Liriodendron tulipifera	Yellow-poplar
Maclura pomifera	Osage-orange

SCIENTIFIC NAME	COMMON NAME	SCIENTIFIC NAME	COMMON NAME
Malus spp.	Crab apple	*Cornus stolonifera*	Red-osier dogwood
Paulownia tomentosa	Royal paulownia	*Crataegus* spp.	Hawthorn
Platanus occidentalis	American sycamore	*Elaeagnus umbellata*	Autumn olive
Populus spp.	Hybrid poplars	*Lespedeza bicolor*	Shrub lespedeza
Populus deltoides	Eastern cottonwood	*Lespedeza japonica*	Japan lespedeza
Populus grandidentata	Bigtooth aspen	*Lespedeza thunbergii*	Thunberg lespedeza
Prunus serotina	Black cherry	*Ligustrum amurense*	Amur privet
Quercus acutissima	Sawtooth oak	*Lonicera japonica*	Japanese honeysuckle
Quercus alba	White oak	*Lonicera maackii*	Amur honeysuckle
Quercus imbricaria	Shingle oak	*Lonicera morrowii*	Morrow honeysuckle
Quercus macrocarpa	Bur oak	*Lonicera tatarica*	Tatarian honeysuckle
Quercus palustris	Pin oak	*Prunus besseyi*	Western sandcherry
Quercus prinus	Chestnut oak	*Prunus virginiana*	Chokecherry
Quercus rubra	Northern red oak	*Rhus aromatica*	Fragrant sumac
Robinia pseudoacacia	Black locust	*Rhus copallina*	Shining sumac
Salix nigra	Black willow	*Robinia fertilis*	Bristly locust
Tilia americana	American basswood	*Robinia hispida*	Rose-acacia locust
		Rosa multiflora	Multiflora rose
SHRUBS		*Rosa rugosa*	Rugosa rose
		Rosa wichuraiana	Memorial rose
Amorpha fruticosa	Indigobush	*Salix purpurea*	Purpleosier willow
Aronia melanocarpa	Black chokeberry	*Sambucus canadensis*	American elder
Berberis koreana	Korean barberry	*Shepherdia argentea*	Silver buffaloberry
Caragana arborescens	Siberian peashrub	*Viburnum dentatum*	Arrowwood
Cornus amomum	Silky dogwood		
Cornus racemosa	Gray dogwood		

Plant Species for Revegetating Coal Surface-Mined Lands in the Western United States (From: Thornburg, Ashley A., *Plant Materials for Use on Surface-Mined Lands in Arid and Semiarid Regions*, USDA, Soil Conservation Service, 1982).

SCIENTIFIC NAME	COMMON NAME	SCIENTIFIC NAME	COMMON NAME
GRASSES		*Agropyron intermedium*	Intermediate wheatgrass
		Agropyron riparium	Streambank wheatgrass
Agropyron cristatum	Crested wheatgrass	*Agropyron sibiricum*	Siberian wheatgrass
Agropyron dasystachyum	Thickspike wheatgrass	*Agropyron smithii*	Western wheatgrass
Agropyron desertorum	Standard crested wheatgrass	*Agropyron spicatum*	Bluebunch wheatgrass
Agropyron elongatum	Tall wheatgrass	*Agropyron trachycaulum*	Slender wheatgrass
Agropyron inerme	Beardless wheatgrass		

SCIENTIFIC NAME	COMMON NAME	SCIENTIFIC NAME	COMMON NAME
Agropyron trichophorum	Pubescent wheatgrass	*Festuca idahoensis*	Idaho fescue
Alopecurus arundinaceus	Creeping meadow foxtail	*Festuca megalura*	Foxtail fescue
Alopecurus pratensis	Meadow foxtail	*Festuca ovina*	Sheep fescue
Andropogon barbinodis	Cane bluestem	*Festuca ovina duriuscula*	Hard fescue
Andropogon caucasicus	Caucasian bluestem	*Festuca thurberi*	Thurber fescue
Andropogon gerardi	Big bluestem	*Hilaria belangeri*	Curlymesquite
Andropogon hallii	Sand bluestem	*Hilaria jamesii*	Galleta
Andropogon ischaemum	Yellow bluestem	*Hilaria mutica*	Tobosa
Andropogon scoparius	Little bluestem	*Hilaria rigida*	Big galleta
Arundo donax	Giantreed	*Leptochloa dubia*	Green sprangletop
Bouteloua curtipendula	Sideoats grama	*Lolium rigidum*	Wimmera or Swiss ryegrass
Bouteloua eriopoda	Black grama	*Muhlenbergia montana*	Mountain muhly
Bouteloua gracilis	Blue grama	*Muhlenbergia porteri*	Bush muhly
Bromus biebersteinii	Meadow brome	*Muhlenbergia wrightii*	Spike muhly
Bromus carinatus	California brome	*Oryzopsis hymenoides*	Indian ricegrass
Bromus inermis	Smooth brome	*Oryzopsis miliacea*	Smilograss
Bromus marginatus	Mountain brome	*Panicum antidotale*	Blue panicgrass
Bromus mollis	Soft chess	*Panicum coloratum*	Kleingrass
Bromus rubens	Red brome	*Panicum virgatum*	Switchgrass
Buchloe dactyloides	Buffalograss	*Pennisetum setaceum*	Fountaingrass
Calamovilfa longifolia	Prairie sandreed	*Phalaris arundinacea*	Reed canarygrass
Cenchrus ciliaris	Buffelgrass	*Phalaris tuberosa*	
Cynodon dactylon	Bermudagrass	var. *hirtiglumis*	Perlagrass
Dactylis glomerata	Orchardgrass	*Phalaris tuberosa*	
Deschampsia caespitosa	Tufted hairgrass	var. *stenoptera*	Hardinggrass
Distichlis stricta	Inland saltgrass	*Phragmites communis*	Common reed
Elymus cinereus	Basin wildrye	*Poa ampla*	Big bluegrass
Elymus giganteus	Mammoth wildrye	*Poa canbyi*	Canby bluegrass
Elymus junceus	Russian wildrye	*Poa glaucantha*	Upland bluegrass
Elymus triticoides	Beardless wildrye	*Rhynchelytrum roseum*	Natal redtop
Eragrostis atherstonei	Atherstone lovegrass	*Setaria macrostachya*	Plains bristlegrass
Eragrostis chloromelas	Boer lovegrass	*Sorghastrum nutans*	Indiangrass
Eragrostis curvula	Weeping lovegrass	*Sporobolus airoides*	Alkali sacaton
Eragrostis intermedia	Plains lovegrass	*Sporobolus contractus*	Spike dropseed
Eragrostis lehmanniana	Lehman lovegrass	*Sporobolus cryptandrus*	Sand dropseed
Eragrostis superba	Wilman lovegrass	*Sporobolus flexuosus*	Mesa dropseed
Eragrostis trichodes	Sand lovegrass	*Sporobolus giganteus*	Giant dropseed
Festuca arizonica	Arizona fescue	*Stipa comata*	Needleandthread
Festuca arundinacea	Tall fescue	*Stipa viridula*	Green needlegrass

SCIENTIFIC NAME	COMMON NAME
Trichachne californica	Arizona cottontop
Trichloris crinita	Twoflower trichloris

FORBS

SCIENTIFIC NAME	COMMON NAME
Astragalus cicer	Cicer milkvetch
Coronilla varia	Crownvetch
Desmanthus illinoensis	Illinois bundleflower
Erodium cicutarium	Alfileria
Eschscholzia spp.	Gold poppies
Gaillardia pinnatifida	Slender gaillardia
Helianthus maximiliana	Maximilian sunflower
Helianthus laetiflorus	Stiff sunflower
Ipomoea leptophylla	Bush morningglory
Kochia prostrata	Prostrate summercypress
Lotus corniculatus	Birdsfoot trefoil
Medicago sativa	Alfalfa
Melilotus alba	White sweetclover
Melilotus officinalis	Yellow sweetclover
Onobrychis viciaefolia	Sainfoin
Penstemon palmeri	Palmer penstemon
Penstemon strictus	Rocky Mountain penstemon
Petalostemum candidum	White prairieclover
Petalostemum purpureum	Purple prairieclover
Salvia pitcheri	Pitcher sage
Simsia exaristata	Annual bushsunflower
Trifolium fragiferum	Strawberry clover
Trifolium hirtum	Rose clover
Trifolium incarnatum	Crimson clover
Trifolium pratense	Red clover
Trifolium repens	White clover
Trifolium subterranean	Subterranean clover
Vicia americana	American vetch
Vicia dasycarpa	Woolypod vetch
Vicia villosa	Hairy vetch
Zexmenia hispida	Orange zexmenia

WOODY PLANTS

SCIENTIFIC NAME	COMMON NAME
Acacia constricta	Mescat acacia
Acacia greggii	Catclaw acacia

SCIENTIFIC NAME	COMMON NAME
Ailanthus altissima	Ailanthus
Amelanchier spp.	Serviceberries
Amorpha canescens	Leadplant
Amorpha fruticosa	Indigobush
Artemisia arbuscula nova	Black sagebrush
Artemisia cana	Silver sagebrush
Artemisia tridentata	Big sagebrush
Atriplex canescens	Fourwing saltbush
Atriplex lentiformis	Quailbush
Atriplex numularia	Oldman saltbush
Atriplex nuttallii	Nuttall saltbush
Atriplex polycarpa	Desert saltbush
Atriplex rhagodioides	Silver saltbush
Atriplex semibaccata	Australian saltbush
Baccharis sarathroides	Desertbroom
Berberis repens	Oregon-grape
Buddleia scorioides	Butterflybush
Calliandra eriophylla	False-mesquite
Caragana arborescens	Siberian peashrub
Cassia covesii	Coves cassia
Ceanothus fendleri	Fendler ceanothus
Ceanothus greggii	Desert ceanothus
Ceanothus martinii	Martin ceanothus
Ceanothus prostratus	Squawcarpet
Ceanothus velutinus	Snowbrush ceanothus
Celtis occidentalis	Common hackberry
Celtis pallida	Spiny hackberry
Celtis reticulata	Netleaf hackberry
Cercidium floridum	Blue paloverde
Cercidium microphyllum	Yellow paloverde
Cercocarpus ledifolius	Curlleaf mountainmahogany
Cercocarpus montanus	True mountainmahogany
Chilopsis linearis	Desertwillow
Chrysothamnus nauseosus	Rubber rabbitbrush
Clematis ligusticifolia	Virginsbower
Cornus stolonifera	Red-osier dogwood
Cowania mexicana	Cliffrose
Crataegus chrysocarpa	Fireberry hawthorn
Cupressus arizonica	Arizona cypress

SCIENTIFIC NAME	COMMON NAME	SCIENTIFIC NAME	COMMON NAME
Dodonea viscosa	Hopseedbush	*Menodora scabra*	Rough menodora
Elaeagnus angustifolia	Russian-olive	*Nicotiana glauca*	Tree tobacco
Encelia farinosa	White brittlebush	*Parkinsonia aculeata*	Mexican paloverde
Ephedra viridis	Green ephedra	*Parryella filifolia*	Dunebroom
Eriogonum fasciculatum	California buckwheat	*Pinus brutia*	Afghanistan pine
Eriogonum umbellatum	Sulfur eriogonum	*Pinus edulis*	Pinyon pine
Eucalyptus spp.	Eucalyptus	*Pinus nigra*	Austrian pine
Eurotia lanata	Winterfat	*Pinus ponderosa*	Ponderosa pine
Fallugia paradoxa	Apacheplume	*Pinus sylvestris*	Scotch pine
Forestiera neomexicana	New Mexico forestiera	*Potentilla fruticosa*	Shrubby cinquefoil
Franseria deltoidea	Triangle bursage	*Prosopis chilensis*	Chile mesquite
Franseria dumosa	White bursage	*Prunus americana*	American plum
Fraxinus pennsylvanica	Green ash	*Prunus emarginata*	Bitter cherry
Fraxinus velutina	Desert ash	*Prunus virginiana*	Chokecherry
Gleditsia triacanthos	Honeylocust	*Purshia tridentata*	Bitterbrush
Isomeris arborea	Bladderpod	*Quercus gambelii*	Gambel oak
Jamesia americana	Cliffbush	*Quercus macrocarpa*	Bur oak
Juglans microcarpa	Little walnut	*Rhus microphylla*	Littleleaf sumac
Juniperus communis	Common juniper	*Rhus trilobata*	Skunkbush sumac
Juniperus horizontalis	Creeping juniper	*Ribes aureum*	Golden currant
Juniperus monosperma	Oneseed juniper	*Robinia neomexicana*	New Mexico locust
Juniperus occidentalis	Western juniper	*Rosa* spp.	Roses
Juniperus osteosperma	Utah juniper	*Salix* spp.	Willows
Juniperus scopulorum	Rocky Mountain juniper	*Sapindus drummondii*	Western soapberry
Juniperus virginiana	Eastern redcedar	*Shepherdia argentea*	Silver buffaloberry
Kochia americana	Green molly	*Simmondsia chinensis*	Jojoba
Krameria parvifolia	Range ratany	*Symphoricarpos albus*	Common snowberry
Larrea divaricata	Creosotebush	*Tamarix aphylla*	Athel tamarisk
Lonicera tatarica	Tatarian honeysuckle	*Viguiera stenoloba*	Skeletonleaf goldeneye
Lycium halimifolium	Matrimonyvine	*Yucca elata*	Soaptree yucca
Maclura pomifera	Osage-orange	*Zizyphus jujube*	Common jujube

Index